BIJABOJI

North *to* Alaska
by Oar

Betty Lowman Carey

Edited by
Neil G. Carey

H A R B O U R   P U B L I S H I N G

Published by
Harbour Publishing Co. Ltd.
P.O. Box 219 , Madeira Park, BC V0N 2H0
www.harbourpublishing.com

Edited by Neil G. Carey and Mary Schendlinger
Page design by Martin Nichols
Cover painting by Harry Heine
Photographs by Betty Lowman Carey unless otherwise noted
Maps by Martin Nichols under consultation of Jackpine Design Studio

Printed and bound in Canada

Harbour Publishing acknowledges financial support from the Government of
Canada through the Book Publishing Industry Development Program and the
Canada Council for the Arts, and from the Province of British Columbia through
the British Columbia Arts Council and the Book Publisher's Tax Credit through
the Ministry of Provincial Revenue.

THE CANADA COUNCIL | LE CONSEIL DES ARTS
FOR THE ARTS | DU CANADA
SINCE 1957 | DEPUIS 1957

BRITISH
COLUMBIA
ARTS COUNCIL
Supported by the Province of British Columbia

Library and Archives Canada Cataloguing in Publication

Lowman Carey, Betty, 1914–
   Bijaboji : north to Alaska by oar / written by Betty Lowman Carey.
   Includes index.

ISBN 1-55017-340-5

   1. Lowman Carey, Betty, 1914– —Travel--Northwest Coast of North America.
2. Canoes and canoeing—Northwest coast of North America. 3. Northwest Coast
of North America—Description and travel. I. Title.
GV776.N76L69   2004   910'.9164'3   917.9504'44   C2004-904600-4

To all persons, ashore and afloat, who welcomed me along the magnificent Inside Passage, to those who made my many side trips so interesting and educational, and to the kind Native fishermen who rescued me in Douglas Channel, making it possible to get to my father in Alaska.

Contents

Acknowledgements 9

Itinerary 10

Introduction: Rowing by Moonlight 13

1: *Bijaboji* 15

2: Ship's Master 29

3: Aquaplaning in Agamemnon Channel 40

4: Deer Hunt at Garden Bay 56

5: Logging Show in Teakerne Arm 69

6: Navigating the Yucultas 84

7: R & R Aboard the *Tyee Scout* 102

8: Gale-Force Winds in Queen Charlotte Strait 119

9: House Calls with Dr. Darby 132

10: Dangerous Waters in Fitz Hugh Sound 150

11: Birthday in *Bijaboji* 170

12: Exploring Gardner Canal 185

13: Swamped in Douglas Channel 201

14: North to the Skeena 216

15: Prince Rupert by Land, by Sea, by Air 237

16: Reunion with Captain Lowman 253

Epilogue: *Bijaboji*—the Next Sixty Years 274

Index 280

Acknowledgements

Thanks to Ray B. Lowman, for the finest gifts my father could provide: my dugout canoe *Bijaboji* (named after my four brothers, Bill, Jack, Bob and Jimmy), years of training in small craft and saltwater swimming, and faith in my health, my ability, and my trust in God; to Neil, my husband, who saw this book, a lifetime wish, to completion; to Richard and Laura Sample for their patience and computer expertise; and to Tevis Sample and Jackpine Design Studio Ltd. for design consultation.

Itinerary

Guemes Island, Washington, to Ketchikan, Alaska
June 15 to August 19, 1937

Day	Date	Start Day	End Day
1	Tues June 15	Guemes Island, WA	Shaw Island, WA
2	Wed June 16	Shaw Island, WA	Johns Island, WA
3	Thur June 17	Johns Island, WA	
4	Fri June 18	Johns Island, WA	Stuart Island, WA
5	Sat June 19	Stuart Island, WA	Saltspring Island, BC
6	Sun June 20	Saltspring Island, BC	Nanaimo, BC
7	Mon June 21	Nanaimo, BC	Lasqueti Island, BC
8	Tues June 22	Lasqueti Island, BC	Vancouver Bay, BC
9	Wed June 23	Vancouver Bay, BC	Princess Louisa Inlet, BC
10	Thur June 24	Princess Louisa Inlet, BC	Garden Bay, BC
11	Fri June 25	Garden Bay, BC	
12	Sat June 26	Garden Bay, BC	Underway, rowing at night
13	Sun June 27	Underway, rowing	Powell River, BC
14	Mon June 28	Powell River, BC	Turner's Cove, BC
15	Tues June 29	Turner's Cove, BC	Teakerne Arm, BC
16	Wed June 30	Teakerne Arm, BC	Yuculta Rapids, BC
17	Thur July 1	Yuculta Rapids, BC	Mainland Beach, BC
18	Fri July 2	Mainland Beach, BC	Port Kusam, BC
19	Sat July 3	Port Kusam, BC	Underway aboard *F.K.*
20	Sun July 4	Underway aboard *F.K.*	Charlotte Bay, BC aboard *Tyee Scout*
21	Mon July 5	Charlotte Bay, BC	Slingsby Channel, BC
22	Tues July 6	Slingsby Channel, BC	Allison Harbour, BC
23	Wed July 7	Allison Harbour, BC	Aboard *Tyee Scout*
24	Thur July 8	Allison Harbour, BC	Alert Bay, BC
25	Fri July 9	Alert Bay, BC	
26	Sat July 10	Alert Bay, BC	Sointula, BC
27	Sun July 11	Sointula, BC	Pulteney Point Light, BC
28	Mon July 12	Pulteney Point Light, BC	Mainland Beach, BC
29	Tues July 13	Mainland Beach, BC	Mainland Cove, BC
30	Wed July 14	Mainland Cove, BC	Stonjalsky Float, BC
31	Thur July 15	Stonjalsky Float, BC	Allison Harbour, BC
32	Fri July 16	Steamer Day, Allison Harbour: SS *Venture*	
33	Sat July 17	Picnic, Skull Cove, BC	
34	Sun July 18	Allison Harbour, BC	Goose Bay Cannery, BC

35	Mon July 19	Goose Bay Cannery, BC	Yacht, Goose Bay, BC
36	Tues July 20	Yacht, Goose Bay, BC	Gillnetter, Rivers Inlet, BC
37	Wed July 21	Gillnetter, Rivers Inlet, BC	Hospital, Rivers Inlet, BC
38	Thur July 22	Hospital, Rivers Inlet, BC	Underway to Addenbroke Light.
39	Fri July 23	Underway to Addenbroke Light	Addenbroke Light, BC
40	Sat July 24	Addenbroke Point lt., BC	Namu, BC
41	Sun July 25	Namu, BC	Pointer Island light, BC
42	Mon July 26	Pointer Island light, BC	Ocean Falls, BC
43	Tues July 27	Ocean Falls, BC	Bella Bella, BC
44	Wed July 28	Bella Bella, BC	Oscar Passage, BC
45	Thur July 29	Oscar Passage, BC	Klemtu, BC
46	Fri July 30	Klemtu, BC	Graham Reach, BC
47	Sat July 31	Graham Reach, BC	Butedale, BC, Betty's birthday
48	Sun Aug 1	Butedale, BC, fish camp and boat	Gardner Canal, BC
49	Mon Aug 2	fish camp and boat	Kitimat Village, BC
50	Tues Aug 3	Kitimat Village, BC	Foch Lagoon, BC
51	Wed Aug 4	Foch Lagoon, BC (Stranded on cliff)	
52	Thur Aug 5	Foch Lagoon, BC, aboard *Kitgore*	Hartley Bay, BC
53	Fri Aug 6	Hartley Bay, BC, aboard *Sherman*	Lowe Inlet, BC
54	Sat Aug 7	Lowe Inlet, BC	
55	Sun Aug 8	Lowe Inlet–Grenville Channel, BC, aboard *Yanagi*	Lowe Inlet, BC
56	Mon Aug 9	Lowe Inlet, aboard *Sidney W.*	Ogden Channel, BC
57	Tues Aug 10	Ogden Channel, BC	Inverness Cannery, BC
58	Wed Aug 11	Inverness Cannery, BC	Prince Rupert, BC
59	Thur Aug 12	Prince Rupert, BC	
60	Fri Aug 13	Prince Rupert, BC	Port Simpson, BC
61	Sat Aug 14	Port Simpson, BC	Wales Island Cannery, BC
62	Sun Aug 15	Wales Island Cannery, BC	Tongass Island, AK
63	Mon Aug 16	Tongass Island, AK	Foggy Bay Fish Trap, AK
64	Tues Aug 17	Foggy Bay Fish Trap, AK	Mary Island light, AK
65	Wed Aug 18	Mary Island light, AK	Libby–McNeil–Libby Trap, AK
66	Thur Aug 19	Libby–McNeil–Libby Trap	Ketchikan, AK
	Fri–Mon Aug 20–23	Ketchikan, AK (Aug 20–21 speaking at theatre), Skowl Arm and Ketchikan, AK	
	Mid-Sept	Skowl Arm, AK, aboard cannery tender *Una Mae*, bound for Anacortes, WA, with father, Captain Ray Lowman	

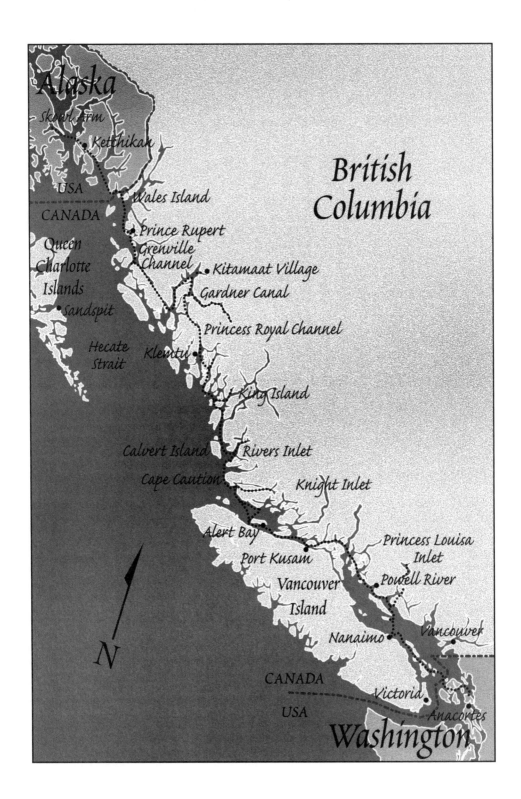

Alaska

Skowl Arm
Ketchikan

USA
CANADA

Wales Island

Prince Rupert
Grenville
Channel

British
Columbia

Queen
Charlotte
Islands

Sandspit

Kitamaat Village

Gardner Canal

Princess Royal Channel

Hecate
Strait

Klemtu

King Island

Calvert Island

Rivers Inlet

Cape Caution

Knight Inlet

Alert Bay

Port Kusam

Vancouver
Island

Princess Louisa
Inlet

Powell River

Nanaimo

Vancouver

CANADA

USA

Victoria

Anacortes

Washington

N

Rowing by Moonlight

As I rowed out of Garden Bay in *Bijaboji*, my little red dugout canoe, I realized that I was completely alone. There was no one to talk to, no one to help me if I got into trouble and no one who might need help from me. But I was free. At last, succeed or fail, I was on my own. The first 10 days of my trip had tested my self-confidence and proved to me that I had the necessary strength of body and mind to row every inch of the way to Ketchikan.

Malaspina Strait, where I had had such an unpleasant crossing just days ago, was now smooth as glass. In no time I crossed the mouth of Agamemnon Channel. The shores of Nelson Island loomed ahead, then receded in the twilight. Where on this island, I wondered, were the remains of the salmon cannery that my grandfather had owned before I was born? All I could see were rocks and trees.

Before I was across the wide mouth of Jervis Inlet, a huge mellow moon rose over the hills behind Pender Harbour and played in and out of the ragged clouds. When the moon was in hiding, I watched phosphorescent water drip from my oars, and gleaming lines spread from each side of the dugout's bow. When the moon shone forth in all its brilliance, the wide stretch of Malaspina Strait looked like crumpled cellophane over black satin. Resting sea birds grumbled noisily before reluctantly flying away from my intruding canoe.

Along the far shores of Texada Island, the running lights of trolling boats and tugs bobbed like a string of Japanese lanterns at a merry garden party. They were 10 or more miles away but the steady drone of the engines carried undistorted across the water. I was afraid to sing for fear they would hear and think I wanted help, but I hummed a favourite campfire song, "Mammy Moon," thinking, praying the words, "Please keep watch until the morning light..." I checked my progress by any mountain peak I was opposite and knew that whatever way the tide was moving, I wasn't standing still.

Finally the moon vanished behind a darkening cloud that grew and spread over half the bowl of the heavens. Every dip of my oars frightened dozens of sleeping salmon, which revealed their presence by leaving twisting phosphorescent trails in their wakes. Occasionally a fish leaped clear of the water and my heart missed a few beats, startled by the unexpected noise and the sparkling light.

At last, wearily, I nosed the canoe into a tiny cove where great granite boulders and stark gleaming tree trunks appeared as weird sentinels, protecting me while I rested. Hours later a wanton breeze, heralding sunrise, set the water in motion and the canoe rocked me into wakefulness. I rowed on, sniffing the salty air joyfully—as though I hadn't grown up with my lungs full of it. I was a happy child again, with a heady sense of freedom—freedom to think on my own and to test myself in a world where material possessions counted for nothing if you did not have brains, strength and ability.

CHAPTER 1

Bijaboji

I cannot conceal a pride of ownership of my cedar dugout,
any more than can the owner of the trimmest gleaming yacht
moored at the best club.

— Betty Lowman, *Pacific Motor Boat*, April 1938

IN 1931 THE CREW OF A COAST GUARD CUTTER found a dugout canoe in Juan de Fuca Strait, near my family's home in Anacortes. For more than a year the Coast Guardsmen endeavoured to locate the owner but with no luck. Perhaps it was predestined that my father should wangle the dugout as a present for me, a teenager and his only daughter, whom he had taught the joys of life on salt water. He placed the painter of the canoe in my hands on my 18th birthday, in July 1932, and said, "Now it is yours, and it is a masterpiece of workmanship. It is like a Grand Banks dory, perfect for survival on the open sea. Be sure that your seamanship takes nothing away from the seaworthiness of this Native canoe." I named the dugout *Bijaboji*, after my brothers Bill, Jack, Bob and Jimmy.

None of the local Natives recognized the style of this superbly crafted 13-foot 10-inch dugout that was equipped for rowing, paddling, trolling, towing or sailing. Empty, the canoe was too heavy for even two people to portage. It was handcrafted from one large log of straight-grained western red cedar; a lightweight wood easily worked or split and reasonably rot-resistant. Its beam had been sprung to 38 inches by steaming the thin wood and carefully wedging the sides apart. Bill, my oldest brother, strengthened *Bijaboji* with four oak ribs. He also nailed a copper strip to the bottom from stem to stern to seal

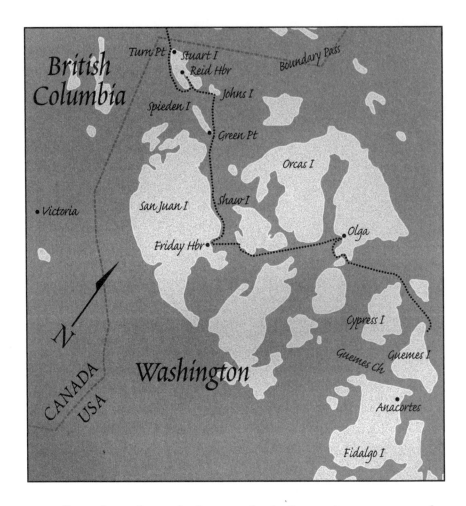

a small crack, and attached two oak chafing strips to protect the canoe from gravel and barnacles when it was dragged ashore. My pride of ownership grew every time I paused to look her over. Rage made a wild woman of me whenever I discovered that someone had used *Bijaboji* without my permission—permission rarely obtained by anyone other than my brothers.

The chill waters of Puget Sound were a playground for my four brothers and me. We enjoyed many exciting summers camped on various of the San Juan Islands while Daddy tended salmon traps that he and Grandfather owned. I was 10 years old, and Bill a year younger, when Mother first told us to row the skiff from our camp

Betty and Bijaboji *in a rare moment of rest.*

at McCracken Point on Henry Island to Roche Harbor for supplies, two miles distant. Throughout my childhood I absorbed knowledge of how to take advantage of tides and back eddies, to use kelp beds for anchorage, where and how to catch wind or not to catch it while rowing, and countless other things that rest in my subconscious. At age 14 I first made the one-mile swim from Anacortes to Guemes Island, where the velocity of bone-chilling currents in Guemes Channel sometimes exceeds five knots. I repeated the swim numerous times after that, during all seasons.

After high school graduation I decided that I was going to row *Bijaboji* up the Inside Passage from Anacortes to Ketchikan, where my father fished for salmon in the summer months. I chose to row rather than paddle *Bijaboji*. A dugout is heavy and responds quickly and positively when oars are used to pull or push—a necessity in rough water. I could face my destination and oncoming waves, or turn around and watch a following sea. I could change course quickly by pulling one oar forward and pushing the other aft, like a boat with two propellers, and oars would be useful in stabilizing the dugout, like instant outriggers.

I had no doubt I'd be able to complete the trip. Daddy, familiar with the Inside Passage, calculated that 10 miles was the greatest distance I'd have to swim in case of mishap. So I swam the 10 miles from Anacortes to Cypress Island through changing tides in water chilled by snowmelt from Mount Baker, while he accompanied me in a rowboat. Even as he helped me prepare myself, he warned me that I had better forget about my plans—he would never let me try such a dangerous journey. But in 1937, after I had completed four years of university, another of his "hope-you'll-forget-it" requirements, I was still determined. I had spent innumerable pleasant hours studying nautical charts and pilot books, planning routes and mail stops, estimating miles per day and tossing in a storm delay factor, and had calculated that I would need 55 days to reach Skowl Arm.

I firmly believed that the hazards of navigating the Inside Passage in *Bijaboji* were negligible. I was strong, and I knew full well what it is to live by the tides and wind; to be lost in fogs, to be caught in countercurrents or perilous tide rips, and of the rapidity with which sunny days can curdle, and serene, friendly seas can change to treacherous enemies. For years I'd practised oar techniques that transform rowing a dugout from drudgery into fun.

At the end of my last year of university I had met Flo, a physical education student who was excited about my plans, and on the spur of the moment I invited her to come with me. We spent the first few weeks of summer quietly making plans for our vacation. For extra comfort and safety we spent $7.45 of our money (about $20 total) on a zippered, kapok-filled sleeping bag that could also be used as a life preserver. Anacortes friends gave me a new set of wide-blade hardwood oars and a good Scout hatchet and hunting knife. We borrowed an old army cooking kit, rain clothes and a canvas tent. For evening warmth I had a pair of dark ski pants. Almost all of our gear was the type we would take on a weekend jaunt, except for an Argus Model A (known as a "candid camera"), writing materials and extra sport clothes.

Flo and I eagerly looked forward to a stimulating and healthy life outdoors, and envisioned adventures, new friendships and the possibility of surprising our university journalism professors by selling an article or two. My father had already left for Skowl Arm by the time we were ready to go. I asked my mother to promise not to write to him and tell him that his daughter was about to go on the adventure he had forbidden. We told anyone who asked that we were going on a two-month camping trip through the islands. To avoid publicity we chose the sparsely settled Guemes Island as our departure point.

On Tuesday, June 15, 1937, Flo and I lifted *Bijaboji* off the seawall, set it on the agate-speckled shoreline of the north beach on Guemes Island, and quickly loaded our supplies and camping gear. Mother, Aunt Nell and a few close friends watched us while chatting nervously. We hurried to be underway and get the full benefit of the falling tide that would carry us westward across Bellingham Channel. With this change of tide the Scotch mist became a chill drizzle. Mother made her final plea to dissuade me from going. I'm sure she knew it was futile, but she had to try. Aunt Nell chose this golden moment to tell me again how senseless and foolhardy I was to attempt so long a journey in so small a craft. However, she did give me one bit of vital advice: "Be sure to clear through Canadian customs in Nanaimo." I hadn't even thought about customs and immigration. Just as I was about to thank her, she killed the thought by adding, "If you're lucky enough to get that far." We stowed the last piece of camping equipment, remembering that "last in is first out," then hooked the shiny, waterproof black Fabrikoid (artificial leather) covering over the bow. Flo hastily patted the folded tent and clothes bag into a comfortable overstuffed seat and backrest before agilely stepping over the bow and into her place at the stern.

Wearing only tennis shorts, shirt, sou'wester and a red silk bow tie that matched *Bijaboji*, I waded alongside the dugout and pulled it into knee-deep water. I swung the bow toward Orcas Island, climbed over the black gunwale and settled onto the rower's comfortable fitted seat. Then, gripping the new broad-blade ash oars—they had a reassuring feel—I leaned forward to take the first stroke.

We were underway at last. Flo and I waved spasmodically until the rain and my tears obscured Mother's misted dark brown hair and bravely smiling face. Flo said little until we were nearly across calm Bellingham Channel. She too must have been dwelling on thoughts of home and loved ones, especially her mother in Madison, South Dakota, perhaps anxious about a lengthy canoe trip for which only she knew how inadequately prepared she was.

A small pod of harbour porpoises leaped and splashed a few hundred feet offshore of Cypress Island, searching for food near the gently undulating kelp bed. While winding among the five Cone Islands, we sighted pigeon guillemots drifting in pairs, silent and content, apparently enjoying the rain. Cormorants perched at attention, alone or in groups, as they crewed drifting logs. With our sou'westers on, it was easier to look at sea life than to look upward at the small fir trees maintaining precarious footholds in the shallow soil of the stubby, cone-shaped islets. Smooth, reddish-barked madrona trees, grotesquely twisted, leaned precariously over the rain-speckled water. We skimmed between small, round Towhead Island and the northern end of Cypress Island before nosing through a bed of slippery bullwhip kelp and into Rosario Strait.

The tide was flowing with us and helped considerably through narrow Obstruction Pass between Orcas and Obstruction islands. A curious seal surfaced nearby. Flo and I whistled in harmony, which seemed to attract him. Each time he poked his head up he was nearer. We named him Christopher and had faint hopes of taming him.

At Olga, a summer resort on Orcas Island, we sent our first postcards home. We studied the big chart tacked to the wall of the community store and asked about tides, though we were well equipped with large-scale charts trimmed to notebook size, and the June–July–August pages from a tide table book that a solicitous tugboat captain had ripped out and given us. I had wondered at Flo's interest in the chart until I noticed that a half box of strawberries in the crate under it had been surreptitiously consumed.

Flo decided that her sweater would be better tucked into her khaki trousers so she wandered across to the hotel's rest room. I heard her shout for help. Rushing in, I found that her khaki trousers had slipped over her hips when she unfastened the belt and she couldn't pull them up. No wonder! Her belt was weighed down by a hatchet, a flashlight, two hunting knives, a ball of tarred twine, a watch, first aid supplies—and a .22 pistol, which she hadn't mentioned to me when we packed. We had a good quarter-hour's tugging and squirming before her trousers were inched into place. For the first time it occurred to me that Flo might not be able to swim if she fell off the dock or tipped out of the dugout.

The water was glassy calm when we skirted the ragged, wooded shores of Orcas Island. Even the seabirds were resting. Gradually the fir and madrona trees lost their individuality of form and colour and became a jigsawed silhouette against the darkening sky. Time to make camp. I thrust *Bijaboji* through the wavelets and nudged onto Shaw Island.

"We've made about 20 miles," I said happily. "Only 630 more to go—if we don't make any side trips."

The temperature dropped with the setting sun and I began to shiver. A southeast wind whipped and bent the tall weeds before me as I plowed through the dense, damp brush to the farmhouse to ask permission to make a fire and put up our tent for the night. A black spaniel rushed at my shins, yapping threateningly until a man ordered him to be still.

"You'd better take your boat into the cove over there." He pointed across a short projection of land. "You can't make a fire without a permit and I doubt if you have one. But if you want to run the risk of arrest, I won't say anything. There's good water at the well."

It was nearly high water and we had no trouble hauling the loaded dugout up the gravel beach and across a couple of drift logs. Dusk was fast overtaking us. Again it began to sprinkle. Flo hurried with supper while I cleared a place for the tent. It was a joy to cut the waist-tall brush with my sharp hatchet. With our tent erected and tied securely with tarred fishing cord, and my sleeping bag and Flo's Scout blanket roll in place, I slithered onto the beach to enjoy the warmth of Flo's fire. We ate ravenously, filling up on tasty bacon and eggs while looking at the lights of Friday Harbor four miles distant. Steam rose from our woollen socks as they dried before the glowing coals. I had not succeeded in getting the well's creaky pump to function so resorted to our emergency water supply in a large thermos. We washed our mess kits in the chill salt water.

"This is just the fun experience I expected a canoe trip to be," Flo said before we crawled into the tent, "in spite of a little rain."

Squirming into our sleeping gear, trying to get settled on our bed of ferns and leaves, we talked long and loud—loud because of the restless swishing of swaying fir boughs on the canvas tent and splashing wavelets washing the beach. We talked about the days of fun to come when it stopped raining and imagined the people we might meet, and we envisioned our rendezvous in Nanaimo with our Seattle friends, who were crewing the *Tyee Scout*, a boat full of Boy Scouts on a summer sea adventure.

The next morning, after a filling breakfast of fresh fruit, we broke camp. The tide was out, so I showed Flo how to place small, round driftwood pieces under the heavy dugout and roll it to the water's edge. The dull grey water was unruffled and *Bijaboji* surged forward yards and yards with every pull of my strong scarlet oars.

Thick mist soon obscured the rocky coves and beaches of Shaw Island. Flo watched uneasily as rain and low streaks of fog moved rapidly toward us from Juan de Fuca Strait. I assured her this was normal summer weather in Puget Sound and began to think that I should have asked her some questions instead of just assuming that a phys-ed major would be able to do anything out of doors.

We pushed on toward the summer resort at Kwan Lamah, on the edge of Friday Harbor. Minutes before we could get there, we were caught in a deluge and only too glad to make the canoe fast to the float and dash for the lodge. I held Flo back just long enough to point out "Cooky Can," a cottage on pilings that had once sheltered Louise Williams, an artist, and me on a weekend canoe trip.

In the lodge's warm and spacious kitchen, a young German girl was carefully mounting bright pictures on stiff cardboard to decorate the walls of the cottages along the shore. She explained that there were no guests on account of the ferryboat strike, so she kept busy doing little jobs to make the place more attractive.

Flo stretched her wool jacket over a chair near the hot cooking range, where it soon began to steam. She warmed her cold, wet legs beside the range, turning forward and back many times. I headed off to the store to get supplies and talk to the store owner, Mr. Carter, about using his family's cabin on Johns Island.

At the store Mr. Carter's son sketched a map of Johns Island on a piece of brown wrapping paper, marking the cabin's location and describing the small gravel beach. The cabin had been built years earlier for any yachting, hunting or camping party needing its shelter. A spring, some distance away, provided pure drinking water. Sloshing back to Kwan Lamah, I contemplated how lovely it was to walk under those stately fir trees, even when they were sodden and dripping.

Soon after we set out for Johns Island the wind rose rapidly and visibility decreased. The channel between San Juan and Spieden islands was uncomfortably rough and we soon became chilled by the mixture of pelting rain and flying salt water. The waves built as we neared the middle of Spieden Channel. Whitecaps and flying scud surrounded us. The dugout pitched and rolled, and breaking waves sloshed aboard. Wind and tide pushed us toward the rocks. "It's better to go on than to turn back," I said, attempting to reassure Flo. The canoe rolled heavily; my oar missed a wave and fanned the air. That threw us off course and a big wave leaped over the gunwale. Flo bailed, tossing water over one side and then the other while I struggled to hold the canoe off Green Point, the eastern end of Spieden Island, where wind and tide fought, creating nasty breakers. Touching the rocks would mean a sure upset, probably a serious bashing. Possibly an ignominious end to our trip. Beyond the point, the sea was a little quieter. Flo's bailing can splashed cold water up the legs of my slacks as I propped my feet on the gunwale to give her room to bail.

As we emerged from a narrow pass between the Cactus Islands we saw our friend, Christopher the seal—at least it looked like Christopher—cavorting with a couple of pals. Flo shouted familiarly to Chris and the three became strangely subdued, staring solemnly at us.

The water was alive with whitecaps between us and the cabin on Johns Island. The wind was rising fast and the rain felt unusually wet and cold. But on we went, bouncing and bailing, until we thrust through the low surf to beach on the gravelly shore of the island.

It didn't take long to find the cozy log cabin, snuggled under dripping fir trees: a safe harbour for two sailorettes, even better than friends had led me to expect. Flo built a cheery fire and heated water and beans while I hauled the canoe high above the noisy, splashing surf, then lugged our clothes and sleeping gear into the living room. We'd start out dry in the morning.

Flo crawled into her sleeping bag on the double bedsprings thickly padded with dry bracken, while I caught up on our ship's log by the light of the fire. Our clothes were drying on the metal beside the fireplace. "Sing!" Flo ordered, and I sang everything from Wagner's *Lohengrin* to "Winter Wonderland." Singing is easy when one is happy in her element, and the sounds of roaring rain and moaning wind disguised any vocal shortcomings. In the morning Flo found that the

Betty Annette Lowman, University of Washington graduate, 1937. She sang Wagnerian opera, played tennis and worked as a newspaper reporter and columnist before leaving on her trip.

gentle firelight had been deceptive—all our clothes were scorched. Then she burned our breakfast of stewed apricots to charcoal on the hot bricks and we laughed at our inexperience.

A strong southeaster bent the small firs nearly double before releasing them, only to bend them again with each successive gust. The sky was dark and foreboding. All day whitecaps raced toward Stuart Island and smashed against the shoreline. Heading out wasn't even mentioned. We made ourselves cozy in the friendly cabin, writing postcards, singing, reading old magazines, relaxing, and taking inventory of our things.

Our inventory included everything from my heavy dugout to Flo's smallest bobby pins. My costume was comfortably scant and I contributed little to the list. Hunting and Scout knives were attached to the belt of my wool ski trousers and a metal waterproof container of matches was in the button-down pocket. On Flo's belt and in the pockets of her khaki outfit we found nearly 200 items: hatchet, knives, cord, iodine, salt, notebooks, pistol, sunglasses, watch, tide chart, strings of safety pins—and bandages, for Flo's smallpox vaccination. She had read of the devastating smallpox epidemic that had killed so many Natives on the coast, and although it had ended decades ago, she didn't want to take any chances. Four days before we departed she'd had the vaccination. I worried that the inoculation would make her sick and delay our trip, but she assured me that she would be fine.

While Flo caught up on her notes I scouted through the woods in hope of finding the spring, wandering farther and farther from the cabin until I knew our half of the island quite well. I was admiring the view from a cliff above Sunset Cove when the bleating of a stray sheep startled me. I turned, and my foot slipped on the wet grass along the cliff's edge. Instinctively I grabbed the wrist-sized trunk of a stunted, wind-deformed tree. Fortunately its roots were firmly anchored in a soil-filled crevice in the rock. I clenched the wood with both hands and searched the rough rock face. Finally I located a short projection and got the toe of my right foot on it. Pulling and thrusting upward, I reached a sturdy bush, then another, until I was again on top of the cliff. With a prayer of thanks, I headed back to the cabin.

That moment of hanging precariously over the rocks made me realize, as nothing else could, the great responsibility Flo and I had to each other not to take chances and always to inform each other of our intended whereabouts.

Talking it over in front of the fireplace, we agreed that as soon as possible we'd each get and always carry a police whistle. Flo suggested that she practise with the oars on every calm day. I agreed, realizing I had been derelict in this important training. Flo was not the rowing, distance-swimming phys-ed major that I had imagined. She was handy with a canoe paddle and could always go for help, but propelling the dugout with a paddle is much slower, more difficult and tiring than with oars.

We carried loads and loads of wood up from the beach so future visitors might find a ready supply of dry firewood. The cabin was swept and scrubbed. Then we cleared the path of weeds and fallen branches.

Our chief hope of earning something from the trip was to write instructive articles for young people's publications. Until darkness and exhaustion made us quit, we read the Boy Scout and Campfire Girl manuals to each other, absorbing what knowledge of campcraft and woodcraft we didn't already have.

The next day we were still stormbound in that cabin, less than 30 miles from Anacortes. Flo was now frequently and apprehensively checking her vaccination scratches. She had to admit that she'd been mistaken — the vaccination was inflamed and painful. We decided the best thing to do was to get to Nanaimo straightaway, where she might suffer the worst phase of the "take" in a clean, warm hotel room and have the reassurance of a doctor.

The next afternoon the storm finally abated, and as soon as the tide turned we loaded up, hooked the Fabrikoid covering over our equipment and pushed off for Stuart Island. The sun was blinding but the day was surprisingly cool. Flo dragged her toothbrush in the salt water, scrubbing her teeth vigorously whenever steering didn't require all of her attention. Throughout the entire trip I kept my toothbrush in a groove by the oarlock and am lucky not to have scrubbed the enamel off every tooth. It seemed a shame not to take advantage of the handy and refreshing mouthwash five or six times a day.

The shell-whitened sand gave the shallow water of landlocked Reid Harbor a grey-green colour. There were no ripples on the surface and no sign of life around the houses along the shore. As we neared the mooring floats a Native man poked his head out of a boat cabin. I had been told that my canoe might have been made in Reid Harbor, so I asked him whether he had ever seen a dugout like this.

He didn't even take a good look. "No," he said.

His heavy brown and white wool sweater with its Native symbols and skilled knitting intrigued me. I asked where such sweaters were made. "My wife made it," he stated proudly before briskly withdrawing into his boat.

Crossing the Canada–US boundary was our goal for the day but the wind hadn't fully abated along the exposed shoreline and our progress was exasperatingly slow. Finally, several miles short of the boundary, we were forced to make camp on Stuart Island's inhospitable rocky beach, a mile south of Turn Point light.

We chose the clean gravel under the sun-bleached roots of an upturned tree for our sleeping place. Flo cut armfuls of bracken from the hillside, showering them onto me while I was busy throwing the bigger rocks out of our bed. On the beach we found two short boards and made a rough trough to run water into our containers from a dribbling spring. Our tasty supper was cooked in a natural wood fireplace that we kept from burning by sousing its sides with salt water carried in an old beachcombed nail keg. Until dark we scrambled through salal, blackberry vines and underbrush on the steep slope, exploring this uninhabited part of the island.

C H A P T E R   2

Ship's Master

I have always said that if I were a man, I would — someday — be a
ship's captain. Well, there I became in a second an honest-to-goodness
master mariner. On paper, at least. I liked the sound of it — Captain
Betty Lowman. Barnacle Betty.

— Betty Lowman, *Alaska Life*, January 1940

THE STRAITS WERE GLASSY THE NEXT MORNING. With a favourable tide we soon reached the farthest point of Stuart Island and looked across the calm water to British Columbia. Flo skillfully steered us through the crosscurrents and mild tide rips off Turn Point. We were well on our way to Moresby Island and Canada, on the northwest side of Boundary Pass.

Crossing what we thought must be the international boundary, we thought a ceremony or celebration might be in order. We ended up splashing each other with a bit of cold salt water in Swanson Channel. Canada! We were finally in a foreign country and now definitely on our way to Alaska. As we crossed the long, open stretch of Swanson Channel to Saltspring Island, we trolled for salmon, hailed men on small tugs and waved at ferryboat passengers.

The day was bleak and I promised Flo we would stop for the night at the likeliest camping spot on the east shore of Saltspring Island. We saw no good camping beaches after rounding Nose Point, only unfriendly No Trespassing signs. Fine pinpoints of rain stung my cheeks and obscured the trees ahead. I held close to the rock shore for miles, but the overhanging trees gave scant shelter. It seemed as though the east side of Saltspring Island was a mammoth moss-covered wall

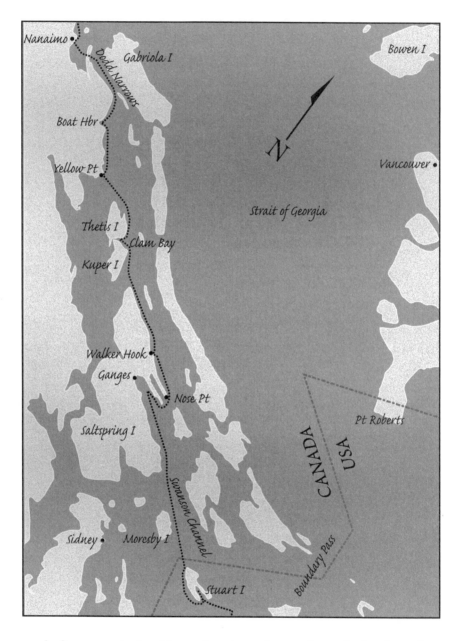

made from square boulders of various size, each perfectly shaped as if cut to build the pyramids. Brilliant blue and green sea anemones and other interesting marine life lurked in the numerous cracks and crannies below the tidemark.

The drizzle was blinding, and we were nearly alongside a couple of loggers before we saw them, labouring on a sandy spit. I ran *Bijaboji* ashore. Flo chatted with the loggers while I walked to a farmhouse on the other side of an apple orchard to ask if we might sleep in the barn that night.

A smiling, hunched-over Scots lady urged me to come in and dry out by her smoke-stained fireplace, heaped with ashes and a small fire. I ran back for Flo. While we were introducing ourselves the lady's bachelor brother entered, carrying an apple box loaded with their week's supply of groceries from the store at Ganges.

Flo and I were charmed by their old-world simplicity, and fascinated to see hot tea steeped over coals scraped onto the hearth. The brother insisted that Flo and I put on huge boots and thick rubber capes and follow him about in the muddy flower garden. He had giant pansies, roses, foxglove and innumerable other lovely flowers. He discussed them at length until a black Model T Ford rattled along and stopped at the gate.

The passengers were the loggers who had been working on the beach. Their wives were with them, and the driver called out: "We're going home for the weekend, on the other side of the island. You girls are welcome to use our tent tonight." In the warm kitchen we enjoyed cheese and bread and home-canned fruit with the congenial Scots couple. The man quizzed us relentlessly about American religion, finance and crime control, and the social problems of industry. We marvelled at the depth of his knowledge, obviously gained from newspapers and magazines. It sorely tested our educations and revealed our ignorance of the world away from the University of Washington campus.

The tent was set over a dry platform, just beyond the seaward side of the farmer's orchard. A small metal stove and plenty of firewood were inside a cedar shake lean-to connected to the tent. We piled the bedding off one bunk and onto the other. While water heated for a wash-up, we spread our bedrolls side by side on the higher bunk.

The next morning we looked out through sheets of water. Flo was wretchedly unhappy. Her vaccination had taken — painfully.

"I'll make Nanaimo today, Flo, or bust trying," I told her, "if you can only hold out till we get to the hotel."

Flo insisted upon cooking a big breakfast, enough for any hard-working seafarer, while I rolled and hauled the dugout over the mud and sand. We ate heartily and were somewhat cheered. The rain ceased just as the Scots farmer appeared and pushed us off. By the time Walker Hook was a half-mile astern, the sun was bright and the day so warm that we had to shed our rain clothes. Except for Flo's dizziness and pain, we were having a wonderful day. The tide was with us and a stiff following breeze hurried us toward Nanaimo. Curling sideways in the stern of the canoe as best she could and with her knees bent over the crossbar, Flo slept.

Off Kuper Island the sea was agitated and we had a rough half-mile. Flo awoke, soaked by the chill salt water that sloshed around our feet. Without a word of complaint she commenced to bail. Natives on the beach below a hillside village looked up from their clam digging to watch us. I was proud of the way *Bijaboji* weathered the cross-chop off that shallow spit of sand, and wished we could beach and ask the Natives where my canoe might have come from. Instead we rowed into nearby Clam Bay, where two tugboats were anchored. We eased alongside the larger, a snub-nosed green and orange vessel whose bow, sides and stern were festooned with bumpers made of old truck tires, and inquired about the tides in Dodd Narrows.

The skipper invited us aboard. The tires made it easy to climb onto the main deck. Pictures of the skipper's handsome wife and children were prominently displayed in his cabin. A glance at the mirror revealed that my sunburned face was as crimson as my silk bow tie. Even a soapy scrub and rinse scarcely dulled the lobster red. Then we had a seaman's hearty lunch in the galley, where the cook hovered over our shoulders, continually refilling our thick white mugs with sweet tea. In the pilothouse the knowledgeable skipper went over the charts, described the narrows and explained how to take advantage of back eddies to get through an hour before slack water.

When we were ready to go again, I found that one of the men had spliced a new and longer painter into *Bijaboji*'s bow. Another crewman had dried my sweatshirt in the engine room. Such kindness! We scarcely knew how to thank these considerate seafarers.

Thetis Island was soon behind us. Yellow Point on Vancouver Island lay ahead. Flo slept again while we passed the low, ragged coast north of Yellow Point. She awoke when we entered the stubby, tree-lined passage to Boat Harbour. The water was a rich uniform green—green as the gushing stream at the far end. Trees of a darker shade overhung the steep banks, and ferns luxuriating from the water's edge to the height of the hills more nearly matched the water. We idled there, resting for a regenerating half-hour before returning to the main channel.

Flo let out our trolling line. We were infinitely surprised just south of Dodd Narrows when a fish grabbed onto the plug and Flo pulled up a lively six-pound lingcod. She had it half over the gunwale when we realized that neither of us had the cold-blooded nerve to whack it on the head, so she yanked it aboard very much alive. The fish flipped and flopped around our legs on the curved and crowded bottom of the canoe. I foolishly rose to strike it with the butt of an oar and nearly brought our vacation to an ignominious conclusion when the fish cast the plug and one of the treble hooks snagged my leg. *Fish catches girl on Heddon plug*—I could almost see the picture and caption.

A couple ashore hailed us. "Come ashore before you tip over!" They insisted we eat with them in their quaint beach wood-shanty. The man skillfully cleaned the cod and within minutes the fish was sizzling on the coals under their campfire grate, and my leg stung from the iodine his wife had liberally swabbed on.

We passed through Dodd Narrows just before dark. I continued rowing, entranced by Flo's stories about her brothers and sisters. I laughed until I could hardly row when she confessed her unrequited love for the high school orchestra leader, and the panic of her first public recital. When it started to rain again, Flo encouraged me to stroke like my friend Don Hume, gold medalist in the Olympics at Berlin the year before and rowing champion from the University of Washington. I tried, but my stiffening fingers were a definite handicap. Flo coxswained wonderfully and shortly there was only a skinny strip of land between us and the lights of Nanaimo. "Oh, why isn't the dugout light enough to portage across?" I moaned. Going around the point would mean at least another exhausting hour in rain and dark.

Just then we came upon a ditch blasted through the middle of that long, thin peninsula. By using the oars to shove against the rock sides of this narrow channel we sped through, then across to the busy waterfront where a freighter was loading Nanaimo coal. Men in shiny black slickers bustled about. Reflections of high-mounted electric lamps danced across the rain-ruffled water.

Shortly after nine o'clock on Sunday night, June 20, we landed alongside a float below the Malaspina Hotel. We were thoroughly drenched and weary. We thanked the tugboat men who helped pull heavy *Bijaboji* onto the float and cover her, then rushed to the hotel, in such a hurry to enjoy the warmth and comfort of a hotel room that we didn't stop to report to the customs and immigration officers.

We entered the Malaspina's lobby without removing our dripping sou'westers and registered, unable to convince the desk clerk that we weren't young men. Our room faced the harbour, but we didn't take in the view that night. Flo's vaccination was making her miserable and she immediately ran a hot tub. I cleaned my face with cold cream and flopped, exhausted, into the springy double bed.

"It will be great fun to be towed to Princess Louisa Inlet for a side trip, won't it, Flo?" I called out, relaxing my tired muscles and luxuriating in the comfort of a bed, while anticipating an easy day or two.

"Are you sure the *Tyee Scout* will be here?"

"Sure." I had coordinated our schedule to be there when they arrived, in case we needed a tow across the Strait of Georgia. I had also expected to arrive two days earlier so we'd have plenty of time to write our articles and send them to the syndicates. I couldn't wait to see the Scouts—it seemed ages since I had seen anyone I knew.

In my sleep that night I rowed the dugout miles and miles and miles and couldn't unclench my hands from the oars or protect my face from the fiery sun.

Flo was still asleep Monday morning when some impulse made me spring out of bed and dash to the window. The first thing I saw was

Tyee Scout leaving the harbour, the boys bobbing about the deck wearing their distinctive white sailor hats. A dozen things to do exploded in my mind. I couldn't run to the wharf in my pajamas, but I could scream and wave my arms. I could wave the scarlet pajama top. I could flap the window blind. Maybe it wasn't the *Tyee Scout* at all. Maybe it was a runaway imagination that made me hear a boy holler, "Hey, Cap'n Art!"

The best thing was to hurry to the customs office to check in and inquire there. The only decent clothes Flo and I had between us were my new wool ski trousers and Flo's blue sweater. I put them on and dashed to the office. I was expected. "Your friend Captain Church told me you planned to meet here," the customs officer said with a smile when I introduced myself. "He and the boys waited overnight anticipating your arrival. They just pulled out. Said they couldn't wait any longer. But he did leave some packages for you." Now the smile disappeared. "Also, it's serious not to report immediately to the customs and immigration officers upon entering a foreign port. You see the problem that created for you?" His voice became almost fatherly as he added, "Now, just run down to the floats. Somebody may be able to stop them."

I ran from float to float and talked to many boatmen, but I got no encouragement because the Scout boat had no radiophone. Dejected, I walked to the post office; perhaps I'd fare better there. Indeed, there was a letter from Uncle Robin and a Canadian 10-dollar bill. Suddenly I realized we had registered at Nanaimo's swankiest hotel—probably without enough money to pay. When I went back to the customs office, the kind officer gave me the packages left for us by *Tyee Scout*. We then started the process of clearing customs and immigration. I don't recall how many forms and papers covered his desk, but there were just as many as for a large yacht. "Nationality? Destination?" I suspected he already knew those answers, having talked with Art Church, but wanted to hear it from me.

"Name, type and length of craft?"

"*Bijaboji*. Indian dugout canoe. Thirteen feet, 10 inches."

He raised his eyebrows and gazed at me for a moment. "Don't believe I'll come aboard to inspect." His eyes twinkled. "How long do you expect to stay?"

I wasn't sure about that. We had been out only five days and already we were two days behind schedule. A quick guess. "It might take me two months to get to Alaska."

"Alaska! In a little dugout?"

"Yes. The Natives used dugouts all along this coast for centuries. I've seen families land on the beach at Anacortes and read about other Indian trips." The insinuation that *Bijaboji* wasn't as seaworthy as any craft in the harbour hurt me. "I was raised in the islands of Puget Sound and I've used rowboats all my life. I've always worked and trained for a life at sea and I can swim at least 10 miles in the salt water. That's enough to get ashore in case of any problem."

For a moment he just stared at me. "Crew or passengers?"

"One crew member. Florence Steele."

"Cargo or goods being brought into Canada?"

"Camping equipment, some food, a few clothes, a fishing line and lure, and Flo's pistol."

The easy, routine atmosphere changed.

"It's a criminal offence to carry any kind of concealed weapon in Canada," the officer stated sternly. "Now, Miss Lowman, you get that weapon and bring it here." Back in our hotel room I took a moment to change clothes and open my packages. In the larger was my leather jacket, which I had obtained in a successful trade with one of my brothers, then forgotten in the excitement of leaving, plus raincoats, paper towels and all sorts of things Mother had thought we might need. The smaller package contained a small camera with cloud filter, zippered case, films and a letter from Roy Bucknell, a camera fanatic at Harborview Hospital in Seattle. The letter was a masterpiece of instruction and encouragement for the trip. Roy had completed plans for the same sort of vacation but been thwarted by ill health.

I changed into our "street clothes" and returned to the customs office with the pistol. There I explained that Flo's brother, a Seattle policeman, had insisted that she take it along for protection. Carefully I placed the .22 and a box of cartridges on the desk. The second officer inspected it with easy familiarity. "Any police officer in Washington should have known handguns are not allowed on this side of the

Betty and her 13-foot, 10-inch-long dugout Bijaboji, *ready to go.*

border," he said, "and obviously he didn't expect you to stop a bear with something this small."

Time seemed to stop while the two officers stared at me, at the pistol, and again at me. Finally they engaged in a short discussion of what sort of permit to give two female canoeists who wished to linger in Canadian waters for two months. They finally gave me the only thing possible — a yachting permit, listing ship's stores as cargo. I nearly burst with pride when I saw my name entered as Ship's Master, and that my 13-foot, 10-inch dugout was classed the same as all those magnificent yachts with varnished woodwork and polished metal fittings, rocking gently at their moorings in the harbour.

I was much less pleased to see that I was recorded as ballast.

"Keep these papers safe and turn them in at the customs and immigration office when you leave Canada," the officer said.

One of the inspectors was carefully swathing Flo's pistol in red tape and dominion seals. That is when I learned the origin of the expression "government red tape." While I was watching, a barefooted young man entered the office. He wore a large belted raincoat and began asking me questions. I suspected he was a reporter and answered ungraciously. I didn't want Daddy to find out that I had disobeyed him until I arrived, and certainly not to find out in the newspaper. But when the man admitted that he was a reporter, I relented. I explained that Flo and I were out for a vacation. "If you tell about us in the papers, it will make us seem like a couple of crazy stunters." He wrote a short and friendly item that appeared on the front page of the *Nanaimo Free Press*, and I decided to hope for the best.

Finally the customs officer handed me the tape-shrouded pistol. "If you need to use this weapon, just unwrap it, but be prepared to satisfactorily explain the circumstances."

"Yes, sir," I replied, eyeing the wad of tape. If we ever need it, I thought, Flo had better just throw it at our attacker for we'll never get it unwrapped.

Flo called on the doctor while I was clearing customs and she was still away when I returned. Alone in the hotel, I enjoyed a luscious cry over Roy's grand, bossy letter and the camera that my family had asked him to send as my birthday present. Flo returned about mid-morning with food and the doctor's report: "A beautiful take, but don't get out in the cold or rain any more than you can help," she quoted him. "He was young and handsome and charged me only a dollar."

So far we had been blessed with very good luck. I slipped into my leather jacket and set out to find a marine hardware store.

With a spare set of 35-cent oarlocks and a copy of *Sailing Directions for British Columbia, Volume II*, bought for two dollars, I returned to the hotel, washed a stack of clothes stained by our Fabrikoid clothes case and sent them down to the drying room. Then I splashed into the steaming bathtub. The hot water hurt my sunburn, but relaxed my stiff hands and lame shoulders. It was a choice place to make plans—which I had to make, because Flo was obsessed with the idea that she was "a drag, a dampener of spirits, a weakling sister." I hoped her mood might change as the vaccination became less painful. Meanwhile, having missed the *Tyee Scout*, I would have to row across the Strait of Georgia and catch them somewhere in Jervis Inlet. I was not delighted.

Out of the tub, I found that Flo had donned our street clothes and disappeared. So I wrote up our trip for the several syndicates that our dean at the university had recommended to us. Then I wrote notes to Mother and to Roy Bucknell and his wife Dubs, a college mate during my three years at Pomona College.

Flo rushed in, nearly breathless. "If we get down to the float right away, a man will tow us to Lasqueti Island. Maybe we'll catch up with the Scout boat and they'll take me back to Seattle."

"Back to Seattle! Don't joke, Flo!"

My better judgment told me to keep Flo in the hotel one more night while I rowed across the Strait of Georgia. But we couldn't afford it, and my hands were still too stiff to handle the oars properly, and I thought that if we caught up with the Boy Scouts they might rekindle Flo's enthusiasm for the trip. I decided to get a tow across the strait.

CHAPTER 3

Aquaplaning in Agamemnon Channel

The fair navigators average about 20 miles per day and make a keen study of the tides and winds to aid them in their trip. Yesterday Miss Lowman caught her first fish, a lingcod, which was enjoyed by the "crew" for supper.

—Nanaimo Free Press, June 1937

WE TOSSED EVERYTHING TOGETHER HASTILY and lugged it to the canoe, and within minutes my red dugout was being dragged ignominiously behind a gas boat. I'd learned that *Bijaboji* wouldn't tow on the end of a rope without lunging radically to the right or left and finally swamping. So I sat in the stern, steering with a paddle when necessary and ready to balance her against any sideswiping waves. Flo huddled miserably in the boat's shallow cockpit, out of the chilling wind.

One can't easily turn when wedged into the stern of the canoe so I didn't get a final look at Nanaimo, brightened by the sun shining intermittently from behind windblown grey-streaked clouds. But I enjoyed the sight of the wooded hills and Vancouver Island's rocky shoreline, and I could take the opportunity to catch up on our ship's log. Already I had nearly filled one notebook.

Several miles up the Vancouver Island coast we turned into well-protected Hammond Bay. The water was scarcely disturbed by the afternoon breeze and a dozen or so anchored trolling boats floated quietly. A few painted bungalows rimmed the head of this modest bay.

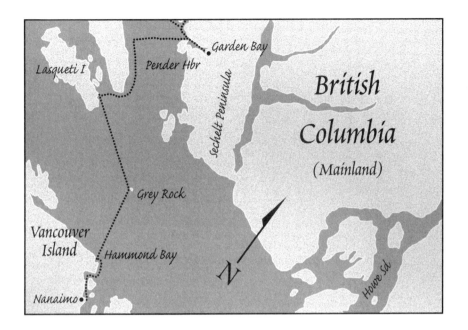

Doug, the man who was towing us, was a fish buyer, and he stopped at troller after troller, rousing the lone fisherman on each boat and buying freshly caught salmon. The fisherman would uncover the fish hold, drop in and, with a fish pugh (resembling a pitchfork with only one short, curved tine), catch each salmon in the gills or head and toss it up onto the deck, where the fish were separated by species. Then each species would be tossed across to the buying boat and put into a scoop hanging from industrial scales. The total weight of each species was recorded and a duplicate signed receipt given the fisherman, who could later collect cash or a cheque from the canning company.

One man rowed out in a flat-bottomed dugout from the beach-wood shanties perched on the rocks. I tried to be as flippant in chatting with him as I would with a college classmate, but as a man who had to fight the elements day and night to eke out a living, he couldn't joke—life was grimly serious.

We approached Grey Rock, small and bleak, where long-poled trolling boats circled slowly. I saw them as graceful water bugs, their sensitive feelers extended, manoeuvring curiously about a tempting but mysterious morsel. A deep gorge split Grey Rock, and silvery tidal

One of Betty's first stops was bustling Hammond Bay, near Nanaimo.
Rare Books and Special Collections, UBC Library, MacMillan Bloedel Ltd. Photograph Collection

water sloshed through, to and fro. Shacks built of rough boards clung on the shrubless crags just above the water's reach. Then, abruptly, Doug reversed his boat. Before I could grab an oar to hold *Bijaboji* out of the way, my slack bowline caught in the spinning propeller. It wound around the blades and *Bijaboji* plunged toward the rudder. I screamed. Fishermen shouted. The rope was hopelessly entangled.

"If you'll let the end go that's tied to your boat, I can dive under and untangle it," I yelled, but Doug cut the rope quickly with a butcher knife tied to a pike pole. So much for my new bowline! We crossed a long stretch of open water before stopping on the lee side of a small island. A tall grey-haired man had pitched a small tent just above the high-tide line. Nearby, four young men were living in a tent set on a flat portion of the grassy bank. All were hand trollers and had nearly two days' catch. Their regular buyer hadn't been around, and without ice or refrigeration they were anxious to sell their fish. Another fisherman in a clinker-built skiff rowed in with an excellent catch. A Native man and a small boy paddled alongside in a dugout loaded with their tent and few belongings. They didn't have salmon, but wanted a ride to the fish camp at Lasqueti Island. We departed with dugouts trailing from both port and starboard quarters, veering back and forth erratically, often coming dangerously close.

When I wasn't bailing, I sang lustily. The sun set and darkness engulfed us quickly. Rain and a boisterous wind lashed the Strait of Georgia into confused, white-crested waves. *Bijaboji* proudly rode the agitated water more easily than the gas boat. I discovered why my dugout often rode contentedly in water that made larger boats wallow uncomfortably. The dugout lifted buoyantly over the top of swells while faster boats usually plowed through them. Except for the welcoming lamplight of a fish camp scow—where fish were bought, groceries and gasoline sold—it was pitch dark when we entered the sheltered cove on the east side of Lasqueti Island. Eagerly we entered the small, warm store, where Doug introduced us to Bob, the soft-voiced storekeeper, and other fish buyers. He anticipated our anxiety about making camp in the dark, wet woods and offered us the only two bunks on the scow. We brought in our bedrolls gratefully while Bob rustled up a hot supper.

During the next few hours, fishermen crowded into the store, making too much noise for Flo and me to think of going to bed. I sat in a corner on a sack of rock salt, studying the instructions for my new camera and tinkering with its various gadgets. Alex, a young, blond, muscular fisherman, left his friends and came over to sit on a fruit crate beside me. He was kind, and his questions showed a genuine interest in our trip. Alex brought a chart from his boat and pointed out the coastline where I could use the tides to advantage in rowing from the fish camp to Pender Harbour. I had concluded that Pender Harbour would offer the best chance to catch the Scouts.

When only two young fish buyers and Bob lingered, Flo and I said goodnight and retired to our cramped bunkroom. The men remained on the other side of the thin partition—a partition with numerous knotholes—drinking beer, smoking and swapping stories until two o'clock. Finally Bob said, "The girls must find it hard to sleep with us gabbing here. We'd better get out."

When all was quiet I began to worry about the canoe. Had I tied it securely? Was it in a place where the trollers wouldn't smash it when they left before dawn? I crawled out of the upper bunk, crept past the counter and tried to open the wide door. It was bolted. I pushed, pulled and shoved but it was securely fastened. In our closet window was one large square pane held in place by six-penny nails. I fussed with it until the pane came loose, then wriggled out and landed in a rain puddle on top of an oil drum.

I saw that one of the men had properly secured the canoe and I mentally thanked Alex. It was so cool and clean outside that I sat a long time on one of the scow's towing posts, refreshed by the night air and lulled by the lapping of tiny ripples under the sloping end of the scow.

Inside again, with the windowpane replaced, I slept so soundly that I didn't hear the Natives depart for Blubber Bay, or other trollers coming and going. It was hours after sunrise when we got up and cooked breakfast for Bob, the fish buyer and a few hungry trollers.

A Union Steamship at Irvine's Landing, Pender Harbour. Alice Wray

After the dishes were washed and dried we bought oranges, jam and bread. I was happily surprised to see that I still had five dollars. We made sandwiches for our lunch and I rolled my blankets on the warm, nearly flat tarpaper roof of the shed. At about 10 o'clock, when we were ready to shove off, "Frenchie," a French-Canadian troller, asked if we would like a tow around the end of Texada Island. Flo went aboard his boat and I got in the stern of the dugout, ready to balance her whenever we got underway.

It wasn't far from the fish camp to Texada Island, and the sunny day encouraged me to experiment with my precious camera. I particularly wanted a picture of Alex and I believe I got a good one of him, shirtless and tanned, scrubbing down the deck of his boat.

On the east shore of the heavily wooded, mountainous Texada Island, the trollers set me loose to row alongside and pick up Flo. "We may see you farther up the coast," Alex called as the three boats chugged away along Texada Island. I pulled toward Sechelt Peninsula and Pender Harbour with high hopes of finding *Tyee Scout* there.

Tugboats and small steamers passed us on their way to and from Vancouver. All but their masts disappeared as they dropped into the troughs between the waves. We sighted a southbound tug that looked as if it might pass near us. Flo urged me to try doubly hard to meet it so that she might hitch a ride to Vancouver. Lifting and dropping as we were, our forward speed was cut in half. The tug passed less than a mile in front of us and Flo's spirits sank as deep as the bottom of the sea. I became cross with her when her steering made us ship water and then was wretchedly sorry because she was so ill.

"If the Scouts aren't yet in Pender Harbour, we'll get you a room at the hotel until they do come," I promised. Water had slopped into her padded seat and she was wet and chilled—exactly what the doctor had told her to avoid.

It was mid-afternoon when we reached the Union Oil float moored inside Pender Harbour. A young man on a yacht said he'd seen some boys in uniform a couple of days ago, and suggested we ask at Irvines Landing.

It was cloudy but not raining, so I let the canoe drift while I ate half of our sandwiches before rowing on. Flo had no appetite. At Irvines Landing, mainland work and pleasure boats were tied three abreast. I pulled alongside the shallow, vacant shoreward side of the slip.

At the post office–general store building we sent cards and learned that the Nanaimo Sea Scouts had been in but not *Tyee Scout*. "Mr. Church brings the boys in here on nearly every trip," a bystander offered. "They might be in today." That possibility encouraged us.

A buxom lady kindly ushered us through the general store to the hotel kitchen where we could get dry. There we met the motherly Mrs. Oulton, busy cutting out spice cookies. She had us hang our wool socks on the pipes behind the hot, black, oil stove, then got out a starchy blue house dress for Flo to put on while her khaki pants dried. The dress wrapped around Flo's lank figure more than twice. She was a forlorn creature as she huddled beside the stove, feet on a three-legged stool, chin on her knees.

Now seemed a good time to study my camera again so I went to the float to get it and a notebook. Along the way I met a pleasant, slim blonde woman in tailored slacks. She'd heard over the radio in their yacht about two girls starting out to Alaska in a canoe and asked if we were the ones. So much for our attempt to avoid publicity.

An attractive woman with long hair fluffed over her forehead in a becoming pompadour introduced herself as Mrs. Lee. She told us that she knew Mr. Church well and that the Scouts had headed up Jervis Inlet that morning. "This is boat day," she said. "The logging tenders will be going back to camp right after the steamer unloads and the loggers pick up their supplies. Just ask one of the logging boats to tow you up the inlet. Then you will have a better chance of meeting them."

Back in Mrs. Oulton's kitchen, she told us that she had emigrated from England in 1907, when there were many men in Canada but not enough young women. "Our country offered to pay the passage for any unmarried girl who could qualify as to health, disposition and character," she said. "For building a new country they didn't want pretty fluffs that would weep and want to go home as soon as they had put up with a little hardship. I met Mr. Oulton at the home of friends in eastern Canada."

Mrs. Lee rushed in, raindrops twinkling in her hair. "If you hurry, a Vancouver Bay Logging Company boat will tow you to their camp. Hurry! Hurry! They will take you 20 miles up Jervis Inlet."

Flo dreaded leaving the warmth and comfort of the kitchen, but she scurried into a side room and changed into her dry clothes. I ran to untie the dugout and manoeuvre it into position behind the logging boat. Flo came a-running, a deep frown of pain between her eyes. The skipper of the logging tender attempted to make her comfortable in the cramped pilothouse, where three new loggers for the camp stood, strangers to each other.

All the way up Agamemnon Channel and into Prince of Wales Reach, I aquaplaned in the dugout, bailing rainwater and the wash spilling in because of our speed. I felt wonderful with rain trickling off the brim of my sou'wester, and leaving behind, for a while, signs of civilization. Rising steeply on both sides were rugged, wooded mountains, their tops hidden somewhere in the swollen, scudding clouds. Uncounted waterfalls tumbled into the salt chuck—white streaks rushing down green mountainsides. Occasionally the hill-sides showed only glistening rock—rock wiped clean by massive landslides. Ahead—only the unexpected. In a way I wished I weren't so satisfied and completely happy. I wished that I might have known more physical pain and fatigue in my lifetime so that I could be more understanding and helpful in my sympathy for Flo, now ensconced in the warm, dry cabin of the logging boat.

One of the loggers, his coat collar pulled high, came out to shout, "We want you to come inside." He hauled the canoe up short, intro-ducing himself as Ronny as I climbed aboard. He and another man pulled and lifted the dugout until it was safely on deck. "We should have done that at the start," Ronny said with a big grin. Then he added, "Gotta watch out for rheumatism in this wet country."

Ronny cleared a place on the bunk for me beside Flo, and we intro-duced ourselves. Then he proudly showed me pictures of the dance orchestra he had toured with and of activities in other logging camps

Betty and Bijaboji *were dwarfed by the surrounding landscape as they travelled north through Agamemnon Channel.* Sunshine Coast Archives

where he had worked. He described logging camp operations knowledgeably, including ones where the great fir logs are hauled from the woods to the booming grounds by steam railway engines. Ronny said that he'd been married six weeks but couldn't realize it because his job never allowed him any time at home with his bride. The dreary rain continued. Dark soon blended sky and mountains as we charged up Jervis Inlet.

At last we reached the logging camp in steep-sided Vancouver Bay. The men put the canoe on a float near the booming area. Ronny overruled Flo's and my protests about imposing any further on the camp and guided us across a trestle and up the steam engine tracks to the mess hall. Ronny was new here, but he'd been in enough camps to know his way around. "There's always plenty of grub for everybody in a logging camp," he assured us. The cooks weren't talkative but they set heavy platters heaped with hot bacon and eggs, thick brown toast and mugs of tea and coffee on the table before the boat crew, the new loggers and us. Poor Flo was so sick that she hardly touched the generous and delicious meal.

The loggers put their city addresses in my little blue book, "Just in case you ever stop over in Vancouver." It was a wonder they wanted to see me again, especially after I told them how disillusioned I was to meet real loggers. "I looked forward to seeing huge blustery brutes with inches of stiff chin whiskers, thunderous voices and a clomping swagger," I said. "Real Paul Bunyan types. You are all rather like my brothers."

Just then the office man came in to tell us that the camp boss wished us to occupy the engineers' vacant quarters for the night. He led us across the tracks to a sizable room where blueprints covered a large worktable. The bull cook had a fire roaring in the pot-bellied stove and set out everything we might need. He had even turned down the bedclothes on the cots set under windows at opposite sides of the big room. The office man backed out before we could thank him.

Heat and rest eased Flo's pain and we whistled in harmony as we jotted notes for our ship's log. Flo dangled her legs over the arm of a wicker chair, her notebook on her knees. When she was too sleepy to write any more she accepted my offer to carry her to bed.

As I tried to lift her, the wicker seat gave way and she sank through. Laughter made us too weak to get her out, and finally the chair toppled, dumping her out. In bed, with lights out, we chatted for hours, she under one window and I across the room. As college girls will when they are relaxed, we got onto topics of a rather intimate nature and nearly collapsed from embarrassment when we heard a man's chuckle nearly in our ears and realized that only a thin board separated us from other quarters. I crawled over to Flo's side and, in whispers, we plotted to escape at dawn, before we'd have to face any of the unintentional eavesdroppers.

At last, despite the pounding rain and frequent rumble of the logging train passing only a few feet from our door, we slept from sheer weariness. Early in the morning we bundled our things together to make a getaway — and bumped into the boss. He waved away our embarrassed protests and ushered us into the mess hall for a superb breakfast.

In the big cookhouse we sat at one of the long mess tables, our heads low and faces red. We gulped down our food, then cut out through the commodious and fragrant kitchen, where bread dough had risen over the edge of the baker's big mixing tub and hung to the flour-dusted floor. We dared not wait to see what the baker would do with it, but rushed to load *Bijaboji* and row away into the impenetrable morning mist as rapidly as possible.

We rowed back through Jervis Inlet, then into narrow Queens Reach. The mountains rose steeper and the falls gained in breadth, height and volume as we skimmed along near the southeast shore. Flo watched the fog mist thin out above, then ahead of us, while I rowed steadily against the ebbing tide. I watched the curling fog disappear behind us, except in gullies and deep valleys, where it hung silent and white among the dull green fir trees. As the dropping tide left more sea life exposed on the rocks, we gave our upward-bent necks a rest and exulted over colourful starfish and unfamiliar seaweeds.

Steep, bare cliffs gave way to boulders. Streams, canopied by great cedars, gushed joyously into the salt water through rocky shores and dusky seaweed. Some of the slopes, speckled with black, charred jags of trees, recorded the devastation and utter waste of a forest fire. Salal, alders and young second-growth fir trees covered the thin deposit of dark earth. A bald eagle glided low over us, searching, anticipating a fish dinner, gracefully fanning broad wings or angling wide white tail feathers to control its turn.

I thought I heard an airplane but I couldn't see one. Then we rounded a point and I sighted a low, white motorboat travelling close to shore. The hum of its engine became louder as it approached us.

The boat, *Irene R.*, slowed and pulled even with us. The operator, Harry, offered us a ride and we were happy to accept. We climbed over the low rail and the men quickly hauled the loaded dugout aboard.

As we proceeded up Queens Reach toward Princess Louisa Inlet, Harry told us about the two bachelors living on opposite sides of the inlet. Major Haddock, a retired veteran, lived on the southeast shore and Harry was sure we could stay with him if *Tyee Scout* wasn't around. He stopped the boat near the major's float and we slid *Bijaboji* over the side.

Flo and I dropped into the dugout, called out our thanks, waved and headed toward shore. The small, white-haired major, retired from the Canadian Army, rowed out from his green and cream painted cottage to help us land, welcoming us with the dignity and cordiality to be expected of a British-trained officer. I asked about *Tyee Scout*.

"They left this morning. You must have passed them in the fog as you came up the inlet. Mr. Church mentioned that you girls might come this way."

"Well, we'll have to get me a ride on a yacht," Flo said, "or else I'll go back to Pender Harbour in the morning on the loggers' boat and wait for something there."

"Oh, Miss Steele, you are in one of Canada's most beautiful and restful areas. Take at least a day to enjoy it before you go back to the rush and confusion of some city. Now, we'll have lunch right away, just as soon as one of you girls cooks half a dozen steaks from this 11-pound coho I caught this morning." The major was justly proud of the bright silver-sided salmon lying on the cleaning table. Flo quickly set to work over the polished wood stove, frying the salmon's red flesh and heating canned peas. We also had boiled new potatoes, dug from his well-tended garden, and finished the last of his weekly batch of homemade bread. The major steeped the tea properly, as only a Canadian or Britisher does.

We were fascinated by his stories of the Great War, and better understood the horror of war when the major told of the wounds that had crippled his arm. "And I am one of the fortunate ones. I'm alive and mobile." He was disappointed that his radio was on the bum, for he enjoyed music and soap operas.

We were curious about Herman Casper, the bachelor who lived on the north side of the rapids. "I need to borrow a loaf of Herman's bread," Major Haddock said. "This will be a good opportunity for you to meet him."

Flo and I quickly rowed across the inlet's narrow mouth. Herman Casper, a large, broad-shouldered man of perhaps 55 years, greeted us with a strong German accent. We learned that his many talents included tool making, logging, playing the zither, making guitars and writing songs. He was happy in his unpainted cabin with 15 or so cats, most of them pure white, and much excited about the heavyweight boxing match of the night before. He quickly found that we knew nothing about boxing.

Casper said the tide was nearing high-water slack, so I headed *Bijaboji* into the rapids at the mouth of the inlet while Flo took the well-worn path through the woods. Some spots in the rapids swung and bounced the dugout about, but I got through without water splashing aboard and picked up Flo, who was waiting on a broad rock ledge.

One of the ladies we'd met in Pender Harbour had told us about James "Mac" Macdonald, the third bachelor of Louisa Inlet, a retired American who spent his summers in a comfortable lodge at the head of the inlet. We wanted to meet him, too, so we rowed toward the roaring, 120-foot Chatterbox Falls. They leapt off the mountainside before noisily crashing near Macdonald's lodge. After shooting a few photos we landed among the yachts moored to the log float. We trudged up the path and across a rustic bridge to the door of a magnificent lodge and expectantly raised the doorknocker and let it fall.

A smiling young man welcomed us inside. "Mac is eating on the biggest yacht down there," he said, waving toward the float. "But I've spent enough time here to be able to show you around." Visitors were apparently an everyday occurrence. "This inlet and lodge would make a wonderful location for a movie," Flo said after our tour.

"Some of Mac's many Hollywood friends agree," our guide replied. "Mac told me a few movie scenes have been shot here."

We accepted his invitation to make ourselves comfortable in the living room. A warm fire snapped and crackled merrily in the fireplace. Flo buried herself in a book while I chatted with the young man.

Soon Mac arrived, a tanned, ruggedly handsome middle-aged man with a quick smile, accompanied by a bevy of attractive young ladies. A natural host, Mac immediately made us feel as though he had always known us. I was happily surprised when he told me that as a young man he had used a dugout canoe in Puget Sound, and had also attended Pomona College. More yachters arrived and scattered about the delightful room. We all laughed uproariously when Mac told about a crab race conducted with all the betting and excitement of a Kentucky Derby—at a picnic he'd hosted for yachtsmen and local loggers.

I was flattered when Mac asked us to sign his much-used guest book. The names of Art Church and other Anacortes friends were among those of visiting yachting parties.

A silver-cream moon swung above the mountains as we rowed back to the major's float. "We'll die of holding our breath if we wait to see anything more gorgeous," Flo said. I agreed. Only a ribbon of star-filled sky was visible overhead between the saw-backed, glacier-fringed ranges surrounding us. A few exuberant salmon leaped from the quiet water and splashed back, creating shimmering rings of phosphorescence.

From somewhere nearby we heard the yodel-like cry of a loon. Flo had never heard that unmistakable call, and I'd heard it only a few times in Puget Sound. I stopped rowing to listen. "Do you realize, Betty, that these three unusual men, each so different, all having served in different armies, each having seen more of the world than most, have found peace and solitude in this beautiful and isolated inlet? So many people come here, disturbing their privacy, and still each man welcomed us like old friends."

"I've been thinking something like that. Obviously these bachelors don't dislike people…women. Think of that flock of beauties surrounding Mac. I guess they just need the feel of freedom."

I was glad Flo had been unable to head home earlier, so she could share this incredible experience. We began to sing. Our voices echoed from the steep slopes of the slender inlet and we emphasized the harmonies by making one voice rebound from the starboard slope, the other from the port side. Never before had the 121st Psalm meant so much to me as it did when I rowed the length of this four-mile inlet. I lifted up mine eyes to the hills and knew that even though Flo was turning back, I was to go on.

Next morning the major had crisp bacon and eggs sunny side up nearly ready to put on the table before he woke us. Even so, I took a few moments for an invigorating dip in the salt chuck. Despite cold streams flowing into the inlet, I found the water there, as everywhere else along the British Columbia coast, decidedly warmer than Puget Sound. I ate ravenously after my swim and had barely started the dishes when Harry arrived with *Irene R.* and shouted, "Shake a leg, if you two are riding in this boat."

Grabbing our gear, we scrambled down the steps and over the rocks to the float. I winced noticeably as Harry and the major scraped *Bijaboji's* bottom as they slid her into the water before loading her aboard. Harry laughed. "Anything that hurts this red scow hurts Betty worse." That was the truth.

I was the last to push off, and the major—a real gentleman—said in a low voice as he bent over the painter, "Never get to know any man on the coast any better than you know Harry right now."

"Thank you, Major Haddock," I promised, and we clasped hands firmly.

To Betty's frustration, she narrowly missed meeting the Tyee Scout *at Irvines Landing on the Sunshine Coast.*

Late in the evening we reached secluded Garden Bay in Pender Harbour. Flo was determined to ride to Vancouver on the *Irene R*. From there she'd go by bus to Anacortes to reassure Mother, then to Seattle. I tried to persuade her to recuperate in Garden Bay, where we could rent a cottage and repaint the canoe. I hiked to the store and bought scarlet and black paint in an effort to convince her that it was a good plan, but it was no use.

"You'll make it better alone," Flo argued. "I'm too much of a responsibility. Yes, even a liability. Just say hello to my father and brother in Petersburg and tell them that I had ten exciting, unforgettable days with you and *Bijaboji*."

I made no more attempts to change her mind. We sat down on the float and divided our equipment. Flo took her red-tape-wrapped pistol. I needed the food, sleeping bag, clothes, charts, hatchet, hunting and scout knives, camera and writing materials, cooking utensils and the spare oar. I put my things into a small pile. Flo had even less. I couldn't trust my words or muscles until the logging boat and Flo disappeared behind the point. Then I dashed into the woods for a frame-wracking sob-fest. It worked wonders.

Now there was no doubt. I was on my own resources, totally. With the dollar I had left after buying the paint, I rented a cottage, where I could stay while I repaired and painted *Bijaboji*.

CHAPTER 4

Deer Hunt at Garden Bay

*Without a compass, without a companion — with only a dugout canoe
and a love of adventure, a 22-year-old girl is rowing to Alaska.
"She loves adventure," says her mother, "and hopes to write up her
experiences to help defray college expenses this fall."*

— Washington Post, September 1937

I WAS SITTING ON THE STEPS of my rented cottage in Garden Bay, cutting leather to wrap around the oars where the wood had worn and frayed in the metal oarlocks, when I noticed a shadow. I looked up and saw a brawny Native youth watching me with a superior half smile. "I guess you know more about this than I do," I said.

He reached for my knife and took over the job, cutting the tough leather easily. "I'm Billy Shields. My father is one of the chiefs here in Sechelt." Billy told me he'd been around canoes and boats since he was a child. After a quick inspection of *Bijaboji* he disappeared, soon to return with tinsnips and clean metal cans. Billy cut the cans into strips and nailed the metal over *Bijaboji's* bow and bottom where I'd rubbed off paint and splintered the soft cedar when beaching on rocks and barnacles. He quickly finished cutting the leather and tacked it around my oars, then painted the waterproof cases and the scarlet part of the canoe. My fishing line was adjusted, lures polished and hooks sharpened. All day he helped me get the canoe ready. That evening he tapped on my door. "I'm going to hunt deer. My cousin can't go. Do you want to?"

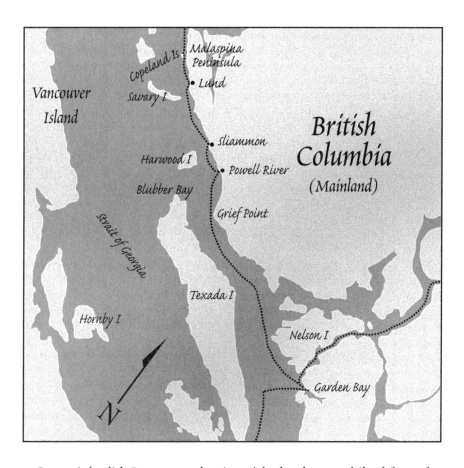

I certainly did. It was nearly nine o'clock when we hiked from the resort and into the forest. The sun wouldn't set for more than an hour, yet I had difficulty following the light-footed Billy in the darkening forest. He paused once in a bit of a clearing carpeted by cedar chips and said, "This is where I dug out my first canoe."

I listened spellbound to his stories, exceedingly well told and embellished with demonstrations of animal sounds and suggestions of their movements in the woods. He told of shooting seals, swimming fast and diving for the dead or wounded animals. He described every detail of a hunting trip with his father and brothers when they shot a dozen mountain goats high in the mountains at the head of Jervis Inlet. His brother once was attacked by a grizzly bear he'd wounded and barely escaped.

We tramped farther into the woods and crossed a marsh, working through a thicket of sharp brush before climbing higher into the hills. Billy frequently had to wait for me to fight my way through or over the limbs of giant wind-felled trees. At last he stopped beside a half-rotted fir log and motioned me to sit on the moss behind him. Laying his rifle on the ground between us, he commenced blowing softly on a deer call his cousin had made with twigs and a thin strip of cedar bark. Just any squeaking sound from the vibrations of the bark wasn't satisfactory. Billy tuned his call to a faint, high-pitched squeak and blew every few seconds. "Sometimes I stay here all night before a deer comes, " he said softly, "but I never go back without something."

For some inexplicable reason I whispered, "I want to try shooting your rifle." I had never fired a rifle. Before I was through shooting there were no more shells. It had not been a conscious plan. "I'm always thinking that I'll have the nerve to shoot something, but I don't believe I could even bear to see anyone kill an animal. I'm no good as a hunting companion."

Billy startled me by saying, without anger or resentment, "The warden may have heard the shooting. We'll have to go back on the cliffs. Quiet."

Suddenly I realized that if I had shot anything I would have broken several laws: hunting on an Indian Reserve, out of season and without a licence.

On the last 500 yards of our hike we edged along a narrow ledge with our backs to the cliff, not making a sound, waves lapping at our toes. We reached the cottage and, without a word, Billy disappeared into the woods. I lit a lamp and wrote up the evening in the ship's log.

Saturday morning I strolled down to the float. The scarlet paint on *Bijaboji* was dry, so I started to trim the gunwales with black paint. The canoe looked so classy that I went all out and painted the ribs, seat, foot brace and crossbars. Billy rowed up in a flat-bottomed dugout just as a purse seiner eased alongside and made fast to the float. "My brother works on that boat," he said, before going aboard to talk with the Japanese owner.

Two little boys were fishing off the float. They hovered about, eager to help, until I allowed them to take turns painting while I fished with their lines. After we finished painting the three of us lay on our stomachs trying—unsuccessfully—to snag one of the countless speckled perch moving lazily under the float.

After supper I gave each of my assistant painters a short ride in *Bijaboji* before pulling away from the summer resort. The beer parlour man who had given me the nails and tin waved. Billy Shields's cousins on the Reserve called out a farewell. The summer resort people stared for a moment or so, then went on with their badminton or card games. I set off for Powell River by moonlight.

It was my first night alone and I rowed out with the tide, through Malaspina Strait, along Jervis Inlet and past Texada Island in the peaceful, enchanted night. Just before dawn, beyond a point and a stretch of water, a square concrete building appeared. It was lighted in every window; below tumbled a foaming stream. The roar of huge turbines carried across the quiet water. A power plant. Objects ashore became distinct as the early morning sun rose above the eastern hilltops. In the far curve of the bay was a village where electric lights gleamed from numerous tall poles. A bright sign identified one building as a general store. A solitary car was parked in front.

Long grey sheds nearly covered a pier that loomed before me as I tried to find an opening in the log weather boom protecting the beach. There was no opening. Day was dawning when I tied *Bijaboji* to a dolphin below the power plant and crawled up the bank in search of the night watchman to ask if I had reached Powell River.

I found nothing and saw no living soul when I peered through the windows. If this was Powell River, I'd have to find some way of getting my mail, Sunday or not. It would be a waste of effort to go on until I had inquired at the post office, so I unrolled the sleeping bag between two logs and wriggled in for a nap.

I awoke with an uneasy feeling and stared up into the face of a big man sitting on the bank above, looking out over the canoe and me. I slipped into my shoes and climbed up to ask about tides and where I was.

Betty stopped briefly at Stillwater, the location of a power plant and logging operations. Vancouver Public Library, Special Collections, VPL 1583

"This is Stillwater," he said gruffly, and added that the plant supplied power to the mills at Powell River by remote control. He was not friendly. I lost no time in finding rollers to put under the canoe left high and dry by the ebbing tide. I rowed far offshore from the modest summer homes bunched along the beach.

While going around Grief Point I got a sample of really turbulent water. For several miles I was forced to row the canoe facing ahead to avoid crashing into ugly brown rocks awash after every breaking, foaming wave. Huge bulbs of bullwhip kelp streaming long, ragged yellow fronds rose and fell with the swells. If I had been rowing then as I was later—sitting in the stern, facing forward and pushing with the oars instead of pulling—I should have had a much easier time of it. Rowing with my back to the bow gave me greater leverage, but to see oncoming waves and obstacles more than compensated.

No high hills glowered over me and no solid masses of greenery covered the slopes of terra firma that morning. Only dead trees, many with trunks stripped of bark, all thrusting broken, shattered limbs to the sky. I kept my attention on what was under the water—tattered strands of amber-coloured kelp moving rhythmically with the waves and tide. Rocks might lurk there.

In a slightly sheltered bight where unpainted buildings told of former human activity, I let the oars drag while I opened a can of beans, poured them onto a paper plate and nibbled at a small portion. It was a case of eating because I thought I should. I wasn't hungry and threw the greater share away. Maybe the fish liked them.

About two in the afternoon my port side was even with the white splotch of the lime kiln at Blubber Bay on the north end of Texada Island. Ahead to starboard, and at least five miles away, Powell River's large pulp and paper mill smoked and steamed lavishly. On the hills above the mill were rows and rows of bungalows. Two stubby Canadian tugs lay at anchor in the bay below Westview, the nearest suburb of the company town. I rowed alongside the larger boat and asked, holding onto the wide fender, "May I tie up and rest here a bit?"

"Sure, come aboard for a spot of tea," a stout, shirtless man invited me. I climbed aboard. Two other crewmen stepped into the galley, and all of them were skeptical of my plan to navigate Yuculta Rapids.

"It's either the rapids or Seymour Narrows," I argued. I said I'd rather go along the mainland coast and see some of the wonderful islands than head for Cape Mudge from either Savary or Hernando Island.

A half-hour later a Peterborough canoe edged alongside the tug and two young men in swimming trunks climbed aboard. "I saw you way out there against the horizon," I told them. "You looked like toothpicks in a pea pod." My frankness betrayed me as an American, and one of the men said he'd been a grease monkey in the United States Army during the Depression's early days.

Wonderfully pepped up by the tea and friendly conversation, I accepted a challenge to go swimming. I changed in the privacy of the engineer's stateroom and we plunged overboard. Off the gunwales and off the pilothouse we straight-dived and jackknifed. Then we raced the length of the towline and back. It was great fun and I forgot how disgruntled I had been with people that morning. The old elation of being alive and healthy surged back.

The sky was momentarily overcast and we—sitting on the stern of the tug, fussing with my camera—began to shiver. As we huddled over the big diesel engine to get warm, Walt Drayton, the older of the swimmers, asked me where I was going next.

"Since it's Sunday and I can't get my mail and what money there may be in it, I'm going to sleep on the beach. And tomorrow, after getting to the post office, I'll head for Squirrel Cove."

"Oh, no, you won't," Walt said positively, glancing toward the boulder-strewn beach. "We are going to fix you up with a place to stay in Westview."

After thanking the tugboat crew for the tea and their hospitality, the swimmers and I headed for shore. They paddled beside me to a beach about a mile nearer the mill, and easily lifted their canoe and carried it into the brush. Quickly finding two other men to help, they carried *Bijaboji* to the logs above the high-tide level. We walked to the large rooming and boarding house in Westview where most of the unmarried millworkers hung out. "Ma," busy in the kitchen, told us all of her rooms were occupied by a circus troupe who were waiting for a boat large enough to take them to Ketchikan. Secretly I was glad, for I preferred roughing it on the beach.

Walt Drayton was of a different mind. That's how it happened that his brother and sister-in-law, the Steve Draytons, invited me to use their spare bedroom for the night. The room was already prepared, so I stopped protesting.

Steve Drayton worked in the Kelly Spruce mill, where lumber for airplane construction was sawed. He put up lunch for the next day while his sweet wife dressed the baby for bed. "The oranges are in the lower cupboard," she called to Steve. "No lunch is complete without an orange," she explained. "Steve uses the juice to take off wood stains."

No one had ever mentioned such a use during my three years in California.

Walt left for his job on the graveyard shift in the pulp mill. I caught up on my notes while Steve and his wife prepared a midnight snack of tea, toast and marmalade. As we ate they urged me to stop at Teakerne Arm to see their logger friend, Barney Smith.

"We named the baby after him and he's never seen it," Mrs. Drayton said.

"I guess he hasn't been away from camp since he gashed his leg in April," Steve added.

Next morning I was wiping the last of the dishes after a filling breakfast of bacon and eggs and Mrs. Drayton was bathing the squirmy baby when Walt came in. "I can get passes to take you through the mill," he announced happily.

Once more we hiked through the woodsy lane, now poignant with a sweet, sharp early-morning forest smell. It was an hour's walk although we didn't loiter on the rustic bridge admiring the tortuous fern-bordered stream, as we had the day before. Walt told me that in the mill I would see the whole process, beginning with unbarked logs and ending with big rolls of paper, wrapped and ready for shipping.

Bright patterns of light shone through the thinning trees, relieving the forest's dark shadows. Soon we saw the white clouds above Powell River pierced by two giant stacks—industry's exclamation marks. Beyond were mountains, some forested, others bare. The town's commercial centre included a two-storey company store, post office, hotel, hospital, taxi office and shops. We signed in at a small building near the mill and were handed blue visitor passes.

Our tour commenced where men using long pike poles pushed hefty floating logs onto a ramp where a moving chain caught and pulled each log up a slick chute. Then great steel arms rolled the log onto a moving platform that rushed it at a large spinning saw, which screamed like a demented creature. The carrier sped back, powerful steel arms rotated the log and again it whizzed into the saw—again and again—each time removing strips of the log's rough surface until the round log became a square. The squares were then sawed into planks. Each plank dropped onto twirling cylinders, where a man quickly determined its quality and dimensions before sending it in one of several directions on slow-moving rollers. An instinctive terror chilled me whenever that whirling saw hit wood, and my eyes became glassy following the motions of those metal arms moving and turning the logs as easily as I would turn a pencil.

It was so fascinating I hated to go, yet I was relieved when Walt guided me away from the controlled fury of the sawmill and across a field riotous with dandelion yellow and green, and thistle purple, to the immense building where he worked. "We had a little trouble here last night," he said, waving an arm toward the concrete floor, soapy with liquid pulp. Walt grabbed a handful of the juicy crushed wood and gave it to me. It was warm and fibrous, and it exuded an odor I couldn't identify. Walt's job was to stoke the big machine with blocks of wood that were pressed against powerful rotating grinders made of stone.

We climbed a metal ladder to peer into great vats of soggy pulp. From there, the pulp moved to a sweltering room, where it was spread out then passed through tiers of speeding rollers that squeezed the liquid out and shaped the pulp to width and thickness. At the far end of the long building, muscular men, whose brown backs gleamed with sweat, wrapped heavy rolls of newsprint for shipping. I stared, fascinated by their muscles flexing under shiny skin as they worked with machine-like precision and efficiency. No motion was wasted.

Outside, blinking in the sunshine, I remembered that I might have mail. Yesterday I'd been anxious for mail from home; today I'd forgotten it. I asked the man at the post office for letters addressed to B.A. Lowman. There were none, and neither he nor his assistant remembered seeing mail for anyone with that surname.

My shoulders sagged. Suddenly I was overwhelmed with the realization that I was 150 miles from home, in an unfamiliar country, unknown, 700 or more canoe miles from Daddy, with Yuculta Rapids and Queen Charlotte Sound between us, and I was nearly penniless. But it should prove no hardship, unless I broke an arm or something.

Walt hailed a bus and we flopped onto leather seats for the ride to Ma's for lunch with Walt and "Scoop" Richards of the *Powell River News*. There I met two more of Walt's brothers and their friends. They marvelled at the paucity of blisters on my hands—I had acquired only three tiny ones during the first days of the trip, and they were caused by seams in the horsehide gloves I wore to prevent blisters. The Draytons again urged me to say hello to Barney Smith, their old family friend, at Teakerne Arm. I promised gladly, happy to repay their kindness even in that small way.

Scoop Richards escorted me on a tour of the *Powell River News* building and presented me with a "slug" with my name on it, set on the linotype machine.

When it was time to go, Walt appeared on the beach in his swimming trunks to help launch the dugout. I wore navy blue shorts, matching tailored shirt and scarlet silk tie. From my belt of white cord with its shiny silver buckle hung my sharp hunting knife. Walt gave me final instructions as he paddled the Peterborough alongside me. "You'll get most help from the current if you stay with it until you pass the Indian village of Sliammon," he said. "Then head out. Say hello to Barney. Good luck to the end." With a broad smile and a friendly wave, he veered off.

It was a sunny day. An unusually bright, sparkling day. The water was calm and I could see far into its depths. The bottom was covered with sediment of pulp fibre and chips from the mill. Far to the right, between me and the great snow-streaked peaks on Vancouver Island, 16 miles across the Strait of Georgia, was the flat, wooded three-mile length of Harwood Island. Close at hand to port was Powell River's 800-foot breakwater reinforced by the derelict steel hull of a navy cruiser, once the USS *Charleston*. Inside the breakwater a few small but powerful boats were breaking up great booms of logs, pushing them here and there, sorting them according to type and quality. The hundreds of windows in the mill buildings glinted in the dazzling sunlight. Three raucous seagulls followed me, hoping for a handout.

Deliberately I rowed into the foamy yellow river-like current churning into the bay from below the mill. I put all my strength into getting through and into calm water.

A mile ahead lay the Sliammon village, a straight row of dwellings dominated by a Roman Catholic church. I resolved to visit the Father to learn how the Natives sailed a dugout. I was weary of explaining to nearly every man I met that I preferred rowing to bothering with the weight of outriggers, mast and centre board or keel, but the Indians might have an age-old trick.

The tide was very low, exposing the beach for yards and yards from the village. I anchored the canoe in the mouth of a stream and

The happy canoeist relaxing in the quiet waters of the Inside Passage.

waded through wet sand and seaweed to a row of drift logs nearly in the rutted road in front of the people's homes. In a field several bronze-skinned men were piling a wagon high with hay. Nearer, and on the upper beach, was a grey-haired woodcutter. He sat comfortably on a sun-dried log slowly pulling and pushing his saw across a small log. I approached and asked about the priest.

"The Father is gone today. Blanket make good sail. Tie cord on corner. Where you go in little red canoe?"

"Alaska," I said, glancing toward *Bijaboji*, now floating as the flood tide swiftly washed over the beach.

"Canoe too small," I heard him mutter as I raced back to my craft before I would have to swim out to it.

A mile north of Sliammon I said hello to an elderly Native hand-troller in a dugout. He looked up from under his broad-brimmed black hat to advise me of the tides to Lund, saying, "Stay out. Water shallow. Tide good."

Facing forward, I rowed in a direct line to the red spar buoy marking Atrevida Reef. Although I was some distance from the wooded shore, too often my oars became entangled with drifting sea grass. An attractive, bright-painted summer cottage broke the monotonous forest green of the coastline as I came abeam of the spar. A barking dog, romping with a small boy, shattered the stillness. I decided to turn the canoe and sight off the stern at the red spar. As the bow swerved I was momentarily headed toward the hazy, blue-white mountain range on Vancouver Island. Soon I was again parallel to the continental shore, low and flat compared to the island's distant snow-patched peaks.

When I was abreast of Savary Island, a chugging tug passed nearby. Men gathered at the rail beside the high pilothouse to stare through binoculars.

"Where are you headed?" one yelled into a megaphone.

"Alaska," I shouted. He must have heard me, for he shook his head in disbelief.

"Lund's a mile ahead," another crewman hollered.

A long streamer of scalloped black smoke from the tug drifted slowly over its tow of five booms of logs tied in tandem. I rowed close to the bold cliffs beyond Hurtado Point to poke into a shaft at the edge of the water. The tug's wake, rushing in and receding, made an eerie sound. A trolling boat moved past at snail speed a few yards away and the putt-putt sounds of the engine reverberated weirdly from within the old man-made cave, once an iron mine.

The sun was close to setting and the ruby flush on sky and water promised a lovely sunset. I pulled hard to reach Lund, where I could send a telegram to Mother.

Lund appeared around the extremity of Hurtado Point's 250-foot cliff. It was a small settlement of low wooden houses, a conspicuous two-storey hotel, a stubby wharf and a modest machine shop. After tying my dugout to the float, I pulled on my ski trousers, climbed to the wharf and went in search of the telegraph operator.

He was busy at something up the road and hurried my way only when he saw two couples enter the beer parlour on the lower floor of the hotel. I followed him inside before realizing that he was also the bartender. I ducked out immediately and sat on the veranda railing until he was ready to take my message. "Have to do that over here," he said, hurrying across the road to the general store. He waited on two women in the grocery section, sold a fisherman a plaid shirt, handed letters to a suntanned boy and finally took my message. He spent some time thumbing through a book, ascertaining if it could be sent collect across the international boundary. Fortunately it could.

The polychrome western sky was dazzling when I undid my square knot, leaped into the canoe and pointed the bow toward the gold rim of the sinking sun. None of the memorable sunsets I've thrilled to in Puget Sound or California compared with this one, suggesting a golden water flower with shading of pink petals. I let the canoe idle in the glimmering rosy waters until a tug, and then a passing troller with a jabbering family aboard, interrupted the God-nearness of my feelings.

When I got into Thulin Passage, between the low Copeland Islands and the mainland, two pugnacious tugs passed, setting the water into a rolling motion. The nearer tug was northbound without a tow. Lights shone from the lower cabin windows; within, men were reading. Soon the tug was out of sight and hearing. The other tug laboured toward Powell River as though it were weary—frightfully weary—of pulling a string of log booms against the hurrying tide. It appeared scarcely to move.

From the north end of the Copeland Islands to Sarah Point I intended to row a mid-channel course, then take the shortest angle to Cortes Island and Squirrel Cove. It was a grand evening for rowing—calm, clear and windless. But twilight deepened prematurely into blackness in the narrow channel between the Copeland Islands and the steep, bare cliffs of Malaspina Peninsula. It would be foolish to look for a camping spot along the mainland. The canoe was responding wonderfully to every stroke and I wanted to prolong that marvellous rowing day.

As all light faded from the sky, the channel ahead held the inky blackness of a cavern. There were millions of stars overhead and a familiar constellation or two. I was alone, ecstatic, free of self-consciousness about my muscular 160 pounds, free of know-it-alls trying to tell me what equipment I would have brought for the trip if I weren't crazy. If I weren't so broke and loving it! With thoughts along this line, I rowed on, past a likely camping spot in a cove where, on shore, a gaslight shone steadily.

Chapter 5

Logging Show in Teakerne Arm

*I had no lofty ambition in making the trip, only a youthful zest for
"roughing it."*
　　—Betty Lowman, *Daily Colonist* (Victoria), December 19, 1937

TWO LIGHTS GLEAMED INVITINGLY IN A COVE beyond the Copeland
Islands, one on an anchored fish boat, another in a lone farmhouse. It
was too black ahead of me to see Cortes Island and be sure of keeping a straight course, so I beached in the cove, intending to sleep on
the fine sand of what was called Turner's Cove, about seven miles
northwest of Lund.

Stepping over the side of the canoe, I was startled by the water's
warmth and the great marbles of phosphorescence that appeared to
roll away from my feet. No princess ever had a lovelier footpath.
From that night on, the warmth of the salt water in these more north-
erly latitudes of British Columbia never ceased to amaze me. I have
shivered and chattered for many hours, both winter and summer,
when swimming in the icy waters of Puget Sound.

Disturbed by my activity in coming ashore and unrolling the sleeping bag, watchdogs on the other side of a wire fence barked menacingly. I was too tired to retreat, so I crouched on my bedroll while one
dog redoubled its efforts to get at me through the wire. Just when it
seemed the snarling hound would break through to leap at my throat,
a woman rushed onto the porch, flashing a light through the trees.

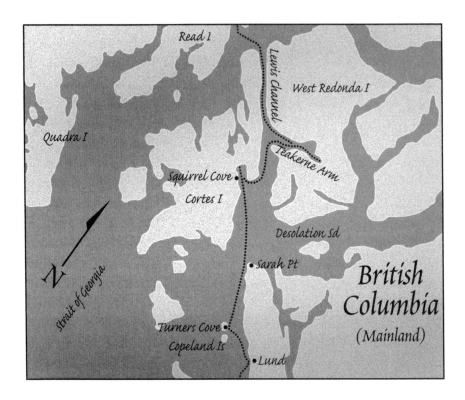

"Sic 'em! Sic 'em!" she ordered distinctly. Then, possibly detecting that the dogs were barking at a human intruder, not a wild animal: "Who's there?"

I wanted to scream: "It's only me from over the sea!" Instead: "It is I, an American girl with my dugout canoe," I shouted above the racket of barking dogs and squeaking, straining fence.

Another woman stood silhouetted against the lighted window. A sharp command and the dogs immediately quieted. "Come up to the house. Please, I'll shine my light on the gate. The dogs won't bother you." The voice now had a friendly tone. I entered the yard and the dogs walked quietly beside me.

When the light glowing from the open door fell on me, one of the ladies said, "Come in. We've heard about you from the radio, but never expected to see you. I'll put the kettle on."

This was the Anderson home. Pete Anderson had gone trolling and Helen Anderson and her friend were my hosts for the evening.

"That fishing boat came in after dusk. The man didn't come ashore first thing, and we wondered about his intentions," Mrs. Anderson explained. They insisted that I bring up my sleeping bag and stay in the cozy house.

It had been a long day, more tiring than I realized. Even the stimulating steaming tea couldn't keep me alert enough to carry on much of a conversation. My sleeping bag was soon spread on the couch and I had a most needed sleep.

The fishing boat was gone from Turner's Cove when I awoke. Before breakfast, Mrs. Anderson proudly showed me her vegetable garden, flowers, fruit trees and long-haired white goats. She told me that it was hard to raise anything on the island, but that the cove was so lovely and sheltered, the sun-warmed beach so fine, the scented woods on the hill and mirrored lake so beautiful that she and Pete hoped to sell the place to someone interested in building a private lodge or constructing cabins for tourists. "Our place is much more promising than the islands across there," she said, pointing at two identical rocky islands several miles away, toward Vancouver Island. "An American millionaire read about them in the paper and bought them sight unseen. Now he's building a 16-room log lodge out there." Mrs. Anderson paused to look around her enticing island. "This is lovely, but I want to live in a floathouse so I can always be near the fishing grounds and Pete. There is nowhere around here for my daughter Violet to go to school, so she has to be far away in Vancouver. At least Pete and I could be together."

On Tuesday, June 29, after an early and hearty breakfast of bacon, eggs, toast and homegrown canned cherries, we all rowed out of the cove, the ladies and the cougar hound in a clinker-built skiff and I, of course, in *Bijaboji*. I dipped my oars once to every three times for the ladies, since *Bijaboji* is built for more speed and ease of rowing than a skiff. Chatting as we rowed, only yards apart, we soon covered the short distance to Sarah Point. That rounded, rocky peninsula sloped gradually from the saltchuck to a 750-foot hill. A little past Sarah Point we separated, they to visit a relative up Malaspina Inlet and I to cross Desolation Sound to Cortes Island.

When I thought the canoe might appear to the ladies as no more than a wee red speck, I tore off my shirt and ski pants, the better to benefit from the morning sun in my rowing shorts. A straining tug-boat with its tow of logs moved slowly toward me from the direction of Lewis Channel. Far behind the tug, snowy, blue-streaked mountains rose irregularly against the lighter blue of the sky. Mountains to the right, mountains to the left, I thought. If I could see Vancouver Island over Cortes Island, I'd see mountains behind and mountains ahead. All this region is just as extraordinary as the purse seine fishermen at home told me it would be. Exultant, I snapped a few black-and-white pictures, wishing I had colour film to capture the unrivalled beauty of the scene. For a while I debated whether or not to take a side trip up Toba Inlet in the direction of the highest peaks. Two things made me row on. I wanted to get through the awesome Yuculta Rapids while the good weather held, and I *had* to reach Alert Bay by July 4 or miss the *Tyee Scout* on its second excursion trip of the summer.

A Native girl trolling for salmon and wearing a floppy sunbonnet approached to ask how many fish I was catching, and she caught me without a shirt on. I don't know what flustered her more — that, or the discovery that I was a white girl rowing an Indian dugout on a long-distance trip. Three nice salmon lay in the bottom of her dugout. "My mother makes pretty baskets," she said. "We live at Squirrel Cove Village."

"Is that where the post office is?"

"No, it's in a bay down that way." She pointed and I stroked twice with the port side oar to head *Bijaboji* onto my new course.

The side of Cortes Island that I was passing appeared to be no more than 200 feet high and could barely sustain stunted trees. There was a noticeable increase in fertility of the land as it gradually gained height. I rowed along some five miles of tranquil shoreline to the post office.

Near the Native village, puffs of steam lifted from a donkey en-gine mounted on an A-frame raft, and a large log came swinging and crashing out of the woods on a taut cable. A lean, sure-footed man leaped from the raft and ran across three or four floating logs to unhook it. The cable whipped and whined as it was rapidly winched back into the woods for another log. Overeager to see what would happen next, I forgot about the tidal current and nearly upset the canoe when we drifted onto a boulder awash from a small wave.

The tide was low when I arrived at Squirrel Cove and made *Bijaboji* fast behind a fuel barge. Access to the pier was by a hinged wooden ramp resting on a roller, permitting the ramp to move along the float as the tide rose or fell. As usual, this ramp was divided, one half fitted with horizontal wooden cleats to prevent slipping while walking up or down, and the other half smooth so that supplies could be slid down to the boats or dragged up to the pier.

A store sign was mounted on a tiny cottage a dozen yards from the land end of the pier. A bell jangled and a baby whimpered when I pulled open the screen door. Inside, shelves were loaded with canned foods. The freighter must have come in with supplies quite recently. At the far end of the small, dimly lit room was the post office window and beside it an open door. A harried young man in a yellow wool sweater appeared and looked at me questioningly.

Betty received her first letter from home at the Squirrel Cove Post Office on Cortes Island.
Museum at Campbell River, Photo No. 17143

"Have you any mail for Lowman or Steele?"

Quickly stepping behind the window, he reached into an unmarked box and thrust two letters at me. "Your mother wrote me asking to help you in any way I can. Just call me when you finish reading your letters. I know the tides and eddies around here."

"Thank you very much. I'll get my chart."

Walking along the pier, I opened Mother's letter. "Dear Balboa," she wrote. "Your daddy is in a frenzy. He heard a report of your trip over a Spokane radio station. He may have the Coast Guard on your trail now. For his sake and yours I'm sorry we couldn't keep this trip entirely out of the papers and off the air. People cannot be expected to understand a girl like you, Bebby, who loves physical accomplishment, as even few boys do, rather than the achievement of sewing a beautiful dress or baking a light textured loaf of bread."

Thankful for the few dollars in Mother's letter, but feeling much disturbed and terribly alone, I went to the dugout for my chart, then headed for the store. While going up the steep ramp I heard the snarl of a powerful boat engine and looked around to see a grey boat speeding around the point. Canadian Coast Guard! Daddy's set them after me, I thought. I streaked to the store with my chart.

I asked the proprietor whether I could possibly get out of the cove through the long, narrow lagoon that nearly separated the island, according to the chart.

"Not possible." He shattered my hopes for an easy escape.

"Then where is the Kelly Spruce camp at Teakerne Arm?"

He marked the place on my chart with a small tick. I hid my hunting knife under my shirt-tail, thinking it might betray me for a camping canoeist, tucked the folded chart under my arm and strolled casually down to the float where the grey boat was tied. Sauntering by the idle deckhand, I stepped around to the other side of the barge, where the canoe was hidden from the government men.

They strode along the pier, and when their backs were turned I set out from behind the barge and across a short open stretch to the shelter of a little island. I rowed away, keeping the barge between the grey boat and *Bijaboji* until I had crossed to the rocky, cliff-rimmed eastern side of Lewis Channel. A great blue heron stood at the water's edge, still and stiff as a statue. Suddenly it jabbed its long beak into the water and withdrew a minnow, its lunch. I was too agitated to want any lunch. The blazing sun was melting the cold cream I had smeared over my face to protect me from sunburn and more freckles. Mirages quivered ahead of me.

A stiff breeze caught at the bow of the canoe and the mirages vanished as I headed into narrow, steep-to Teakerne Arm. "Too deep for anchoring," according to my well-used *Coast Pilot*.

When I had so gladly promised the Draytons to visit Barney Smith and bring news of his namesake and Powell River friends, I had taken for granted that "Arm" meant a protrusion of land. The arm would be a sheltered spot where I might pause for a half-hour or so before rowing on to the Yuculta Rapids. According to the postmaster's tick on my chart, the logging camp was at the far end of what I'd call an inlet. And that inlet was nearly four miles long. I would have reconsidered my promise to the Draytons, but going into the arm would get me safely out of sight of that grey government boat. Almost four blistering hot miles of rowing in the seclusion of the arm was as nothing in my mind to the disappointment of being apprehended—on orders from my father—and being ignominiously hauled back home.

Only wooded hills lay ahead in the arm. No signs of logging activity. Rough white-grey rock, an ideal reflector for the sun's searing rays, rose from the water's edge to 30 or 40 feet above me. I took off my sweat-soaked short-sleeved shirt and gave three cheers for the sunglasses that Flo had not exchanged for linseed oil. The current seemed to swat back and forth across the arm, and when that wasn't making it hard to steer, strong puffs of an afternoon breeze tossed the dugout like a chip. During a lull in the breeze I stood up to stretch my cramped legs, and sat down—on the sunglasses, smashing them. Just lovely! What next? The sun's rays reflected by the water stabbed at my unshielded eyeballs. A large sunburn blister rose across my left upper arm. A screw working loose from one rowlock socket squeaked irritatingly.

A plane roared somewhere overhead but I couldn't see it, and I didn't care much. No aviator could see my little canoe sneaking in and out of every nook and cranny of that ragged, desolate shoreline. A speedboat zoomed by with spray flying over its windshield. So anxious was I to get into my shirt that I got tangled and couldn't handle the oars to get the dugout pointed into the boat's mean swell. Seawater hit us broadside. Cold water poured in over my feet.

By that time my slumbering temper was ignited. I was angry at that Barney Smith for being the kind of old bachelor that fine people name their babies after, and a girl goes through all this just to say hello to.

Before embarking on this trip and after hours studying my charts I had checked the dictionary definition of various terms used to describe the land's diverse forms. That swelteringly hot row gave me time to mentally review some of these and to find out where I had erred. Yes, *inlet* and *arm* were nearly synonymous. Even a few long, narrow bays could have been called inlets or arms. I now realized that various European explorers had used the broadest definition of these terms in assigning names to the remarkable configurations of this coast.

Finally, around the last point of rock, a low green building came into view. With renewed vigour I continued and soon identified it as a cookhouse. Still nearer, I saw that it was shielded by a weather boom. Wavelets splashed harmlessly over this string of large, slick boomsticks and into the quiet water inside. Snuggled against the ragged shore and to one side of the floathouse was a shingled green and white cottage where boxes of luxuriant red geraniums sat between slim white veranda posts. From a gorge behind the camp, a waterfall thundered as it leaped from rocky shelf to rocky shelf, culminating near the shore in a foaming outrace of clear, fresh water.

The appealing cottage suggested that a married couple lived in this camp. I felt an awful sight to meet a happy young wife who might be wearing a clean, crisp housedress of tiny blue and white checks with a white ruffled collar. The sight of the speedboat at the floathouse terrified me. Was it a government boat with orders to pick me up? I was all ready to throw a tantrum, to scream and wail, when the husky redhead who'd nearly swamped me with swells from his speedboat nonchalantly walked along a slippery boomstick to grab my rope. "We can see now that you aren't an Indian, but you sure are a redskin," he said with an amused smile. The camp cook, wrapping a heavy white apron around his lean middle, leered from the cookhouse door. Obviously the boat crew was not the Coast Guard. I relaxed a little.

They told me this was a womanless camp, "just eight men and the redheaded boatman from headquarters in Powell River." The cottage was not for the loggers, but for prospective buyers of aircraft spruce, or friends of the big boss. "And," they added, "Barney Smith won't be around until suppertime."

Ignoring the two men, I unfastened my wide cord belt, heavy with two knives, and let it drop into the canoe, then dove off the cookhouse float in shorts and shirt. The camp mascot, a tan and white dog of uncertain ancestry, barked frantically as it raced back and forth on the wet boomstick. The cook and Red were staring in consternation when I finally hauled myself up to sun on the flattest boomstick. I could smile again and felt cool and sweet-tempered enough to laugh at their expressions.

Red escorted me to the green cottage beside the waterfall, where I showered and sang until he threw in the cook's dry shirt and a towel. "The boss wants you to stay to supper. I'll take any message you have back to Powell River."

"Just tell the Draytons that I carried their message." I stepped into the living room wearing my navy slacks, the cook's striped shirt and my scarlet tie, looking and feeling like a new person.

The cookhouse door was held open by a butcher knife flung into the floor. Scars and slivers were evidence that this was a daily ritual. I was relaxing, dropping bits of wood into the water and counting the ripples when Jim, the Londoner cook, announced, "Here's Barney."

I turned hesitantly, not knowing how to greet a rough old logger for whom fine people would name a baby. Suddenly he loomed over me—a tall, swaggering, brown-eyed young man. He gazed at me, obviously wondering, "Who is this freckled lunatic who hasn't the sense to tuck in her shirt-tail?"

I wanted awfully to prove my sanity but I could only splutter something senseless about his friends the Draytons sending me to say hello. I patted the dog vigorously.

Jim set my place next to Barney's at the table. I was too confused to look at the other loggers. The conversation lagged and I avoided them after supper by helping the cook with dishes.

"You aren't going to try to make the rapids tonight, are you?" asked Ernie, the boss. It was more statement than question. "It's blowing up a bit outside and you can stay here. The cottage is for guests, and it's all yours tonight."

I definitely wanted to get away from Teakerne Arm, but after one look at the ruffled water I gratefully accepted his invitation. I would need my strength for the rapids, and with the wind and tide against me, I'd not make it before dark, as I had hoped.

"There's good fishing above the falls," the cook told me. It would be a pleasant hike, and after sitting in the dugout all day I needed to exercise my legs. The two Scots carpenters, casting rods in hand, joined us as we tramped to the lake where they would troll for trout. They took one leaky, flat-bottomed rowboat moored on the edge of Cassel Lake, and Jim and I took the other. I cast and reeled in a million times, it seemed, but never got a nibble, so we tied the boat to a snag on the far side of the lake.

"I've always wanted to follow that stream to its source in behind these hills," Jim said, indicating a spot where pure water gushed from the forest above a logged-off clearing.

"Let's find it now," I urged. "I like hiking better than fishing anyway."

We picked our way around stumps and snags, and over or through the debris of recent logging, following the winding stream upward. Below us the lake mirrored the first pastel tinges of sunset. It was hard going and we stopped short of our goal to rest on a mossy bank. I sat with my feet on a rock where cool water rushed around, clear and gurgling. Jim leaned against a giant cedar.

"We can see everything right here," he said, waving his hand around the refreshing woodland scene—lacy cedars and ancient moss-sheathed logs lying like jackstraws across the tumbling stream. Jim talked of his youth in England, of spring in Kew Gardens with the smell of lilacs in bloom, of a wise father and stepmother, of his job taking orders through the voice tube in the kitchen of a London railway terminal. Then he wandered in Canada after the Canadian Pacific Railroad's enticing literature convinced him to leave England during the early days of the Depression.

The first vagrant stirring of the evening breeze ruffled the warm water of the lake as Jim rowed back and tied our boat alongside the other one. Shadows accompanied us along the rough trail to camp. There we wearily flopped on the dry grass by the carpenters' cabin and found that they had returned with five nice trout. They had also seen two deer.

Barney and Ernie and sandy-haired Walt sat on the cottage steps, clouding the air with cigarette smoke to keep the mosquitoes off. I refused their offers of smokes. They pretended astonishment that any American girl would prefer not to smoke. "Most of the American girls that come here on yachts are asking for a light before they even know our names," Barney said.

Their conversation drifted toward yachting visitors, and I learned that three months earlier the beautiful blond personal maid of an English woman guest at the cottage had devastated every heart in camp. "But Walt's the only one she writes to," Jim mourned. "And he was the only one that ignored her."

"That usually provokes a girl's interest, doesn't it?"

"That's right...I think," Barney agreed with a smile.

I asked them about the grey boat without saying why I was interested, and learned it was a Forestry vessel stationed at Squirrel Cove.

"So far on this trip I haven't seen even one Canadian Coast Guard vessel."

"And you won't," Barney said positively. "We don't have such an organization."

That's a relief, I thought. And the American Coast Guard can't search for me in Canadian waters. I remembered that during the years of Prohibition, Canadian rum-runners were safe after delivering booze to US shores if they could get past the US Coast Guard and return to the Canadian side of the border.

It was nearly dark when Ernie came to get his things out of the cottage and move into the bunkhouse for the night. After showing me about the guest cottage, he left me complete mistress of the six well-appointed rooms and luxurious living room with white pine furniture covered with brilliant cushions. Matching drapes hung at the windows. There was a stone fireplace with kindling ready to be lit, and split wood nearby. The evening was warm so I didn't light a fire, nor did I use the battery radio. I did enjoy some of the outdated — but new to me — magazines: *Saturday Evening Post, Time, Life, Atlantic* and *Good Housekeeping*. This was luxury. You ought to go after your sleeping bag and drag it up in the woods for your bed, I told myself. You'll be too soft for the long, hard stretches if you keep on accepting hospitality like this. This luxury was too much and I fell asleep while reading.

During our substantial breakfast of bacon and eggs, washed down with scalding coffee, Barney suggested that I stay for another hour or so to see the Kelly raft (a variation of the better-known Davis raft — a type of boom invented in 1911) of spruce and cedar logs broken apart with dynamite.

After a peaceful night's rest I was much more at ease and sure of myself. "If I stay, do I get to help?"

The crew quickly agreed.

Jim found a pair of caulk boots and insisted I wear them even though they were too large. "You'll need them to climb over the logs."

Ernie helped me aboard the gas boat, *Leaping Lena*, and we all putt-putted several hundred yards to a gigantic cigar-shaped bundle of massive logs. The boots were heavy and tired me as I climbed to the top of the anchored log raft. I noticed that a string of boomsticks was now secured across the open end of the bay. "That's to prevent any logs from drifting away," Ernie told me. The men scattered, scrambling around the fat raft of logs bundled together by many wire cables, each thicker than my wrist. While they worked I carried the

Two photographs of a Davis raft. Betty detonated the dynamite charge that broke apart a Kelly raft — a variation of the Davis raft — in Teakerne Arm. Rare Books and Special Collections, UBC Library, MacMillan Bloedel Ltd. Photograph Collection

detonating cord ashore, crossing on a broad boomstick that was well chewed by countless caulk boots. Walt and I sat on the rock ledge talking about strikes, unions and communism while the experienced men set the charges in place, inserted the blasting caps and then connected the electric detonating wires.

No one ran, but they didn't waste time getting off the raft. Someone waved the all clear and ready signals and Ernie told me to shove down the detonating plunger. That set off the electric blasting caps and the dynamite blew the shackle pins out of the heavy cables, binding the logs into a giant bundle. Great logs erupted from the water. Some leaped straight up, others dashed sideways. All the logs moved wildly. Those held underwater by the weight of logs atop them sprang to the surface. Those that had been on top tumbled and jostled their way to the water. The cigar-shaped raft was now a frolicking accumulation of logs surrounded by foaming, agitated water. Many minutes elapsed before the water quieted and the pile settled into a disorganized mass of floating logs. That explosion set 512 mammoth logs—1.25 million board feet of cedar and spruce—loose to float over the bay.

For minutes afterward I quivered, thinking of the immensity of what one short, easy downward stroke of the plunger had accomplished. Each log weighed thousands of pounds—more than any leaping grey whale.

The excitement was over. No more logs popped from deep underwater like living things suddenly freed. I had no strength to move when Ernie returned. He shouted twice before I snapped out of it enough to drag those heavy caulk boots over the rocks to a place where I could get into the boat. What an experience! I could never forget it. It occurred to me that no other woman had been privileged to push a plunger and free hundreds of logs in the thrilling breakup of a great Kelly raft. How thankful I was that the Draytons had asked me to say hello to Barney Smith.

My canoe was aboard the gas boat. Jim had thoughtfully put up a big sack lunch for me, and now Ernie was taking me to the main channel. Suddenly I was ashamed for having rowed in to see Barney, and then ignored him through the whole visit.

"Ernie, let me off at the end of the boom for a minute, will you, please?" I asked impulsively as we headed out of Teakerne Arm. "I have to see Barney."

"Sure."

Before he could stop me, and ignorant of the danger, I ran across the slimy, precarious boomsticks to a small platform where Walt and Barney were drilling large holes in the ends of spruce logs, making new boomsticks.

"Barney, the Draytons were grand to me! I'm so glad they sent me here. I'll probably never see any of you again. Thanks for everything. I just want to kiss you goodbye."

"You do?" he asked quietly, and he kissed me goodbye, but it was more of a bear hug.

When we reached the main channel Ernie slipped the canoe into the water, and after a hasty thanks and farewell, I pulled away on a good tide toward the Yucultas. I'm one lucky person, I thought. What a fantastic way to end this month!

CHAPTER 6

Navigating the Yucultas

I expected hardships and I looked forward to them as a chance to find myself out. Haven't I read somewhere that only knowledge of oneself is possible?
— Betty Lowman, *Daily Colonist* (Victoria), December 19, 1937

BETWEEN WEST REDONDA ISLAND and the northern shore of Cortes Island I sighted a swimming deer and approached quietly from behind. The doe finally saw me and attempted to leap through the water. She would soon have exhausted herself. I slackened my pace, content to observe her from the gradually growing distance. She clambered ashore on Cortes Island and shook — just like a dog — then sunned for a few moments. I marvelled at the strength of her lean legs, which could propel her through the water at such speed. Too soon she leaped out of sight among the trees growing out of the hillside at odd angles. I pushed on.

The shores rose gradually, becoming steeper and rockier as I proceeded northward through Lewis Channel. At last I could look northeast into Deer Passage and southwest into Sutil Channel. Throughout the day numerous gillnet boats and several tugs passed going north or south. One or more boats were in sight nearly all the time. The tide was favourable and there was no wind. Calm Channel was appropriately named. I didn't exert myself to hurry because whenever I arrived I'd have to wait overnight at Stuart Island for slack water in the rapids. I was so insignificant in that narrow channel, where timbered hills rose thousands of feet on each side, and behind them, snowy mountain ranges glowered.

While exploring the irregularities of the Rendezvous Islands on the western side of Calm Channel, I studied numerous large starfish and seaweeds that waved gently beneath rippling water. I practised bird whistles and was exceedingly proud when my imitations brought answers. Won't it be wonderful, I told myself over and over, when I am in the really uncivilized country, where there are hundreds more wild animals, and I will have to live somewhat as my pioneer ancestors did.

Then past the three low Rendezvous Islands. To the east, bold, cone-like Raza Island blocked my view up Pryce Channel and the glorious high peaks of glacier-carved Toba Inlet.

The distinctive narrow entrance to Hole in the Wall gave me a reliable navigation check. I was making excellent time on this exquisite day. The high hills of Johnstone Bluff and Henrietta Point kept me from seeing much of the water in the long arm of Bute Inlet. But I could see the tops of stupendous snow-crowned mountains and was inspired to sing Grieg's "My Mind is Like a Peak Snow-Crowned." My voice was feeble in that vast expanse of winding waterway trapped between lush forests and high mountains. I was happy, yet singing didn't seem appropriate.

It was near suppertime when I tied up at the float of the Yuculta Traders (a modest store on the southwest portion of Stuart Island) amidst many gillnet boats, all waiting for the morning slack tide. After speaking to a few of the fishermen, I proceeded to the store, and in the registry appended my name to those of the Tyee Boy Scouts. "I believe they were on the way back to Seattle," Mr. Willcock, the store owner, told me.

With money from Mother's Squirrel Cove letter I bought the large-scale chart Queen Charlotte Sound to Smith Inlet. The friendly clerk shook the curls back from her forehead and found sunglasses for me. She led me to the store's limited produce section and insisted that I accept some lettuce and oranges for supper. "You'll have trouble getting fresh vegetables and fruit from here on north," she said.

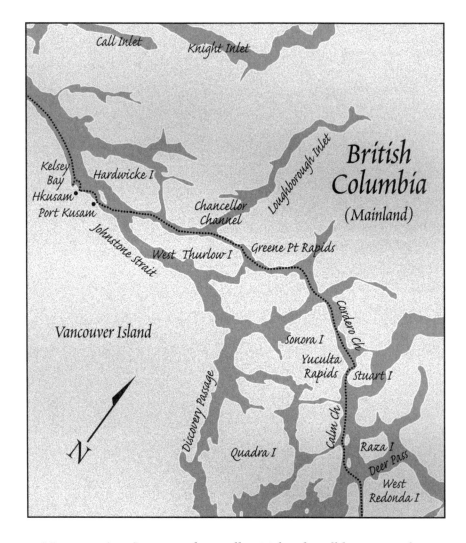

Near evening, I prepared to pull a Richard Halliburton (a daring American adventurer, lecturer and author of the 1920s and 1930s) by unrolling my sleeping bag on the highest rocky ledge I could climb. "To see the sunrise better," I explained to the traders, declining the comfort of the spare bedroom they offered me. I was enthralled with the panorama of pink-tinged wooded slopes and slow-moving trollers below as I sat tailor fashion on my bed-throne, nonchalantly tossing orange peels and outer lettuce leaves into the swirling waters of the lower rapids. I had a powerful longing to dive after them, to

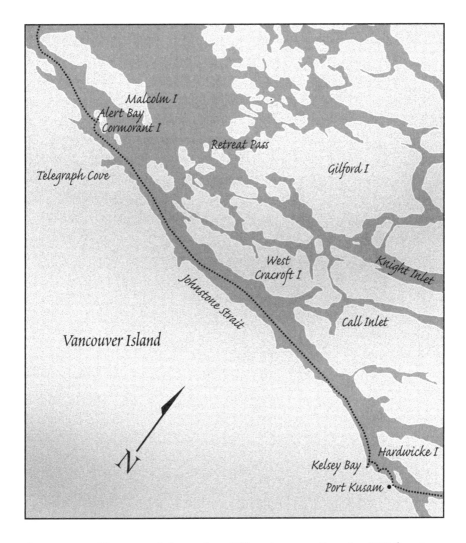

throw myself outward from the cliff and swan dive the 200 feet into the reflecting water.

Before I could act, a speedboat roared up to the float. It was Red, the logging camp boatman from Powell River and Teakerne Arm. I scrambled off my perch and down the steep, overgrown trail. Red had a piece of equipment to be repaired at the machine shop beyond the channel's bend. "Come along with me on a side trip," he invited. "Travel at 20 miles an hour for a change. Maybe you'll get a look at the whirlpools in full force."

Betty needed to be careful in timing her passage through the Yuculta Rapids, one of the most dangerous stretches of water on the West Coast.

"Thanks. That's a marvellous idea." And the breeze might save me from the miserable, hungry, biting blackflies.

It was fun racing along with spray flying over the windshield, some dripping on us. "Should have more speed," Red grumbled. "I'll get the mechanic to check the carburetor." I was disappointed not to get a clear view of the rapids and whirlpools in action, for I had heard plenty about the damage they could do to boats and logs—even swallowing them, and moments later spitting out the remains some distance away.

The machine shop man and Red fussed over the engine while discussing the recent news about the Archbishop of Canterbury and ex-King Edward VIII, now the Duke of Windsor.

"Tide's running at about six knots," Red yelled, as with spray and white water flying we returned at full speed to the Yuculta Traders' float and my dugout. It was 11 p.m. and nearly dark when we tied up.

It had been another long day. Wearily I climbed the cliff for a grand rest—and overslept the sunrise.

I might have missed the slack tide, too, on Dominion Day, Thursday, July 1, if I hadn't hastily thrown my things together and set off without breakfast. The fearsome rapids were tamed during the short period of slack water and I covered the two miles in a few minutes. The Whirlpool Rapids were reasonably calm. My *British Columbia Pilot* stated that the tidal stream could rush through the rapids at five to seven knots. The tide was changing, carrying me into Gillard Pass at good speed. I was thankful that Red had given me a lift through last night when they were in spate. Now it was much different. I raced through three more rapids with their cross and circular currents, eddies and whirlpools before passing the Dent Islands.

Thirty or 40 gillnet fishermen passed me during that row from Stuart Island and through Cordero Channel. Nearly every one of them stepped out of his little pilothouse as he ka-chugged by and shouted, "Want a tow to Rivers or Smith Inlet?"

"No thanks," I assured each, "but I'll be seeing you up there before another month."

I was nearing the northwest end of Sonora Island when my leg began to feel as though a sliver was sticking me. But this was no sliver. It was a little black bug. It wouldn't shake off and it wouldn't brush off. Its head was under my skin. I tried to pull it out. The body broke, leaving the head embedded in my leg. In my haste to depart and the excitement of navigating the rapids, I had not discovered this wood tick burrowing through the skin on the underside of my left thigh. Within hours a red welt rose around the insect's head. It wasn't painful and I forgot about it in the fun and challenge of getting through Greene Point Rapids. The tide was running strong there—perhaps as fast as seven knots. Eagles circled low over the stark trees on slopes partly cleared by logging operations or forest fires. I had to be constantly alert to prevent *Bijaboji* from pirouetting helplessly like the many bits of driftwood that caught in the whirlpools and eddies, or bouncing in overfalls.

That was a long rowing day. It might not have been if, after I got into Chancellor Channel, I'd found even the tiniest landing spot on

West Thurlow Island. Mel Payne, a fisherman I'd met at the Traders' float, had warned me of the miles of precipitous shoreline beyond the Yucultas. I had to see it myself before I'd believe that a canoeist could not find an anchorage or landing beach there.

At twilight, as I battled against the strong flood tide off West Thurlow Island, a streamlined eastbound yacht streaked by, whistling a salute. As the wind picked up and the tide ran stronger against me, I wondered if instead of a salute the signal hadn't been intended to warn me of a rapidly changing barometer.

There was nothing to do but go on, even though deepening twilight made it even more difficult to catch sight of a possible landing spot. I strained to catch sight of the tiniest patch of shoreline less inhospitable than a sheer stone wall. Waves slopped over *Bijaboji*'s stern, which I was shoving foremost. The squeaky screw in the rowlock socket worked its way up alarmingly—up and wobbling until I grabbed the hatchet and pounded it down. "I'd be helpless against this tide with one oar," I muttered, eyeing the turbulent waves during the seconds before I got the canoe in forward motion again.

Waves washed over a rock ahead. Even though it was too small to camp on, I decided to make fast for a while, eat something for the first time that day and put on sou'wester, ski pants and jacket. So I did, but the tide rose fast and I got away quickly when a seal poked up its dark, sleek head about 20 feet away.

Off again. I headed toward the middle of the channel to avoid the backwash and tide rips where back eddies fought with the main current. This is an uncharted channel, I remembered from my studies of the *Coast Pilot*. Anything can happen here. Chill waves continued to wash over the stern. The seconds I needed to bail were precious seconds lost from rowing. I made no headway against the tide, and the calm of hopelessness settled over me. Thinking of the gillnetters I had promised to meet again in the inlets above Queen Charlotte Sound, I chided myself. Spoke too soon, big mouth.

Jabbing the oars into wave after wave, I found myself involuntarily singing—singing Dudley Buck's "Fear Not Ye, O Israel." Almost as soon as the wind drowned out the last words, I was strangely impelled to row away from West Thurlow Island and cross Chancellor Channel to the mainland. There, a mile out of my way and in pitch dark, the canoe nudged onto a bit of sandy beach. Thanks for that quick answer to prayer, I thought. Rest and safety at last.

Wearily I stepped ashore, pulled *Bijaboji* out of reach of the troubled water and secured the bowline to a small tree. Then I tossed my sleeping bag onto the sand beside the dugout and crawled in. I was exhausted. Too exhausted even to take off my sou'wester and leather jacket. Until daybreak, when the rhythmic pounding of a passing gillnet boat's engine awakened me, I slept the sleep of a happy, weary girl canoeist. There was nothing like it. Life was good.

The sky was clear and there was no wind. After spreading my sou'wester and jacket on the sand to dry, I leaped into the salt water for my usual refreshing morning swim and wash. Then a quick cold breakfast before rolling the canoe to the water's edge on small logs. In the morning light I discovered that this tiny beach was the only safe and sandy shore for miles. To me, that was surely answer to prayer. Or a miracle. Perhaps both.

I set out in a glassy calm to the western end of Chancellor Channel. Thence into Johnstone Strait, passing south of Helmcken Island and across to Port Kusam on Vancouver Island, my next mail stop. It was a magnificent day for canoeing. I felt wonderfully alive.

I learned that Port Kusam had been included in my itinerary only because I had an out-of-date chart showing a post office there. One of the Seattle skippers who had helped me plan the trip tried to persuade me not to go back to Vancouver Island after getting through the Yucultas. I insisted that I would be crazy for mail about that time in my travels and I left Port Kusam on my list of mailing addresses for Mother.

"The sea is as fickle as a woman," I muttered as a strong, favourable tide swiftly pushed me over the water—water sparkling and bright as burnished silver—to Vancouver Island. Small powerboats passed a mile or more away and I seemed to have as much speed as they.

Now, rowing along the shore of Vancouver Island, parallel to the crude telephone line strung on trees, stumps and poles, I had time to enjoy the unusual beauty of this quiet island. The favourable tide gave me enough leisure to occasionally poke an oar at a large, prickly sea urchin. There were hundreds of them, red and purple, living on rocks only a few feet under the surface. Nowhere in Puget Sound have I seen sea urchins to match them in brilliance of colour or length of spines. Sometimes I'd nudge the flower-like sea anemones and watch them quickly close.

It was mid-morning when, according to my chart, I was at Port Kusam. It consisted only of a white house, a log cabin, a boat shed and a float walkway extending over the broad tidal flat. Hardly what I would call a port.

Bewildered, I pulled in the oars and studied the charts. They were no help. I was flipping through the pages of my *British Columbia Coast Pilot* when a man and a small curly-haired boy came alongside in an outboard skiff.

"I think I'm lost, unless this is Port Kusam."

"This is Port Kusam," the man assured me. "Just tie up to the float."

They made fast to the float in front of me as a slight brunette lady walked out on the gently undulating float and eagerly reached for the mail the boaters had brought from Kelsey Bay.

"I'm Mrs. Kohse." She greeted me with a smile. "We heard about you over the radio again last night. We've been getting mail for you and couldn't imagine why. It has been many years since this was a post office." Then, quickly looking through the few letters in her hand, she exclaimed joyfully, "A letter from Freddy!"

Eight-year-old Gerald Kohse clambered out of the skiff and hurried after his mother to the lattice gate, where the tall grey-haired Frederick Kohse met them. Bill Green, the sea-going mail carrier, also rushed ashore. "Well, what does that boy of yours have to say?"

"He's going to troll longer out of Bull Harbour," she said sadly. "Fishing's good so he won't be here tonight."

Before luncheon I learned that the Kohses' lives had been indelibly affected by the six years they spent in Canadian relocation camps during the Great War. "My husband was born and raised in Germany, so was interned," Mrs. Kohse said. "I'm English-born and had my choice of being in camp with my husband or living outside with little Freddy. We stayed together as a family."

"The war still goes on," Mr. Kohse said quietly.

I agreed with him, thinking of the war veterans I knew in Anacortes, and those I'd met on this trip: the Major, Ernie and others, physically scarred by shrapnel or bullets. And others mentally scarred by trauma and disillusionment; more at peace in sequestered cabins or isolated camps, away from people who hadn't lain in muddy trenches, been sickened by poisonous gas or endured the indescribable stench of rotting human bodies.

After lunch, despite the Kohses' protests, I prepared to head out again. "If I don't plug on, I'll never meet *Tyee Scout* in Alert Bay on July 4th," I explained. "I missed them on their first cruise and I need the clothes and money they have for me."

"Johnstone Strait's the most heartbreaking stretch on the coast," Mrs. Kohse said. "You'll make double time by waiting for the strong morning tide." With that statement she persuaded me to accept their gracious hospitality for the night, promising an early morning send-off.

During the afternoon, the Kohses' Irish friends from Quadra Island arrived and moored alongside the float and I was interested in their conversation about the difficulty of schooling children along this sparsely populated coast. "It's hard enough on any mother to do all her housework, gardening and canning," Mrs. Kohse said, "plus educating one child by correspondence, let alone trying to teach two or three children."

"When you do live near enough to other families to have a school-teacher," said the Irish woman, "you're always on edge for fear one family will go away and the school will dissolve for lack of having the minimum eight children."

Later a young German couple from a logging camp down the coast stopped in to pass along a few recent issues of women's magazines, which were gratefully accepted. The guests departed before the afternoon winds and changing tides agitated the water and made it too rough for safety. Only a week earlier, a boat carrying teachers and children on their way to an examination centre had been forced to land at the Kohses' and stay until the weather calmed.

As Mrs. Kohse made supper, Mr. Kohse asked me about *Tyee Scout*. "You are very eager to meet that boat. You must have a boyfriends on it."

"No, I'm a career-minded girl who's never had boyfriends," I confessed. "I do have four brothers, plus many cousins, uncles and neighbours."

"You'll want a husband someday," he predicted. "Then you come up here. Women are scarce. Why, some of the most hopeless old maids get married off after coming here on vacations or visiting relatives," he said kindly, if not diplomatically.

Just at suppertime Freddy's boat entered the open harbour. In two seconds the table was deserted. Gerald eagerly led the delighted family to the end of the float, where he waved both arms as his 23-year-old brother eased his boat alongside the bouncy float-walk.

Gusts of fresh wind seemed to rush into the great kitchen-living room along with six-foot, curly-haired Freddy. His lean sun- and wind-browned face lighted in a flashing, friendly grin when he saw a stranger in the room. His mother listened eagerly to the story of his unexpected return while I tried to reconcile this rugged seafaring man, his chest exposed by a half-buttoned red flannel shirt, with the diminutive name "Freddy."

Mrs. Kohse loaded his plate with food, but he had so much to tell and so many questions to answer about trolling at Bull Harbour that he ate much less than I. He told jolly stories, obviously revelling in the good fellowship of his fishermen friends. After supper, with Gerald and me tagging after, he made light, quick work of tasks about the place, driving in and milking the cows, then getting his gillnet boat ready to return to the fishing grounds. My admiration grew by leaps and bounds.

That night I slept on the top floor of the Kohse residence—called, for some reason unknown to me, Ruby House—in a room facing the water. I was awakened sometime during the night by Fred's happy singing. He was spending the night aboard his gillnet boat, *F.K.*, watching for leaks.

The prevailing July wind and rain churned up the salt water enough the next morning to disrupt my going-away plans. The Kohses' neighbour Mr. Green, one of the first black settlers in that area, generously offered to show me some of the nearby sights. So we rowed to the Salmon River, shooting along at great speed on the flooding tide, with me pulling on one set of seven-foot oars and Mr. Green, sitting on a higher seat in the stern of his sturdy clinker-built boat, pushing on the other set. Because we sat facing each other, talking was easy, until we jolted into a sandbar in the mouth of the river. At high water the area appears to be a large bay, but at low water there are many shallow or drying bars near the river's mouth. We rocked the boat from side to side until it broke free.

The outflow of water was against us when we entered the river. To one side was a small islet, on the other side and about a half mile from the mouth were the few remains of Hkusam, an abandoned Native village. Now cows grazed there, somewhat protected from the wind and unmindful of the steady drizzle.

"You're a logger of many years' experience," I said. "Tell me about the trees around here."

He obligingly pointed out and named the various species: fir, spruce, hemlock and yew, and estimated the age of the larger ones. "During the spring floods, lots of the land you now see is covered by the river." He told me that lots of people stopped to see the Kohses and were welcomed with a big meal and even a place to sleep, just as I was. "Mr. and Mrs. Kohse are always pleasant to each other, like a couple of honeymooners," he said. "And do those boys think a lot of their folks? Say! That Freddy sends every dollar he earns home to them, and he earns plenty. Earlier this year he was the highliner on the trolling grounds for a couple weeks."

A curve in the river brought us in sight of a high wooden bridge, where a young boy raced across on a shiny bicycle. A little farther upriver we moored to a float tied against the dark dirt bank of the stream. A man and a young boy on a 40-foot launch were talking to

An abandoned Hkusam village that Betty visited with Mr. Green, one of the first black settlers on the coast. Courtesy Eric D. Sismey

three women on the float. The ladies were obviously disappointed when the man told them, "We're sorry but our permanent wave operator is sick today." I'd never heard of a floating beauty shop.

We visited the general store, which was dimly lighted; flies circled dizzily around a tiny flyspecked bulb. Gunny sacks of feed and sugar were piled about the small store, leaving only a narrow aisle by the counter. I went outside and talked with the man and boy on the beauty shop launch.

"We have general merchandise for sale and our beauty operator can do all the styles women want," the launch owner said. He was wearing one of those tan and brown sweaters woven with Indian symbols. "During the summer we travel to all of these out-of-the-way places. Also furnish music for dances and put on movies. It's a pretty good life. Interesting, too."

He reassured me about the inflammation left by the wood tick. "I had one once. It wasn't nasty at all after I dug out the head with a jackknife."

Why hadn't I thought of doing that?

The ladies who had been waiting for a permanent were now chatting about Amelia Earhart, who had been reported lost in the southern seas. "Such a fine woman," one said, "a man's courage and no bunchy masculinity."

Mr. Green rowed us across the river to a little post office building, where I shoved letters to Mother and Flo through the slot. I wondered how long it would take the letter to reach Mother. We walked some distance along the riverbank to a small mill, where four men were sawing cumbersome cedar logs into rough, thick planks. As we returned to the boat we stopped for a few minutes to watch two men rolling sawlogs off a large truck and into the river.

"Some veterans settled here after the war," Mr. Green said. "Those two men fought in France." As we drifted downstream he remarked, "Usually I have an awful time talking to women, but you seem to loosen my tongue."

He told me that Freddy Kohse had rolled and dragged a lot of logs off the beach that spring. "They'd broke loose from a flat boom during a winter storm," he said. "There's money in them. And he built that trolling boat of his from an old burned-out hulk he got for nothing."

When we returned to the Kohses' float, Fred and his father were busy working on his gillnet boat. I went on to the house. Mrs. Kohse told me that Freddy was to leave that night for Smith Inlet, and she urged me to ride as far as Alert Bay with him.

"My conscience would burn up if I did, Mrs. Kohse," I said. "I'm just wondering if I hadn't better start out in the canoe right now. The strait isn't rough."

"No, but the tide is against you," she argued, pulling a well-worn tide table book off a hook beside the kitchen door, then pointed to the day, time and direction of flow. "The tide runs up to six knots. You'd be going backwards."

It was Saturday, July 3, and I couldn't resign myself to missing *Tyee Scout* again. So, squelching my conscience, I walked out to Fred's boat. Mr. Green was fixing the loose rowlock screw in my canoe.

"May I ride with you to Alert Bay?"

"If you want to," Fred smiled. "Then I can give you pointers on crossing Queen Charlotte Strait. I rowed across the strait four times in a fishing dory before I got this power boat. And your dugout will sure row easier than a dory, especially if there's any helpful wind and tide."

I felt sick about not rowing the northern portion of Johnstone Strait, and firmly resolved to navigate Queen Charlotte and Johnstone straits before a year passed.

During the afternoon I helped churn—the first time I'd seen butter made—jotted notes for the ship's log, cut asparagus, washed dishes while Mrs. Kohse kneaded bread, and stood by Gerald on the float while he fished for perch. I realized that I lacked many domestic skills. And now I felt somewhat ill because the tick's head had infected my leg. Mrs. Kohse tried to pry it out but couldn't budge it.

At suppertime Gerald came in with a bucket of strawberries. "For you, Freddy," he said to his big brother adoringly, his face aglow. Table conversation centred on the fishermen's strike of the previous year, which had been disastrous for the gillnetters in Rivers and Smith inlets.

While the men tended to the cows, Mrs. Kohse mended her son's trousers and shirts and packed fresh bread and canned supplies for him. She also wrapped up a hot loaf of German-style brown bread for me. After the farm chores were done she quickly sheared off several inches of Fred's tight curls, then neatly trimmed my bob.

It was dark when we all struggled down the float-walk with our bundles and equipment. Every step bounced the walk, disturbing the water and surrounding the float with brilliant phosphorescence. We pulled the canoe aboard *F.K.* and quickly said our goodbyes. Fred and I were off for the short trip to Kelsey Bay to fuel his gas boat and pick up two passengers, the couple who operated the Pine Island light.

Fred landed expertly alongside another fish boat tied behind the short end of the L-shaped wharf, then went ashore to find the man in charge of the fuel dock. Thirty minutes later he returned with the agent. They fuelled the boat, then walked to the office. When Fred reappeared he had half a dozen candy bars and disconcerting news. "Martha and her husband can't get here from upriver until four a.m. We'll have about three hours of waiting. You can sleep on that boat next to mine...or shall we talk?"

"Wouldn't you like to go to the dance and see your friends? You don't need to entertain me, Fred."

"I haven't any clothes for dances."

During those next few hours of waiting we nibbled on candy bars and talked—about conditions on the fishing grounds, the prospect of Japanese fishermen taking over the industry, strikes, Skeena River scab fishermen, and why men will blow many months' pay in two weeks in the city. Fred was curious about American university students. "Don't they run around drinking and smoking a lot down there, and all that sort of thing?" he asked. "I suppose you've seen quite a lot of that during four years in college."

"I've seen much less than many high school students. Most of my friends were Campfire Girls and Boy Scouts and other upstanding people. Not many of them smoke and few of them drink. And I certainly don't do either."

Just before four o'clock the lightkeeper couple and a 16-year-old nephew arrived. Somehow the husband stumbled overboard almost as soon as he stepped aboard. There was much excitement and laughing while getting him back aboard and finding some dry clothes.

We left Kelsey Bay at four o'clock with a silvered pink dawn blooming astern, over the Thurlow Islands. To our left a continuous range of high, steep mountains rose abruptly from the water's edge, appearing nearly as high as the mountains surrounding Princess Louisa Inlet. Numerous valleys of varying width and length slashed through these forested ranges. Several miles to the northeast the shore was outlined against the pink sky, less rugged, less mountainous and broken by channels and inlets.

Just outside Kelsey Bay we broncoed through a heavy tide rip. Fred, sensitive to every wild movement of the boat, gripped the wheel firmly and confidently. I crawled through the passage to the bunk behind the engine and slept for two hours. I awoke much rested and stepped out into full daybreak. The lighthouse man was steering and his wife Martha nursed a bump over one eye. "Stumbled against a board when the boat lunged in that tide rip," she laughed. It was too much work to shout over the noise of the engine, so we went outside to sit on the forward deck and gaze at the superlative scenery.

Martha was much in love. "He went overseas. We were engaged seven years and I worked in San Francisco most of the time. Soon after he came home, a good friend at Pine Island appointed him assistant keeper. We've had dinner guests only twice in six months. Many boats go by a lighthouse but few stop," she sighed. "We appreciate having this short visit at Salmon River. Freddy was good to bring us."

Fred went below to get some sleep and it was my turn to steer. I set a course for Cormorant Island and Alert Bay, some 15 miles ahead. I enjoyed handling the boat, which now rolled gently and bowed easily as we sped along. Gulls winged by, always searching for food, and cormorants rode drifting logs, standing tall and formal in their shiny black plumage.

Fred came up when we were about seven miles from Alert Bay.

"Did my zigzagging steering awaken you?"

"No, I came up to see who was doing such a good job at the wheel."

Only one other boat was visible on this long, unwavering stretch of Johnstone Strait, and as our courses slowly converged, I thought the boat looked familiar. I told myself it might be wishful thinking, but when we were about two miles from Alert Bay, I was positive and shouted joyously, "It's *Tyee Scout!*"

Fred offered to take the wheel so that I could wave to my friends, and suddenly I was conscious of my sunburn, of my shaggy stand-up bob, of me generally. I raked out a lipstick and smeared scarlet thickly on my lips. It looked ridiculous when I glanced at the small mirror hanging in the pilothouse. I dimmed each lip with the tip of a little brush. Fred was amused. I tossed the lipstick overboard.

"I don't like make-up. It's hopeless to think I can look like a coed while I'm a canoeist."

Shortly before nine o'clock the two boats entered Alert Bay on a parallel course with only a few feet of foaming water separating us.

In my excitement at seeing someone from the States, I shouted my adventures over the water to the teenage boys on *Tyee Scout*. All were strangers except Captain Art Church.

"Your canoe was green the last time I saw it a year ago," Art shouted, grinning in his inimitable way that lights a person's soul. "We'd never have spotted you in that red thing!" Only then did I stop feeling guilty about accepting the lift on board *F.K.* I'd never have made connections with the Scouts if I had rowed that 30 miles from Port Kusam. *Bijaboji* was unloaded at the red and cream Imperial Oil dock and the Scouts flocked around with box cameras. "Get in the dugout and row," several called out. I was embarrassed. White, Native and Slavic fishermen stood in wonderment on the decks of nearby purse seine boats. "Sure, give the boys a break," Art said, grinning broadly.

"Well, if it's action snaps you want, I'd better get into my rowing suit, hadn't I?" I kicked off my ski trousers in the canoe as it whirled on the current and struck crosswise against the pilings of the dock. I had a bad few minutes getting turned around and out of the tide, and the Scouts hovered over the rail above snapping pictures of me in that unseamanlike predicament. Fred and Art, on the float, offered no advice until I was within their reach. By then the Scouts had discovered new interests and were racing off to take pictures of totem poles in the Native graveyard.

"Thought you were going to tip over," Art said quietly, holding the canoe steady.

"You're having lunch with us, aren't you?" Fred invited me.

"She'd better eat on the ship," Art said. "We'll soon be crossing the strait."

Fred traced a route on my chart for crossing Queen Charlotte Strait. "I see your chart ends at Smith Inlet," he said, handing it back. "Maybe I'll see the girl in the red canoe up there."

"I hope so, Fred." *F.K.*'s lines were cast off. Fred and the lightkeepers were underway for Pine Island.

CHAPTER 7

R&R Aboard the Tyee Scout

*With the exception of the officers, the Boy Scouts were all under 16
years of age. During the five days they were stranded she did not hear
a "swear word," shady remark or slightest sign of lack of discipline
aboard the boat, and it was with regret she told them goodbye.*
— *Anacortes Mercury*, July 14, 1937

AS FRED AND HIS PASSENGERS CHUGGED out of Alert Bay, I stepped
into *Bijaboji* and grasped the oars. Art eased into the stern and husky
Chuck Day—"Cookie" to all hands—piled atop the Fabrikoid covering at the bow for the ride. *Bijaboji* had little freeboard as we headed
for *Tyee Scout*. Art introduced me to the 19 Walla Walla boys who had
been ashore photographing the town's numerous totem poles and
were now clamouring for lunch. Dick Hill, the engineer, introduced
himself.

Art and Dick were a bit taken aback by my determination to carry
on with my plan to row across Queen Charlotte Strait, the widest
body of water I had yet to cross, rather than being towed. "I want to
row every inch of it myself," I assured Art. "But I'd like to ride across
today to look it over."

The boys invited me to come along and assured me that I'd not
spoil their fun.

After a short session at the Alert Bay hospital to have the wood
tick's head removed from my leg and the infection treated, Art and

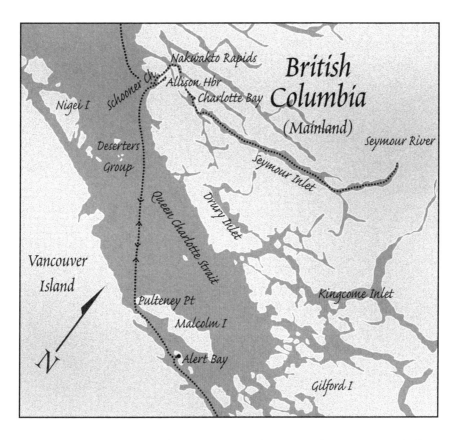

I mingled with the bustling tourists who were chattering and photographing each other around the intriguing totems. Painfully conscious of my ski outfit and shiny red, freckled face, I urged, "Let's go down to the waterfront. I want to see the *Cardena*." *Cardena*, a coastal supply and passenger steamship, had just disgorged local passengers and tourists. Booms were rigged yard and stay and the deck crew was busy unloading freight. A ship's officer told us that this vessel served some 200 ports, including logging camps, canneries and mines, and could carry 250 passengers and 350 tons of cargo, plus 30 tons of refrigerated boxed fish. *Cardena* was indispensable to all persons living and working on this coast.

About one o'clock *Tyee Scout* pulled out of Alert Bay. There was no room aboard for *Bijaboji*, so I had reluctantly left her on the float near some of the local purse seine fishermen, who promised to guard her.

Shortly after a mid-afternoon lunch of gallons of fruit salad we rounded Pulteney Point and headed northeast across Queen Charlotte Strait for Seymour Inlet. Far to port was the northeastern tip of Vancouver Island and westward, beyond the vast Pacific, China. The many islands scattered across the northern entrance to Queen Charlotte Strait slightly calmed our rolling and pitching. We passed the Deserters Group of islands to port as we pitched and swayed through Ripple Passage. For the first time I saw only open water to the northwest. Big brown groundswells rolled in on the back of the flooding tide. *Tyee Scout* was now vulnerable to the capers of the open Pacific and her vigorous movement became uncomfortable for a few Scouts from eastern Washington.

I spent most of my time in the small pilothouse, out of the boys' way. A little Scout, Frank Howard, who could barely see over the wheel, was helmsman. Skipper Art, Engineer Dick and Cook Chuck made plans at the chart table for the evening fireside. Unobtrusively, Art checked on his wheel watch at least every 10 minutes. He also superintended fun aboard ship. When there was a lull in the boys' activity, Art hauled out his big white and gold accordion, apologized effusively for lack of training, then filled the ship with lively Scout songs, popular songs and classics.

Late in the afternoon I heard a shout from outside: "No bottom at 40." Chuck, standing on the starboard side, was hauling up the lead line. For the next half-hour, as the boat moved slowly among the maze of islands off the entrances to Schooner Channel and Allison Harbour, Chuck's or Dick's shouts rang out: "Bottom at..." Eventually we worked past all rocks and reefs encumbering the entrance, found the channel and chugged into a cove just inside the entrance to diminutive Allison Harbour.

As soon as the Scout ship was moored alongside the extensive log float supporting a small store building, the boys leaped onto the float and rushed for the store. Most were soon chewing bars of English toffee and grinning happily. Their attention soon shifted to a couple of young swimmers; a boy and a buxom girl throwing jellyfish at each other. A few moments later the girl slipped off a slimy log and disappeared in the deep, jade-green water saturated with translucent jellyfish. She came up screaming and brushing herself off before hurling herself onto the float and running to wash off the stinging slime.

A salmon troller was also moored to the log float. Art and I asked the owner, Tom Oien, a middle-aged Norwegian, about the rapids. Then Tom introduced us to Frank Bellham and his wife Vi, a tall, slender, red-haired Vancouver girl. They owned and ran the general store, post office, warehouse, fish- and fur-buying post, fountain and lunch counter service. All this on a float secured in a tiny cove no larger than an acre. They also seemed to have a monopoly on buzzing, biting mosquitoes. Their two handsome little boys rarely set foot on land except at low tide when they went mussel gathering. "One or the other falls off the float nearly every day," Vi told us. "They wear life jackets all the time except when they're in bed."

We waited three hours until slack water in Nakwakto Rapids, British Columbia's swiftest tidal stream. "Just follow me," Tom offered, "and I'll lead you through the rapids and on to Charlotte Bay logging camp, where you may lay over for the night."

It was near dusk when we followed Tom's trim troller with its long, limber trolling poles, now pulled straight up, into Schooner Channel and toward the rapids. On the way Art told me what he knew about the rapids from hearsay and the *Coast Pilot*. Nakwakto Rapids, connecting Schooner and Slingsby channels to Seymour Inlet, are a quarter of a mile wide, but the tidal current rushes with great fury against Turret Rock (often aptly called Tremble Island) in the centre. That and rocks two fathoms below the surface cause heavy and dangerous overfalls. The ebb tide may attain a velocity of 16 knots—one of the highest rates in the world—and the flood tide slightly less. Mariners have to await the turn of the tidal stream and make the passage at slack water, which lasts for only six minutes. That is the only time to get through safely.

The rapids were all the book said—and more. Never before or since have I seen such acres of roaring, brawling hills and gullies of treacherous water as I did while transiting Nakwakto Rapids at the beginning of the flood tide. Tom's little boat was a crazily bobbing cork. And *Tyee Scout*, although larger, was equally unsteady. A good experience for these boys from the dry, rolling lands of eastern Washington. Safely through, Tom waited for us to tie alongside for the remainder of the trip to Charlotte Bay in the western end of Seymour Inlet. As we moved toward the dusk-blackened forests, I looked back, thankful to have been guided through those dangerous rapids by an experienced fisherman. Now I knew the rapids deserved their fearsome reputation.

Foam in the wake of the two boats formed a lacy pattern on the pinkish silver waters of early dusk before being swirled into the currents of the rapids. As the boats wound their way between high purple hills, the roar of the rapids diminished gradually and the water lost its silver sheen, except in the centre of the channel, where the great shadows of mountains did not dull the surface.

Finally the two boats reached the calm water of Charlotte Bay. Tom wanted to tie up for the night beside one of the several floathouses, where light from gas or kerosene lamps shone through the windows, so the boys cast off the lines to his troller. We made fast to an outer boomstick, and Cookie set off in the skiff with several of the boys to locate a clearing for an evening campfire. With Tom at the oars of his rowboat, Art, Dick and I went to invite Ray, the Scandinavian boss logger, and his pretty wife Mary to be guests at the Sea Scout fireside. Theirs was the most brightly lighted floathouse in the tiny bay.

In a cheery living room, with a floor covering of green and yellow Congoleum, we were introduced to Mary and four or five loggers. The men were bent over the battery radio, intently listening for news of Amelia Earhart. Mary was curled comfortably on a wicker settee, smoking a cigarette. "Let the boys have their bonfire without you," she said. "Stay here and have cupcakes and coffee with us." Art thanked her but urged her to accept his invitation, and finally Mary and Martin, one of the weather-bronzed loggers, said they would come with us on condition we'd first visit for a while with them.

"So you're the girl we heard about over the radio," someone said. They seemed disappointed that I wasn't a tall, khaki-clad, gun-toting, cursing, smoking female. I felt strangely naive among them.

After a short visit we set out in the rowboat to join the boys, but nowhere along the dark shoreline could we see the light of a fire. "All of *Tyee*'s lights are on," Art said. "They were off when we left."

We went aboard to locate the boys. "They're in their bunks," Cookie said. "We couldn't beach anywhere. It's either cliff or tidal sand flats all around here. There will be no campfire or Fourth of July celebration tonight. Besides, the boys were pretty well worn out."

"You'll have to see our ship now that you are here," Art told Mary.

Dick and Art helped her aboard. Cookie made Tom's rowboat fast then hurried below to fix a tasty midnight lunch while the rest of us made ourselves comfortable in the pilothouse.

Art was eager to find a Native burial ground to show the boys and asked our guests about it. Tom, whose late wife had been a Native, mentioned a few likely spots on islets dense with tangled thicket and brush. Mary was irritated by the question. "Maybe I am a breed Indian," she said indignantly, "but I'm no savage, and I don't know anything of savage ways."

Dick and Art tried to pacify her tactfully but she was off on what must have been a favourite tirade. "I don't care who knows that I had to fish with my father, and haul lines and clean fish and do lots you wouldn't understand. It's no disgrace. And my little girls are well-mannered, white, brighter and better educated than most kids around here."

In an attempt to placate Mary, I mentioned that one of our most loved vice-presidents was part Indian. That only made her turn on me. "You, rowing an Indian dugout up here. Novelty! Sensation! That's all!"

"Not at all," I said quietly. "My father gave me an Indian dugout because the Coast Guard stationed at the Anacortes base happened to find it drifting and couldn't locate the owner. I would never have started up here in any other type of canoe. A skilled Indian made it for safe use in the ocean waters and weather around Vancouver Island and the Inside Passage to Alaska. I pray to find him. I know my dugout's quirks and what it will do. It's wonderfully seaworthy."

Fortunately, Cookie entered the pilothouse just then with a tray of luscious food and a pot of tea. I believe all of us were relieved to have our attention diverted. Art played his accordion while we ate, and it was well after midnight when Tom rowed Ray, Martin and Mary back to camp. I made up my bed on top of the pilothouse. Hundreds of no-see-ums—devilish black gnats—drove me into the Cocoon, as I had begun to call my sleeping bag, and I wished I had a zipper at the top of it, or the courage to dash into the midst of all the sleeping Scouts to find some citronella—sure protection.

In the morning, rubbing my bumpy face, I crawled out to find myself the centre of attention for the men of the logging camp, who had gathered for an early breakfast at the nearest floathouse. Such was my haste to get out of sight again that I nearly went through the bottom of the sleeping bag.

By the time the loggers had gone off to work, the Scouts were milling around. I wiggled into a bathing suit and dove off the top of the pilothouse for a morning dip. The boys were busy with breakfast when I finished, and I dressed quickly in navy blue flannel slacks, sailor blouse and pink sweater.

It was Monday, July 5, and legally our Fourth of July holiday. This was the first time I had been outside my own country for a Fourth of July, but I was with a super troop of Sea Scouts. At the Chinese store in Alert Bay the boys had bought piles of fireworks, which they were saving for the evening fireside.

With the boys taking turns on wheel and lookout watch, we cruised eastward in the deep, ugly brown water of Seymour Inlet. The inlet is only about a mile wide and most of us were topside admiring the scenery as we ran between rugged, densely timbered shorelines, wanton green against the bright snow-draped mountains. But my recollections of the scenery along those miles are few, because I spent a lot of time laughing over the boys' horseplay. It was so enjoyable being with those jolly, good-natured, typically American young fellows about the same ages as two of my younger brothers.

We were only four miles from the head of Seymour Inlet, where the Seymour River pours in, cold from the snowmelt of the Coast Range, when Art took the wheel and turned us about and announced that we would go back and stop at a small logging camp we passed on the way.

He eased us alongside the largest of the three buildings of the float camp and had one of the boys tie the bowline to the eye of a boom chain. He then leaped onto the float and headed toward the bunk-house. He was gone only a few minutes, then we were underway again, heading westward toward Nakwakto Rapids. Art told us that one of the Native loggers had been helpful after he had explained that the Scouts were interested in seeing some of the Native burial spots and would not be after "souvenirs."

"The Indian burial boxes are hidden under a tangle of brush on an islet separated from the site of a long abandoned village, well this side of Charlotte Bay," Art informed the eager boys.

We anchored and the boys went ashore, breaking trail over the top of a knoll barely connected with the old village at low tide. At the base of the knoll was a cedar shack where numerous bird feathers were strewn about a heap of stones blackened by many cooking fires. On top of the knoll were two larger than life-size carved cedar figures representing a man and a woman. Salal grew from the woman's head like bushy green hair. Art spotted a chunk of green-painted wood partly buried in the black soil with smashed clamshells along the water's edge—a broken piece of a dugout canoe. The boys didn't find any burial boxes, so we went to an islet on the other side of the passage.

The islet had no beach—it poked up abruptly from many fathoms of water. Art eased *Tyee Scout*'s bow against the rock and we leaped ashore. The first boys off broke trail through and under the brush to a crude shelter. Many square coffins made of wide slabs of split cedar were piled here. Coming along at the end of the line, I found the boys staring into some of the hand-hewn boxes whose ends or sides had crumbled from age. I shuddered at the sight of fairly well preserved— almost mummified—corpses. Dry sinew clung to the bones. Hair and red paint darkened the skulls. Maggot shells spotted a few faces and garments. A faded and tattered red bandana hung from one box.

I was the first to leave. My conscience makes me miserable over anything like sacrilegious observation of the dead. Maybe I am a bit superstitious, too. Certainly the events of the following night and day gave me grounds to believe in the fateful "finger of the dead."

When the skipper had checked the last ones aboard, the boy on watch set a course for the mouth of the inlet. We passed the placid waters of Charlotte Bay, waving, although probably no one saw us. Art checked the tide book, then his watch, saying, "It's near the end of the ebb. Just right for safely going out through the rapids…Cookie, pass the word for all hands to stay well inboard of the lifelines while we're in the rapids. We'll roll and bounce some. If anyone falls over the side, he's a goner."

We swept through the Nakwaktos without mishap.

Beyond the rapids, whose roar was louder than the chug of the boat engine, Dick came up from below. "Art, do you hear that miss in the engine?" Art listened a moment, then nodded. "Come down and see if you can make it out." But before they could get to the engine room, we were stunned when the engine suddenly went silent—more noticeable because of the riotous bellowing of the rapids only a mile behind us.

The ebbing tide carried us along the channel as it willed, regardless of any angle of the rudder. Art and Dick tried to determine the mechanical problem. We drifted near shore, where were no beaches, only rocky banks. The boys dropped an anchor. To our surprise it caught—and held. Dense forest growth overhung the water. Dusk turned to dark and the boys clamoured to have their Fourth of July celebration. Chuck Day, the versatile cook, led them to a rocky point with enough space for a bonfire. Two boys climbed dead trees and hacked off firewood. Three or four worked up a blaze. Other boys made soft places to sit padded with spruce boughs. They found a moss-mottled wooden cross set in a crack in the rocks, which Cookie said marked the spot of an old shipwreck.

Packages and packages of firecrackers were lit, one by one or as strings exploding like machine-gun fire. Singing and storytelling had held no charms until that wild, remote bit of Canada served as background for a noisy American Independence Day celebration. Cookie led the crew in singing sea chanteys and the song "Three Crows," which ends: "Caw! Caw! Caw!" It was a great favourite, and after it the boys always gave a Sea Scout cheer—"Thar She Blows!"—three times. They gave the same cheer of tribute after Cookie's two ghost stories.

Rain finally drove us back to the boat, where Art and Dick had engine parts spread over the whole engine room deck. "It looks like an all-night session," Cookie commented before counting the bolts and whatnots strewn around. "Sixty-one, sixty-two…" The boys rigged a pulley to the mast and another ashore to a tree. A line much like a travelling clothesline was run through and tied to the skiff so they wouldn't have to row back and forth to the boat. Aboard, they clambered down the pilothouse companionway instead of taking the usual path through the galley and engine room, so as not to scatter engine parts or otherwise disturb the repair work.

"Well," I said finally, realizing I couldn't be of any help, "if you two are going to work until morning, I'll sleep on the pilothouse deck, out of the rain."

Two of the boys helped me with my sleeping bag, saying, "Good-night, Mama," as they went below.

At daybreak Dick and Art stepped over me and climbed into their bunks, greasy clothes and all. Shortly after, I dove from the pilothouse for a morning dip and was startled by movement of the boat as I leaped. As I surfaced I wondered about the menacing roar of the rapids and the nearness of the trees overhanging the rocks. I wondered until I saw that *Tyee*'s keel rested on a short and narrow rock shelf; rudder and propeller projected over seaweed-covered rocks, all visible above the fast-ebbing tide. The boat shifted abruptly, listing sharply to port, when several of the boys came to the rail to joke about joining me for a swim.

"You'll all be joining me if you don't keep a trim ship until high tide," I warned.

Cookie's Jell-O slid off the outside refrigerator and the crowd at the rail tripled to see what red Jell-O might do under water. I put all my strength into a strong crawl stroke that would get me out of the way of the leaning ship. Skipper Art ordered the boys ashore, where

The Tyee Scout *was left aground by a fast-falling tide.*

they'd be safe if *Tyee Scout* rolled over and sank.

I thought it a miracle when a ship came through the rapids and headed our way. It was *Columbia*, a 102-foot mission hospital ship. As it approached and slowed, Captain Godfrey stood on the bridge studying our situation, then called through his megaphone, "We will stand by until high water sets your vessel afloat."*Columbia* manoeuvred into Slingsby Channel and drifted while the boys, a skiffload at a time, went aboard to see the operating room, engine spaces, sitting room, pilothouse and galley. Art boarded and used *Columbia*'s radio to call Alert Bay for a tugboat and a new engine head.

After midday the westerly breeze began to stiffen. In large black letters the boys painted "Tyee Scout 1937" on a prominent boulder to mark the spot of our mishap.

"The sign your boys painted marks two wrecks," Captain Godfrey told Captain Church of *Tyee Scout*. "A larger vessel than yours went down there years ago."

The tide was flooding, rapidly lifting and righting *Tyee Scout*. After a short discussion between Captain Godfrey and Art, *Columbia* sent over a towline. Dick secured it to the bow and the powerful *Columbia* easily hauled *Tyee Scout* clear of the rocks without damaging her hull.

Skiffload by skiffload the Walla Walla boys returned to *Tyee Scout*, now ready for a slow tow to Allison Harbour. Shortly after ignominiously getting underway on the end of a towline we were passed by a pleasure launch. Three girls in colourful nautical clothes reclined on the forward cabin, and they waved languidly as the boat headed in the direction of Queen Charlotte Strait.

In the two-by-four galley, Cookie, our "one-man-band," created such din with his ladles, cans, jars and raucous song that the skipper's brow took on a few more furrows. In good-natured self-defence Art hauled out his accordion and we co-operated in drowning Cookie out, I at the keyboard, Art at the bass buttons.

We were still going full blast when Cookie climbed up the companionway carrying a big bowl of applesauce. Nearly at the top, he slipped and landed on the deck below, wonderfully disguised by the applesauce streaming through his hair, down his face and over his chest.

"So much for our late afternoon snack," was Art's only comment.

At Allison Harbour, *Columbia* tied alongside *Tyee Scout*. Art invited the Bellham family to be on hand for the evening sing on *Tyee*'s afterdeck with *Columbia*'s doctor and cook as featured attractions. As yet no tug had been located by radio and it looked as though the Scouts might get to know Allison Harbour all too well.

The doctor, who had been with the Royal Northwest Mounted Police, told bloodcurdling stories of adventures such as trekking into the far North to aid a wounded captive. The roly-poly cook, once a sea captain, recounted the horrors he had seen in Japan after the great earthquake, fires and tidal wave of 1923 that struck Tokyo and surrounding cities and killed some 143,000 people. Each speaker was cheered with "Thar She Blows" three times, as were Cookie, and Art, who was dressed as a girl for the act, with the help of some rouge and lipstick Flo had left with me. Eventually the mosquitoes furnished noise and discomfort enough to drive everyone under cover. The Bellhams insisted that the crews of both boats and I come to their house for coffee, and that Art bring his accordion.

We sang and played the piano, accordion and violin. Vi told about the Native masks displayed on her wall, which were given to the

The Columbia *mission ship, which came to the rescue of the disabled* Tyee Scout *in Slingsby Channel.*
Harbour Publishing archives

family at a potlatch. "Of course, there's a law against potlatches," Vi explained, "but no law can keep the Natives from celebrating birthdays and weddings after the manner of the old potlatch. Sometimes we sell a hundred sacks of flour for one affair."

While helping to serve coffee and cookies and going back and forth to the piano, I began to get the feeling that I was the brunt of a joke. Cookie looked a bit embarrassed and Art offered me a straight-backed chair as I started across the room, and when I sat down, I knew at once from the feel of the cool, slick varnish against my bare skin what the joke was. There was a hole in the seat of my trousers where my shorts left off.

"Oh, gosh, Art," I whispered. "How much sailcloth have you got aboard ship? I need a patch."

The whisper carried all over the room and *Columbia*'s engineer boomed out, "What are you worrying now for? Your pants were like that when you visited our ship this morning."

My face grew hotter and hotter and I wanted terribly to crawl under the table. Art came to my rescue by suggesting we get back to our ships.

He suggested that I sleep on the floor of the pilothouse, and Scouts Dick Clarke and Gordon "Froggy" Livengood cleared a space for me. I was dying of embarrassment as I wiggled into my sleeping bag in the dark. Why hadn't someone told me about the hole and saved me from being a spectacle all day? Why? Oh, why?

I pulled the sleeping bag out on deck where I wouldn't disturb Dick and Art. Mosquitoes came in clouds. I drenched the kapok around my head with citronella. The smell kept the mosquitoes away and also kept me awake to worry about the morrow.

Eventually I dozed off a bit—and woke up in a puddle of water. Rain was pelting down. The deck was a stream. The edge of the pilot-house roof was a miniature Niagara and I was under it.

Cookie's alarm went off and I heard him banging about in the little galley. His hands were full of eggs when I stepped into the galley with my soggy sleeping bag. "Crawl into my bunk, Betty. It's dry and warm. You ought to get a little shut-eye!"

So I climbed over the younger boys on the floor of the amidships cabin and had a few hours' sleep in Cookie's bunk before breakfast. The boys were up and dressing when I got out for my usual dip. Dick, the engineer, went swimming with me and we had a fun time. Cookie Jr., Jack Ingham, rushed out on deck, not even half-dressed, to ask "How's the water?" His buddies laughed and when he saw me, he got under cover in some confusion. "Gosh," he told me later, "you play with us like a boy and go around in pants. I was just thinkin' of you like one of us."

During the next two days of waiting for a tug, the boys had to confine their activities to the area of the floats. That was much too restrictive for 19 exuberant Scouts. Someone fell or was pushed in nearly every hour. Cookie was the main entertainer. On the first day the boys addressed him formally as "Chuck—oh, I mean Mr. Day, sir!" and saluted stiffly whenever he hove into sight to assign them to various KP duties. He played his part wonderfully, so the boys tried to get his goat on the second day by falling to their knees in front of him, bowing, pleading, "Allah! Allah!" When he ran they pursued him, a grinning, howling mob. Cookie dashed for the floats. He slipped, perhaps intentionally, on a rolling log and retaliated by pulling several would-be rescuers into the water.

To me fell the task of mending numerous torn trousers and shirts after the skipper put a stop to the tussle and roughhousing. On our last day in Allison Harbour, drying, mended clothes flopped from every available line and rail.

At the last evening fire on a bit of rocky shore, Mrs. Serge Stonjalsky and her dark-haired, eight-year-old son Dmitry, two floathouse residents of Allison Harbour, were guests of honour. Mrs. Stonjalsky sang melodious songs she had learned as a child in Russia. Though the boys did not understand the words, they appreciated this rare treat and gave numerous loud cheers of "Thar She Blows." The boys were unusually noisy about getting into their bunks below decks that evening. Dmitry autographed a card or paper for each Scout. All were amazed by his precocious knowledge of boats and scientific phenomena—an outstanding example of home schooling.

They were noisier than ever when Dmitry rejoined his mother so I lifted the companionway cover and called down, "Boys! If you don't go to sleep quietly, Mama won't kiss any of you goodnight."

The joke turned back on me when Teddy Rich, the youngest, piped up, "We're waiting, Mama."

"Oh," I floundered, "Cappy says I mustn't kiss you all goodnight."

"That's all right," answered the little voice, "if you can't kiss all of us, just leave Cookie out."

In the morning of the third day Art hired Frank Bellham to tow us to Alert Bay with his small troller, *Belize*. It took seven hours, and when I wasn't scrubbing the Scouts' dirty sailor hats I was busy studying the sea and coastline, anticipating and planning my own crossing of Queen Charlotte Strait.

The engine part from Seattle had arrived in Alert Bay, and Art and Dick immediately set to work installing it. The boys took advantage of this extra time and were soon scattered throughout the town, sightseeing and picture taking. Dick Clarke, Froggy Livengood, Orville McCarroll, Red and I climbed up to the radio station. Dick asked many technical questions of the man in charge. I understood few of the questions and none of the answers. For a short time we watched men and women playing tennis on a fir plank court built out from the side of a hill. The unusual location and construction of the court interested us more than the game.

Downtown, Froggy and I each bought a pound of watermelon. That nearly flattened our pocketbooks. We got more than our money's worth eating it before the other boys and doling it out to our favourites bit by bit.

By nightfall *Tyee*'s engine hummed like new. Art and Dick were happy. They were behind schedule but could now get underway. The older boys moved my things to the Nimpkish Hotel.

From my waterfront room in the hotel, I watched *Tyee*'s lights disappear down Johnstone Strait, toward Seattle — and home. I swallowed lumps. Right then I wasn't sure about the Queen Charlotte Strait crossing and I didn't expect to see anyone from the States again until the end of my trip.

Nimpkish Hotel (c. 1967), where Betty stayed in the summer of 1937. BC Archives E-05281

Early in the morning I was awakened by the cacophony of many dozens of crows. Their caws seemed always to come in threes, just as in the Boy Scouts' cheer, and I was lonesome! I think I have never had such fun as those five days with the active, wholesome Scout crowd, or such a low feeling as when I again had to depend on myself for entertainment.

Through that day and the next I spent hours, exhausting hours, writing to all the friends to whom I had promised letters. Two English ex-soldiers, who had served for years in India, sat in the small Congo-leumed lobby and warned me endlessly of dangers ahead. One was in charge of tarring the dirt roads and the other was a surveyor. The more they expounded, the more I suspected they weren't as familiar with the sea as they claimed. They predicted the most horrible things would befall me. At luncheon and dinner they spoke of nothing but the frightful ends I might meet: wrapped in the tentacles of a giant squid, blown into mid-ocean, dead of starvation and exposure from drifting helplessly in dense fog—there seemed no end to their imagined exotic dangers.

I was flattered by their concern, but not swerved from my determination to row across Queen Charlotte Strait. Every other white person I knew of who had gone north in a hand-propelled craft had taken a steamer across the strait from Alert Bay. Afterward, all said they could have rowed or paddled across.

I wanted to do it. Not to wish I had.

CHAPTER 8

Gale-Force Winds in Queen Charlotte Strait

Loggers and fishermen, who often gathered together around the radio late at night to gather news of the outside world, told her the disturbing story of Amelia Earhart. They also told her that ferry captains were reporting the whereabouts of "the girl in the red canoe."

—River Magazine, 1999

AFTER A LONG DAY OF WRITING LETTERS and recording notes in my ship's log in Alert Bay, I was lonely. I missed the jolly good times I had enjoyed so much with the Sea Scouts, and I was impatient to be testing *Bijaboji* and myself on Queen Charlotte Strait. So shortly before five o'clock in the afternoon on my second day in Alert Bay, I put my equipment in order and pinned an extra blanket inside the sleeping bag. I even explained to a few curious ladies that I was not an orphan. There was time to get a haircut from the big Japanese barber whose little shop was in a shack on pilings. Then I bought two loaves of bread from the locally renowned Scots baker and loaded the dugout. The two ex-soldiers helped carry my things to the Home Gas float.

This was Saturday, July 10, and many seine boats were tied up for the weekend. The crews stood about talking in various languages. Numerous young Native children plus a few Japanese and Chinese

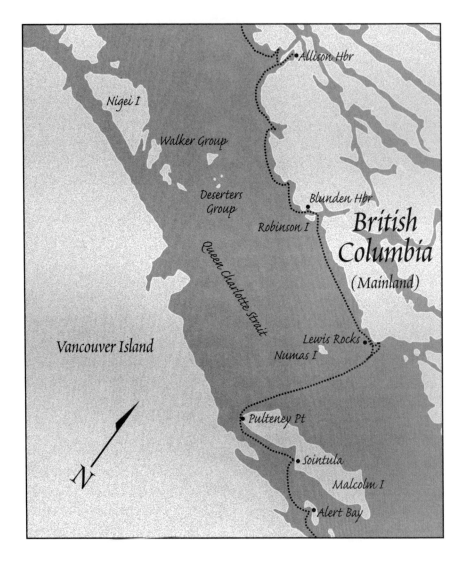

youngsters stared in open-mouthed wonder at me in ski trousers, pink sweater and cord belt with hunting knife dangling accessible to my left hand. I stared back, wondering just what mixture of Oriental, Native and European some of those children were. Whatever, they all seemed happy, healthy and full of marvellous youthful curiosity.

The battered scarlet bailing can had disappeared. In its place was a large, shiny applesauce can with a folded note held together with a screw. It was a note of encouragement from the thoughtful Cookie.

I would have shouted the Scouts' tribute, "Thar She Blows," three times if all the men weren't already looking at me as though speculating on my sanity.

It was early evening by the time I departed. Accepting the advice of a shoe salesman who had stopped at the hotel and of Cecil at the Home Gas float, I decided to row to Sointula, the co-operative commonwealth of Finnish settlers on Malcolm Island. Some miles away, Malcolm Island was the only land between the open waters of Queen Charlotte Strait and me.

After pausing alongside the USS *Swallow*, an old minesweeper, to chat with my countrymen who complained that naval and international regulations kept them aboard in a foreign country, I rowed into the low-lying fog streaks hiding Sointula. To keep a straight course I sighted off the higher hills on Vancouver Island. Several times I bumped into large chunks of driftwood. *Swallow* slowly overtook and passed me. The dense, low fog concealed her grey hull, making it appear as though the mast top was floating through space. A weird sight.

Shortly after seven o'clock I reached the point protecting Sointula's harbour. Just inside the point and several hundred yards inland was a graveyard, then neat homes appeared, and soon a well-built pier.

Betty departing Alert Bay, BC, about halfway through her solo rowing trip to Alaska.

After hauling *Bijaboji* onto the float I walked to the Co-op store to see if there was a shelter I might sleep under. The storekeeper, Frank Kiviharju, offered the hospitality of his home; I accepted the use of his steam bath house for my shelter.

Back at the float I was sitting in the canoe making up sandwiches for supper when a smiling young fisherman leaped from one of the purse seine boats tied side by side. "My name is Spain. We have lots of coffee in the galley. Come aboard and have some."

The row had been pleasant, but as the sun dropped into the horizon the evening turned cool. The promise of a warm galley and hot coffee was irresistible.

"This is the *Lake Como III*," Spain said as we climbed aboard. Men from other purse seiners soon joined us to ask about my trip, then gave advice on crossing Queen Charlotte Strait and Queen Charlotte Sound. They told of many transits—a few smooth but most rough, with cups and other loose gear flying off the mess tables.

When it was time for the evening news broadcast we crowded into the pilothouse to hear the latest about the search for Amelia Earhart. She was still lost. Scotty, a huge, handsome individual, shook his head over how much money she was costing the American government. "No woman is worth it. You'd better hitch a ride across the strait with us or there'll be planes and cutters out looking for another dizzy dame!"

"Oh, no, they won't! I'm not making history, I'm on a vacation." I was not favourably impressed with his attitude.

Several men left the boat with colourful towels tossed around their necks, heading uptown for their Saturday night steam bath. Such happy-go-lucky fishermen I had never met. All but Spain and Scotty had been born in Italy. Scotty made up for his unkind words by inviting me to see the weekly movie shown in the dance hall. It was a Russian film depicting how the Soviets brought begging gypsies under government control and forced them to do their share to create a strong and modern nation. The faces, dances, songs and costumes in the film were new to me and extremely interesting.

Before the Saturday night dance the Finnish women provided coffee and cake. Scotty, big and strong, always made sure I got a giant share. At the dance, the dark Italians were in striking contrast to the blond Finnish girls, adorned in lovely white sports frocks decorated with assorted colourful embroidery. Nicky and Bob entertained the Finnish girls and me with "O Sole Mio," "Dream Boat," "Blue Hawaii," "Rose Marie" and other fine songs. Nicky also did a cute dance. No one disregarded the placards over the dance hall doors: Be a Man. Don't Come Here Drunk.

Toward evening the women provided more refreshments and again Scotty smuggled in enough chocolate cake to sink a ship. On the floor he was a wonderful dancer and the life of the party. Some of the other men said Saturday nights in Sointula were always twice as lively when Scotty's boat arrived.

Shyness kept me in the balcony for more than half the evening, talking with little girls, their mothers and a fisherman who wouldn't dance because he was self-conscious of his six-foot, five-inch height. I think of that evening as one of the grandest of my entire vacation.

Once, Scotty and Archie and I went down to the pier to see if their boat was to sail before dawn. "Our skipper wants to test the fishing around Cape Caution," Scotty told me while Archie was aboard the boat. We stood in the damp fog counting to 37, the interval in seconds between blasts of the foghorn at Pulteney Point. "Anyway," Scotty said, "if that horn is blowing tomorrow, you'd better stay at the lighthouse until Shorty Maisonville tells you to go."

On the way back to the hall Scotty put his arm across my shoulder boyishly and roughed my short hair. "Nice curly top you've got," he said.

"Don't be so friendly, Scotty," I said, wishing big fellows didn't turn my heart over so easily. He took his arm away.

Later in the evening when I was sitting on the sidelines among some of the Italians, I dropped my head for a second on my knees, which were braced high on the rungs of the next chair. "Scotty's dancing makes her seasick," one of the fishermen said. Scotty didn't dance with me again that night.

About four o'clock in the morning, when most of the mothers had gone home and the two pianists were completely exhausted, one of the Italian men escorted me to the Kiviharjus' gate and said goodbye, then rushed to the pier to get aboard his boat ready to pull out.

The foghorn at Pulteney Point was still noisy at 10 o'clock on Sunday morning when I came out of the steam bath to poke my sleeping bag into its Fabrikoid covering. *Lake Como III* was the only purse seine boat remaining at the float and Spain insisted that I have breakfast with the boys. It was fun and I lingered afterward to read a magazine story. I noticed that all literature aboard was of the pulp or *True Romance* type.

Too soon it was time for *Lake Como III* and *Bijaboji* to get underway. Calling out "Thanks for a great time!" to the fishermen, I dipped my

Betty and Bijaboji *alongside a purse seine boat crewed by Italian fishermen and moored at Sointula, Malcolm Island.*

oars into the water. Two of the fishermen took pictures. Some 12 or 15 Sointulians gathered on the dock to wish me a safe trip as I rowed off into the dense fog.

Later *Lake Como III* passed close, heading for Vancouver Island. I rowed near to the shore, where the fog became merely a thin haze, and saw several unpainted farm homes abandoned by Finns who couldn't make a go of it. The sun burned off most of the fog and just before I reached the lighthouse, six American destroyers, bound for Alaska, passed far out around Pulteney Point. Seeing those US Navy ships while in a foreign land filled me with pride.

The fog was still thick in Queen Charlotte Strait and the horn was going strong when I landed on the beach by the lighthouse. The northern extremity of Vancouver Island and the mainland were entirely concealed within that damp, soupy whiteness.

Mr. Maisonville, a short, jolly man, welcomed me warmly. "Heard about you over the radio, dearie. Hoped you'd come this way and stop by. And now you're trapped by this summer fog."

"I've heard so much about you that I'd have stopped to see you and your lighthouse even without this fog and rough water, Mr. Maisonville."

"Everyone calls me Shorty. You just do the same."

The dense fog convinced me to accept Shorty's cordial invitation to enjoy the comforts of the lighthouse until visibility had improved. Before going to the lighthouse, I rowed to an American troller anchored in a cove off the foggy south shore. The two young Seattle fishermen were bound for the cannery at Skowl Arm, where my father worked.

The two other boats were Canadian. One of the middle-aged fishermen was fortunate enough to have his wife aboard. "She handles fish lines and shoots like a man," he told me with great pride. He was leery of my sanity since I travelled without a gun.

Shorty Maisonville was preparing supper when I returned—fresh oysters, fried chicken, biscuits, mashed potatoes, gravy, tea and fruit. "My French grandmother in Quebec taught me to cook," he said. "I'll manage this meal while you have a steam bath."

So I had my first steam bath in a little double-walled shanty built of beachcombed lumber and snuggled against a grassy bank. A booming wood fire burned in an oil drum under a heap of rocks. The room was sweltering when I disrobed and climbed to the high shelf with a bucket of water. Hissing, scalding, invisible steam rose about me as I threw handfuls of water over the hot rocks. I kept that up until I was weak and the blood pounded in my head. Then I gave myself a cold rubdown and after a short rest went back to the lighthouse feeling cleaner than ever in my life. Now I understood why steam baths are so popular with Scandinavians.

The meal was marvellous and Shorty's conversation lively, charming and most interesting. He'd studied art in Paris, then served as a machine gunner on the Western Front until a bullet in his right wrist ended a promising art career. He has welcomed many individuals and groups to the lighthouse, including screen stars, representatives of the National Geographic Society, the crew of the scientific vessel *Catalyst*, the staff of the biological station at Friday Harbor and other equally interesting persons or groups. Shorty was one of those rare, surprising and fascinating individuals who could converse easily with kings and commoners. After tea he hauled out his can of Comfort tobacco and pondered, "Shall I have an orange or a lemon-flavoured smoke?"

I'd never heard of such a thing and watched with great interest while he cut a generous square from the tissue used to wrap an orange, and rolled a cigarette as fat as a cigar. Puffing contentedly, Shorty led me into his marvellous library, saying, "The kids from Sointula often come here to study or just read for pleasure." They had had to row five miles to get here, I realized, and they must have found this place as fascinating as I did—it was the best library I'd seen on this trip. The books' subjects ranged from Canadian birds to Irish art and much more. Throughout that night of being fogbound I had no trouble keeping myself occupied.

During the few hours when Shorty turned off the foghorn, there was excellent radio reception, and we talked about Wagnerian opera, vegetable gardens, hunting big game, Shorty's work on tugboats and in logging camps, even the work of the missionaries in Alert Bay.

"The more missionaries in a place," he contended, "the more sin." I couldn't agree with him on that.

After sundown, during the long dusk of mid-summer, the sea calmed some, and the trollers pulled their anchors and headed northwest toward Queen Charlotte Sound. Sometimes I'd lose sight of them as they dropped into the deep trough behind a fast-lifting breaker. Not long after their departure, Shorty had to start the foghorn machinery again. I wondered about the safety and comfort of those small trollers on that broad expanse of wind-agitated Pacific. Shorty never left his post in the machinery building until 10 o'clock the next morning. I believe that I slept only seconds at a time, between blasts of the great compressed-air horn, and wondered how long it had taken Shorty to get used to such an infernally loud signal. It was a great relief when Shorty shut down the foghorn.

The fog was roving along the mainland shore, some 30 miles across the open water in a direct line from Pulteney Point to Seymour Inlet. Shorty said the fog always lingered over there and advised me not to leave when I had the canoe loaded and ready at about 11. "It is a traditional and delightful part of the lighthouse service to shelter ones like yourself who are too poor to travel in decent-size boats," he assured me with a big grin.

"Don't worry, Shorty," I said, cinching up my cord belt before he lent a hand in getting the canoe off the gravel spit. "I'll make it and you'll be getting a letter of safe arrival from me, postmarked Ketchikan, within a month."

"Well, take this anyway," he said, pushing a bag of dried prunes, oranges and honey under the Fabrikoid covering.

Shorty stood in the tall grass by the lighthouse, waving until I rounded a rocky point that cut the lighthouse buildings from view. On the north side of Malcolm Island I began to feel the force of the ocean swells. Chunks of driftwood were large and ungainly, a danger for persons in any size vessel. On a particularly large log, three seals steamed in the sun, slithering into the water as I drew near. A float plane swooped over, heading in a direct line for Rivers Inlet. Within the hour it flew back and soon another one passed high overhead, going north. A week later I learned that the first plane had carried Vancouver officials to the cannery at Namu to settle a strike.

Some eight hours—I estimated by the sun—after leaving Pulteney Point, I was still in wide Queen Charlotte Strait and more than three miles from the mainland, sore and a little more sunburned but having the time of my life.

A strong westerly blowing in from the Pacific nipped the tops off the rising swells. Every breaking wave that I didn't catch skillfully enough slopped into the canoe. My bailing can drifted from side to side in the water. The paper bag disintegrated and dried prunes swashed around my legs. The prunes began to swell.

Suddenly, Numas Island was blotted out by fog. It had been my prime reference point and I planned to camp there for the night. I was thankful for the strong westerly blowing me toward the mainland and not out to China. But I had to fight the wind, keeping the same angle to the waves as I had before the fog rolled in. It was such a powerful gale that I kept my direction best by rowing with only one oar. That left a hand free to bail while I studied every rambunctious hill of sea-water rushing toward me. My wits worked overtime to figure a way to meet each successfully.

One spot low on the northwestern horizon was so bright it hurt my eyes. The sun was near sinking, but I wasn't afraid. My heart and mind were exhilarated with the excitement and pleasure of this life-or-death challenge. Fog obliterated the shore, but I knew that I couldn't be too far from land. I kept rowing. The mainland was now my destination. Soon, perhaps another hour or so, *Bijaboji* and I would have crossed Queen Charlotte Strait, one of the most danger-ous portions of the entire Inside Passage.

Neither wind nor waves relented. Dusk settled in early. Too early. I had to continue rowing. Somewhere I would reach the mainland. I prayed that I'd find a beach, even a beach of stones, anything except sheer cliffs.

At last the waves became smaller, less forceful, and they didn't leap aboard. No longer did I have to row with one hand and bail with the other. At last! In the dim dusk I saw the shore, painted by the yellow-green phosphorescence of frisky waves. There were no noisy breakers. I turned straight for the beach, caught a wave and thrust *Bijaboji* ashore. Quickly, but wearily, I stepped out of the canoe. Small, smooth stones lay underfoot. This tiny cove was piled high with drift logs as though for a game of giant jackstraws. A lively stream ran under them. I pulled the canoe high over two of the largest logs pointing seaward and well above the battering waves. I don't know what time it was but guess it must have been near midnight when I made camp.

I have no idea just how far south of Blunden Harbour was this drift-log-covered beach where I landed, but I believe it was a cove near Lewis Rocks. It could have been any of the many tiny indentations along this ragged, rough and poorly charted coastline. Many miles of the British Columbia coast were only roughly dotted in on the charts, including some of the numerous small bays and inlets. Fortunately the wind and tide had not carried me farther south and east into Wells Pass.

In a cleft in the rocks I built a fire with one match and no paper, thus sustaining my campfire record. The cove sheltered me from the wind and pocketed the fog so it was impossible to see the tops of the scrubby spruce and cedar trees above me. I hastily removed my clothes and laid them near the warm coals to dry. Flapjacks and thick, juicy slices of bacon were soon ready for supper, all eagerly devoured. This was ideal! No class at Pomona College had prepared me for this exciting life.

I spread Cocoon on the logs dried by my fire and slept soundly until raucous crows awakened me sometime after dawn on Tuesday, July 13. Tiny Numas Island was covered by thick fog and the westerly was still blowing strong. I was glad I hadn't found a landing place there the night before. I could have been stranded for days waiting for the fog to lift and reveal the mainland. The tide was low and I struggled to get the canoe off the logs and to the water's edge.

Since I had successfully made it across notorious Queen Charlotte Strait I could row on at once, staying out just far enough to avoid the great breakers shattering against the jagged rocky shoreline and their equally dangerous backwash. Yet I had to hold close enough to shore not to be lost in the heavy, empty whiteness that hid sun and trees. I chose my theme song that day, Mana-Zucca's "I Love Life," and sang it hundreds of times during the next two days, rising and falling on spectacular swells in bucking wind and tide.

For most of that day I was buffetted by wind and waves, unsure of my position on the chart until I recognized the shape of a bay formed by two islands and the mainland as Blunden Harbour. In the calmer waters behind Robinson Island, the harbour divided into a sheltered bay to the west and, to the northeast, rapids connecting to Bradley Lagoon. The rapids were navigable by canoes only at slack water. Shorty Maisonville told me that a dead walrus had been seen in the shallows of the islet and rock-choked waters near the rapids.

I was relieved to be out of the wind for a while, though the tide ran with lavish strength against me as I strained to reach the unpainted houses of this Native village snuggled along the curving shoreline. Extending out 25 yards or so from the homes and over the water, even at low tide, were outhouses built on pilings, flushed by the changing tides. A rough float ran from in front of the best-built house and across the tidal flats but no one came to greet or deter me when I pulled the dugout onto the log float. It had been nearly two days since I had seen another human, and I would have been glad for the sight of anyone, even a person coming out to chase me away for trespassing.

The doors of the houses were all double padlocked. Nailed on one house were two cloth posters, threatening anyone selling liquor to Indians, or disturbing the material property or natural resources of an Indian reserve. I wandered through the ghost-like village on a crude plank walk. On both sides and throughout the clearing were stinging nettles that grew higher than my head. Most of the houses were little better than crude shacks, evidence of unskilled carpentry, and now dilapidated. There wasn't even a dog to bark at me. I felt lonely, as if I were the last person on earth. A plane roared overhead, and just a glimpse of it through wisps of blowing fog reassured me that I wasn't alone in the world.

Back on the float I prepared a bit of lunch and slept for a few hours. All day the tide rushed in the wrong direction as though it couldn't change. Late in the afternoon I impatiently pushed off against the tide and out of Blunden Harbour. I was lucky in only one slight way: the tide had risen sufficiently to separate Edgell Island from the mainland by a foot of water, enough that *Bijaboji* could skim over the rocks and straight into the battery of breakers that I had to fight through before I could get into the open Pacific.

It was foolish to waste my strength bucking wind and swells while making no more than a mile an hour, so I put ashore on the first bit of beach I found and got some rest. It wasn't long before the wind died slightly. I put out my campfire and went on. Just after I was nicely started, the wind rose. Soon it wailed. I rowed on, only to the next beachable tract, a shore I would have scorned anywhere in Puget Sound. By the time I had a good fire going and eaten a little, I was anxious to go on, and did, though it was getting toward sundown — not that I had seen the sun all day.

Green curlers crashed against the rocks and rose white and snarling in the cracks and crevices before receding. Always there was that rising, falling, tormented roar of water in my ears. The air was cool and deliciously salty as night came down.

Fog and darkness forced me to land for the night in a jot of a cove. There was no way to make the canoe fast so I pulled the bow over the highest rock, built a fire on the rock's lee side above the tide level, and went to sleep on the accumulated driftwood cast there by many storms.

Hours later I awoke to find the fire flickering merrily over a five-foot area. With the applesauce can, I rushed water to the fire until it was out, condemning myself for nearly setting the forest aflame. I then slept without the warmth of a fire until noisy crows and oyster-catchers aroused me. An eagle sat still and ominous on a snag, but that didn't give my heart half the jump the height of the water did. The tide had flooded in and the canoe was floating out. Away...

By scrambling out on a wind-toppled tree and grabbing the loose Fabrikoid, I caught my precious canoe just in time. A few more minutes of sleep and it would have been out of sight in the soupy sunrise fog. For years *Bijaboji* has been almost a living thing to me. Out in the canoe alone, I talk to her as to another person. When I had her safe again, my knees jellied and I flopped on the rocks to await new strength.

CHAPTER 9

House Calls with Dr. Darby

Betty writes home of shooting her frail craft over open stretches of water, battling wind and fog, camping in secluded coves, being entertained at logging camps and by former acquaintances along the route, and of wandering in a deserted Indian village, "nothing breaking the stillness," she says.

— *Washington Post*, September 1937

I WILL NEVER AGAIN KNOW THE THRILL of accomplishment I knew that day in reaching the Stonjalskys' floathome, just beyond Allison Harbour. *Bijaboji* had proved her seaworthiness. She had weathered Queen Charlotte Strait. We had only the southern tip of notorious Queen Charlotte Sound, then the exposed Cape Caution and the wide open Smith Sound to conquer before reaching Smith Inlet.

Before reaching the Stonjalskys', I ate hot vegetable soup with the Bellhams at Allison Harbour, talked with Tom Oien, who had guided *Tyee Scout* through Nakwakto Rapids and was the Stonjalskys' neighbour, saw Reggie, who had been at Charlotte Bay, and met Gus Ericson, a blue-eyed Swede. Reggie invited everybody around to his and Tom's floathouse for supper that night. He'd been preparing food and cooking all day.

At the Stonjalskys' I was welcomed most hospitably—and scolded, "Oh, you have arrived in such a dampened condition." Getty Stonjalsky repeated that many times as she unpacked everything I had

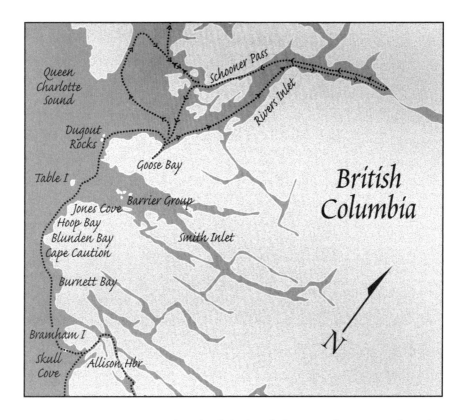

and strung lines under the shed, behind the wood stove and in the warming oven. "You, too, are invited to Reggie's dinner," she assured me, and promptly got out a clean white shirt for me to wear with my ski trousers.

The weather was clearing and Serge, her husband, decided he must be off to the trolling grounds. We all stood on the float waving until his small, sturdy boat rounded the point. Getty stood a few minutes with such a sad expression on her fine, pleasing face that I put my arm around her. "It makes you very sad to have him go. Is it always so?"

"Many times fishermen's wives must be sad, but they have more happy homecomings than sailors' wives."

Upon entering Reggie's and Tom's three-room floathouse I had an overwhelming sense of having been there before. Tom laughed when I mentioned it, then explained that I really had—at the logging camp in Charlotte Bay. He had traded houses with Mary after the Scouts had visited.

Reggie's whole dinner was tasty and the raisin pie especially luscious. We played games and phonograph music before going home to listen to the nightly news broadcast, saying that Amelia Earhart was still lost and that the search would soon be abandoned. I did not know the famous aviatrix, but felt a kinship, plus respect and admiration. My prayers were with her.

Thursday morning Tom removed the worn, splintered oak strips on the bottom of *Bijaboji* and screwed on some new ones. Then Dmitry and I painted the canoe. To pass the time when not working, we rowed up the inlet in Tom's skiff to pick blueberries and huckleberries. Dmitry's police dog ran through the woods in pursuit, swimming where he couldn't run.

That evening, after Dmitry had finished his nightly task of rowing to the stream for a barrel of fresh water, we celebrated with a beach fire supper that included egg sandwiches with catsup and a juicy wild-berry pie. Tom told of leaving his home in Norway and entertained us with thrilling tales of his experiences working his way around the world aboard sailing ships.

Friday, July 16 was steamer day in Allison Harbour. Loggers, fishermen and everyone from miles around arrived to pick up mail and freight from the small Union Steamship Company vessel *Venture*, northbound from Vancouver. A few loggers asked for my autograph. I noticed a slim, young red-haired woman in a tan polo coat leaning on the ship's rail. Well-dressed men stood on each side of her. There was sweetness and a self-reliance about her that attracted my attention. She looked my way suddenly, then turned back to one of the men who was evidently telling her about me. I realized that to them I was an oddity.

On Saturday, Tom and Reggie took us on a picnic to Skull Cove. They chose a sandy beach protected from the wind and hidden behind scattered islets and rocks. Tom pointed out one tiny islet covered with broken clam shells and explained that it was an old Indian midden. Far out on the water, it was too foggy to see Cape Caution, but Tom and Reggie told me exactly how I should row around it next day.

For lunch we roasted kebobs over the campfire. Tom went swimming while Reggie and I sunbathed on opposite sides of the cove. Reggie had an overstuffed couch of moss on top of a sloping log, rather like Cleopatra's lounge. He assumed that role and before long my sides hurt from laughing at his antics. Getty gathered wildflowers until Tom announced it was time to go home.

That evening she played many of her Russian records, translating the lyrics for me. When Dmitry was snug in his boy-size bunk and I was on the guest cot, she played the piano and sang Russian lullabies. The news broadcast came on and we heard that Amelia Earhart was hopelessly lost. Without being morbid, I wished then that I could die someday in the canoe — off by myself, without any Viking ceremony.

Getty said proudly that Serge had, from memory, done the oil painting of a Russian landscape hanging above the piano. She also told me that he had a talented daughter by his first marriage, who was prominent in theatre at the University of Washington.

It was at five o'clock on a bright Sunday morning, four days after I had arrived, before Getty Stonjalsky and her floathouse neighbour Tom Oien would let me push off again. In those four days my pile of notes about the trip grew tremendously. All of my scant equipment was thoroughly dried, the new grub box was filled and *Bijaboji* glistened with fresh paint. Reluctant to leave such fine friends, yet eager to continue my trip, I shoved away from the floathouses and pointed *Bijaboji*'s stern toward the open ocean. With both ends of my dugout pointed, I could row with either end forward. It was easier to hold a straight course pushing the canoe than pulling it. I hadn't yet got into the Native way of sitting in the stern and rowing facing forward.

Oystercatchers circled over me all day, excitedly rendering their short, strident peeping calls. My fingers itched to tape a dozen or so of those bright orange bills fast shut. Beyond Murray Labyrinth — a confused maze of rocks, islets and islands with a canoe-size channel leading from Allison Harbour — the ocean swells lifted and dropped *Bijaboji* as though she were a peanut shell.

With Bramham Island on my starboard hand, the low swells rhythmically rolling in from Queen Charlotte Sound flowed under us comfortably. Rowing was relatively easy, though the blades of my oars were rarely even when I stroked in this undulating ocean. I was thankful that my friends had kept me in Allison Harbour until the Pacific was friendlier.

The northern extremity of Vancouver Island now lay southwest of me. Ships on the horizon seemed distorted—some appeared to be sinking with bows high in the air.

Sunday afternoon I entered Burnett Bay, an open bight south of Cape Caution. Anchored purse seine boats nodded lazily, waiting for the 6 p.m. opening when the crews could commence salmon fishing. I passed close to a seiner and the men shouted greetings. "You were reported lost," one fisherman called out.

I decided not to stay at a cabin in Indian Cove on the north side of Cape Caution, but to go on to a settlement where I might send word to Mother and Daddy in case either of them had heard the report.

Rowing and bouncing through the tide rips off Cape Caution didn't shake me up too alarmingly, although I felt the untiring power of those confused and conflicting currents. I feared what this part of the Pacific might become in bad weather. No one had hinted that the journey around Cape Caution could ever be anything less than brutal and ter- rifying. The wave-battered white granite headland, washed clean to heights of more than 100 feet, showed me how lucky I was. Spruce and cedar trees, high on the cape, contrasted strikingly with the blue and white of the shore-charging breakers. Miles to the southwest stood the bold, timbered, snowy ranges on Vancouver Island. All of that was be- hind me, another part of the trip I didn't have to worry about anymore. Ahead lay mountains heavy with deep green virgin forests.

Dark forests rose everywhere around that wild serrated coastline. Blunden Bay, Indian Cove, Hoop Bay, Jones Cove and other smaller unnamed indentations rimmed the shoreline as I headed into Smith Sound. Close by were conspicuous, worn rocky cliffs, now pounded by frolicsome green waves that broke into a necklace of foaming silver.

I decided to continue on to Smith Inlet. My large-scale chart ended there and Fred would be laying over, awaiting the next Fisher- ies opening. He would help me get in touch with my folks by coast grapevine or otherwise. They must not worry while I was having such a grand time. I hoped that Mother would get my letters from Allison Harbour in the next day or so.

At last I got a favourable tide. I stopped rowing to eat sandwiches and fruit, letting the tide carry me farther into Smith Sound. Drifting a half-mile or so offshore and with time to study my chart, I found that I was on a direct course for Table Island, where gillnetters some-times anchored. I considered stopping at Egg Island lighthouse, but I could see no place on the east edge to land, nor could I find the shel-tered bay at Table Island or any gillnet boat.

I pointed the canoe toward the Barrier Group in Smith Sound. So far as I could see after an hour's rowing, I was the only living be-ing for miles around. Ahead was truly savage splendour unmarred by ugly dwellings, canneries or other scars of civilization. This huge waterway wound its way through purple hills, gradually losing shape and colour behind mist and rain. Finally I sighted an approaching gillnetter. Maybe it's Fred, I thought.

The boat passed by, a green and white company flag fluttering gaily from a stubby mast. The skipper seemed not to notice me. At the stern a boy waved both arms. (Many years later that boy came back into my life as John F. Parker, captain of a British Columbia ferry in the Queen Charlotte Islands.) Then a rain squall added to my depres-sion. What's come over you, Betty? I asked myself. You're ready to depend on Fred too much. Better row on to Rivers Inlet.

I turned northwest, skipping the busy Smith Inlet, to take advan-tage of a wonderfully helpful tide. "Maybe the god of tides has tested us and is now helping us," I muttered to *Bijaboji*. The nearer I got to Rivers Inlet, the more boats we began to meet. All the gillnetters looked alike and each had just one man aboard.

We passed between False Egg Island and the mainland. At Dug-out Rocks I let a swell throw us through a cut-off pass between high, bare rocks and into a tiny cove. My sudden entrance as I shot out from behind the rock on the crest of an incoming wave brought a relaxed, tea-drinking Finnish fisherman near to heart failure. He had believed me to be a rainy day mirage.

During our hasty introduction, I learned that his name was Jacobsen. He found it hard to acknowledge my very existence, let alone my claim of rowing from the States, until I had had a cup of tea and eaten crumpets with him. He told of his mink ranch in the Fraser River valley, gave explicit directions to the cannery at Goose Bay six miles distant, and insisted I accept some of his large-scale charts showing the coast to Prince Rupert.

I mentioned a strange smooth mound I'd seen in the water a few hours earlier. "And it moved with a vaporous cloud above it."

He laughed heartily. "That was a whale, a common sight around here. And those flags flying above floats that you saw far out in the sound are markers where skates of halibut hooks are stretched out, deep on the sea bottom."

After all my years around salt water I hadn't had enough hours in the open Pacific to know that.

I donned my oilskin and sou'wester, spread the leather jacket over my knees and, with thanks and a wave, I set off from Jacobsen's boat toward Goose Bay. *Bijaboji* was pointed into the swells rolling into Rivers Inlet, for now I was rowing with my back to my destination. A launch bounding in the waves came near enough for the skipper to offer me a lift. I shook my head and he went on. At last, I thought. I'm definitely across Queen Charlotte Sound! Now Fred and I can compare our experiences in ocean crossing — if I ever see him again.

Hours later, after making a gooseneck turn — I'd failed to see the entrance and passed it — *Bijaboji* entered the harbour. Ahead were the lights and white-painted buildings of the Goose Bay Cannery. The launch was moored to the float. So was *Chinook*, the seiner that had passed me near Table Island. Two men in dark raincoats and sou'westers, working on the cannery dock, paid no attention as I made the canoe fast and worked the kinks out of my legs and arms. But they did look my way when I called out, "Do you suppose I could sleep under one of the cannery sheds, out of the rain?"

"You'll have to see the manager," the older man said with a distinct lack of enthusiasm.

I climbed the ladder and asked directions to the manager's cottage. Two Native women kindly showed me the way. One said, "If he won't fix you up, we will." It made me feel warm despite being rain-soaked and chilled.

In a snug little cottage built on the side of the hill, Francis Stone, the manager, and his lovely young wife made me welcome. I was introduced to Catherine, the red-haired business girl from Vancouver whom I had noticed on *Venture*, and who was enjoying her holidays in the north as the Stones' houseguest. After lingering in a relaxing hot bath, I joined the Stones and Catherine for steaming tea, and savoured my first beef drippings on toast. They had many questions about my trip.

That night I slept soundly and comfortably aboard the Stones' pleasure launch. When I awoke Monday morning I heard and saw a crowd around the dugout. Five Native women were quietly discussing *Bijaboji*. I enjoyed listening to their low yet expressive voices. They agreed that none of them would row anywhere in such a small dugout. (Years later, I learned that the dugout was designed as a woman's craft for family use.) The wiry dark man from the launch who had offered me a lift off Dugout Rocks cross-examined me antagonistically.

Later in the day as I rested on the yacht, I was disturbed when I overheard a grizzled ex-Newfoundland gillnetter say as he folded his measuring stick, "That hollow cedar log lacks two inches of being 14 foot long. It's barely 38 inches across. That girl got here on a luck charm."

The wiry dark man added, for the benefit of everyone around, "Aw, she's got a screw loose. This morning she told my permanent wave operator and me that she crossed the strait and came in here without a compass. Last night I tried to pick her up inside Dugout Rocks because the swells were breaking bad on the reefs. We lost sight of her every time she went down in the trough of the waves, but she signalled and hollered that she wouldn't take a lift. She was just robbing Davy Jones' locker when she rowed in here a couple hours later. Do you know that she hasn't a watch, compass, money, mirror or gun? She's daft!"

Shortly before noon, that same launch skipper invited me aboard for lunch. I accepted in hopes of defending myself. During the meal I reminded the skipper and beauty operator that for many years the Indians had roved these waters in much frailer canoes than mine and managed to go as far south as Panama, without even knowing about compasses, charts, tide tables or watches. I said I was sure my life on Puget Sound had fitted me to navigate these waters, although they were admittedly more challenging, without having my sanity questioned. We lingered over tea after a pleasant lunch and parted friends.

Returning to the Stones' home I met Faith and Kay, two Vancouver women spending the summer on a launch with a photographer and his wife. They sold knives and magazine subscriptions wherever the boat stopped, at canneries, logging camps, mines and any other inhabited place. "It's a wonderful way to see the coast, meet new people, and pay for our vacation," Faith said.

They told me they were the girls who had waved when *Columbia* was towing *Tyee Scout* in Slingsby Channel. After their rough and uncomfortable crossing of Queen Charlotte Strait, they were amazed that I had survived and asked all kinds of questions about my experience there. I mentioned that I had really got the courage to do it from meeting Fred, a young German fisherman who had crossed four times in an open dory in the broad stretch past Pine Island. Kay and Faith looked at each other knowingly, and Kay said, "Yes, we met him at Boswell Cannery in Smith Inlet. He bought knives from us."

Catherine and I visited the cannery, where I learned that Canadian canneries were still operated as my grandfather's cannery had been operated 20 years ago, and Mr. Stone made arrangements for Catherine and me to go out next day on a fish packer.

Dawn was just breaking at four o'clock Tuesday morning when Catherine boarded the launch and shook me awake. I dressed hurriedly. Bill Shannon, skipper of the 50-foot vessel, mug of steaming coffee in hand, met us on deck. Catherine introduced me to Bill and his lone crewman, Jimmy Darby. He was the son of Dr. George Darby, the dearly loved mission doctor of Bella Bella who maintained a summer hospital at Brunswick Cannery, close to the head of Rivers Inlet.

Our delicious breakfast of crisp bacon and eggs sunny side up was ready for us in the tiny galley. It took me a long time to finish because every time we made fast to a gillnet boat to buy fish, I dashed outside to watch. The fishermen were sleepy and exhausted after a long night of gillnetting salmon. I think no two were of the same nationality or Native tribe.

Shannon's buying territory covered the east side of Calvert Island as far north as Safety Cove, then turned east to recross Fitz Hugh Sound and enter the lower half of Schooner Passage. He bought fish only from those boats flying the New London Fish Company flag. Jimmy pitched each man's catch into a great scoop suspended from Fairbanks scales hanging from a boom near the fish hold. Shannon marked the weight and number of each species of salmon, and initialled this entry in the little black record book that each fisherman carried.

We stopped for a while in a quiet bay where *Pender*, the government survey barge, was anchored as headquarters for the detachments surveying busy Rivers Inlet. Catherine and I sunbathed on top of the pilothouse, but the chill of the wind was more powerful than the heat of the bright sun. Reluctantly we gave up and slipped into warm clothes. During the day I heard that Jacobsen, who had given me the charts at Dugout Rocks, and his brother were considered the best fishermen in the inlet.

"It isn't so much how good your nets are but how good they are for where you fish," Jimmy said. "The Jacobsens know the best colour and mesh size for nets to catch fish in all the different places around here."

Catherine was eager to return to Goose Bay and again meet Jack Horan, a gill net salesman who had been one of *Venture*'s passengers at Allison Harbour. In fact, he was the one who had explained my presence aboard *Tyee Scout* to her and other *Venture* passengers.

At the cannery, Mr. Stone said that his Vancouver manager, with whom he communicated daily by radiophone, would telephone my mother and let her know that I was well and had arrived safely in Rivers Inlet. I couldn't thank him enough.

That evening I decided to visit Dr. Darby's hospital at Rivers Inlet, so left Goose Bay an hour after the packer had landed at the white-painted cannery. Many cannery workers stood on the dock to see *Bijaboji* get underway. Behind them, steep misted green hills climbed into the scudding, low-hanging rain clouds. Pelting rain danced on the salt water. My rain gear kept me dry, but too warm. Jimmy Darby had drawn a rough map for me of the 20 miles to his father's hospital. It would be an easy row and I should arrive sometime around nine o'clock, well before summer dark.

About midnight I had to admit that I was hopelessly lost among the lights on hundreds of gillnet boats and the kerosene lanterns set on floats marking the seaward ends of their nets. I headed for a light looking most like a shore light. It wasn't—it was another gillnetter. The fisherman, well past middle age, had just set his net. "I'll be out here on deck, fishing all night," he assured me, "so you might just as well come aboard and enjoy the warmth of my tiny coal stove, get a bowl of fish stew, and rest 'til daybreak. Then you can see where you're going."

With a grateful "Thank you!" I climbed aboard.

He tied *Bijaboji* alongside where it would be out of his way. I didn't need to introduce myself because he recognized me as the "girl canoeist" whose progress was reported daily from a Vancouver radio station. "I'm Jim Smith," he said, "from Stuart Island."

"That's the island where I got a wood tick."

"Plenty of them around all this area. I knew the Gilkey brothers, Walter, Mark and Charlie, from your town. We logged together in Bute Inlet. Then they went into tugboats."

"The Gilkeys are relatives of mine, but I never knew about their years in BC."

Jim showed me into the warmth of the small pilothouse and galley. I relaxed and enjoyed a scrumptious bowl of hot salmon chowder, then looked at his magazines. In one of them, a *True Story* or *True Romance*, I found an article by Kate Smith that did me good. Her theme was that she had made it to the top despite being a large woman. Contented and warm, I fell asleep.

I awoke at dawn on July 21 to the rattle of wooden floats dropping on deck as the long net was hauled in by hand. The rain had ceased and the sky was clearing. Jim was pleased with the night's work and pointed to the many bright salmon in the hold. "We drifted seaward on the ebb tide during the night. I want to deliver my catch to the buyer. He's up the inlet…nearer the hospital. You cook breakfast and I'll get started." I boiled coffee and fried eggs and thick slices of bacon. We were almost to the buying boat by the time we'd eaten. As I thanked him and cast off, I realized that for him and all the other gillnetters, daylight would bring a few hours of much-needed rest before another long, exhausting night of fishing. For me, it would mean a day of new adventure.

Below the hospital buildings, partially hidden by trees, was a great, long, unpainted shed. Two boats were tied alongside the float. A stream of rust-coloured water gushed over the rocks beside the shed. The worn wooden walkway led to the modest summertime hospital. When I entered, Dr. Darby was extracting metal filings from a Native man's eye. His assistant was cordial and I accepted a chair near the wall, out of the way. The shelves about the office were crowded with labelled bottles of assorted sizes and contents. There was an inspiring poster on the wall telling how a father had grown to understand his son.

When the doctor was free he called Miss Barner, the head nurse, and three people of the hospital staff, and they ushered me into a sitting room to relate my experiences while enjoying tea and cookies or, as Miss Barner called them, "biscuits." The doctor took a few minutes to tell me a little about his work in Rivers Inlet. That was inducement enough for me to eagerly accept his invitation to spend the afternoon travelling about the inlet aboard his small launch while he made "house" calls.

I gladly accepted an invitation to lunch with Dr. Peter Kelly, his wife Gertrude Russ Kelly, and Jim Smith, the gillnet fisherman, aboard the United Church mission vessel *Thomas Crosby*. Dr. Kelly, a sturdy, handsome Haida man just over age 50 would later become the first Canadian Native to earn a doctorate. We had fried salmon steaks, canned raspberries and other delicacies.

Betty visiting with Mrs. Gertrude Kelly and head nurse Ms. Barner after lunch aboard the United Church mission vessel Thomas Crosby.

Early in the afternoon we got underway, with me acting as Dr. Darby's "nurse" for the day (my qualifications included a first aid ticket and Campfire Girl water safety cards). We visited Native and Chinese homes, and workers' quarters at the canneries. Twice I held a man's hand while the doctor yanked out an ulcerated tooth; one fisherman had travelled 20 miles to be relieved of his pain.

Far up the inlet, where snowmelt from the glacier tinted the water blue-white and the highest mountains punctured the white billowing clouds, we stopped at the Kildala Cannery. The cannery was idle, the many buildings vacant, but the Natives' rough cabins, set in a row on a hillside, were occupied and the doctor was needed. Brown-skinned boys tagged after us from house to house, talking in their own language. Some sat on the wooden railings along the walk, others peeked through windows as the doctor examined children and elders. Two little girls had to have teeth pulled. A little boy sat primly on a low stool waiting for his turn to be looked over. "He's not a bit afraid," Dr. Darby said. "We pulled him through a rather serious illness at the hospital one summer. He likes us." The little fellow held his mouth open long before the doctor was ready to look at his tonsils and he sighed with pleasure when he became the centre of attention.

All of the two- and three-room shacks had the pungent smell of fish in various stages of drying. Some of the dwellings were dirty, and the babies had skin eruptions and whimpered constantly. In the cleaner homes, the babies were lively, kicking and smiling. In a house set apart from the others, the doctor left pills for an ailing Spanish American War veteran tended by a sweet-faced Native woman.

As we walked toward another section of the village I commented on how calm and strong the Native women seemed, even when they or their children were unwell.

Jack Horan, the rather handsome gill net salesman whom Catherine had spoken of at Goose Bay, was on the wharf when we returned to the boat. He wanted a ride to the Brunswick Cannery and the doctor welcomed him aboard. We called at a number of other canneries, all with adjacent shacks for Native workers, before returning to the hospital. I tagged close after the doctor into every one of these huts, which seemed quite wretched to me.

Late that night I fell asleep on a bunk below decks. Soon Jack and the doctor shook me awake to see one of the most gorgeous sights on Canadian waters. The night was clear and the sky alive with stars. A mammoth burnished moon rested atop a ragged mountain peak, saturating the snow and dark greenness below with atomized silver. In the black recesses between the mountains all the stars seemed to have fallen out of heaven into the reflective headwaters of Rivers Inlet. The "stars" were kerosene lanterns, marking the far ends of gill nets fastened to hundreds of invisible boats, all quietly drifting with the tide. Somewhere a fisherman blew plaintive melodies on a harmonica and the haunting sound carried miles over the calm water. I thanked God for the privilege of tingling from the thrill of such a spectacle.

Dr. George Darby, famed for his work at the Bella Bella Mission Hospital, maintained a summer hospital at the Brunswick Cannery. Harbour Publishing archives

At the hospital Nurse Barner appeared in a trim red satin blouse and dark skirt to announce that we would have hot chocolate in the kitchen, and then she led me to a bed with clean cool sheets and said I must sleep there for the night.

Next morning I had a hot soak in a zinc-lined bathtub followed by a breakfast that included hot bran muffins and applesauce. I must have been a satisfactory nurse for Dr. Darby suggested I travel with him again that day, and then have a lift out to the main channel. Before we started, Nurse Barner showed me over the entire hospital from the children's ward on the third floor to the supply room and badminton court on the ground. Along the way I met a Scots woman who offered to tell my fortune in cards, so I asked if there was going to be a curly-haired young man in my future. "I don't see him," she said sympathetically.

Jack Horan, the always-on-the-move gill net salesman, came aboard Dr. Darby's boat with us. He planned to get off at every stop to spread company goodwill among the cannery net bosses and fishermen. Jack told me about his two weeks of halibut fishing in the North Pacific. "That's a life for tough men. A fellow has sure got to take it when he goes after halibut. The boat is never on an even keel. That's why I'm a net salesman."

At our first stop, an oil barge and store, I sat in *Bijaboji* catching up on the ship's log. A big packer nosed up to the float and Doug Nicholl, the fish buyer Flo and I had met in Nanaimo and had last seen at Lasqueti Island, came out on deck. You'd have thought he was my brother the way I scrambled out of the canoe to visit with him.

Our next stop was Beaver Cannery. It was a beastly hot day and large flies buzzed around in hordes. The scraggly cedars and spruce trees seemed to be withering before my eyes. The adult Natives were all working, and the children were together in one shack where babies squalled, sick ones whimpered and older ones talked in their own language. Diarrhea was rampant, and so were bad teeth. The doctor pulled four abscessed teeth from one little girl's mouth, and she screamed, kicked and howled so that I found it painful even to help him hold her.

In another shack was a courageous old woman who years before had fallen and broken her hip. At that time there was no doctor to care for her, and now the leg was misshapen and unwieldy. Every day she practised diligently without her cane, and she was overjoyed to hear Dr. Darby's encouraging comments about her progress.

As we plodded back to the cannery store, the doctor mentioned that I must meet Mrs. Elizabeth Wilson. He said no more, but those few words revealed his respect and admiration for her. We stepped into her store, filled with well-ordered arrays of foodstuffs, utensils and attractively displayed clothes for men, women and children. A lovely, dignified woman came forward, her arms outstretched in a charming welcome. Immediately I knew why one should meet Elizabeth Wilson. The first thought that filled my mind was: "This is the sort of poised and graceful lady my mother hopes I shall become."

She led me back to her spotless apartment to show me the many interesting items that people had given her. The treasure that I remember best was an opened oyster with a pearl, sealed in a glass sphere filled with colourless preserving liquid. She gave me a finely woven Indian mat and a picture of the cannery. Later one of the store employees told me that Mrs. Wilson was very sensitive about her Native blood. "She feels it keeps people from liking her," he said, "but she certainly is liked everywhere." After many years at Beaver Cannery, she was planning to return to her home village. "We'll miss her," the man said.

The bookkeeper in the office asked me to say hello to the Jack Calvins in Sitka, whose article about their canoe trip up the coast had been published in July 1933 in the *National Geographic*. He knew them because "they dried out one night at our place."

A Vancouver boat was moored alongside the float and some men were busy transferring salmon into a green and orange painted cold storage building. The net boss greeted Jack Horan and gave us a royal treat—fresh milk. Not merely that, he sent me off with a fresh apple pie and some California grapes and plums. Jack bought us each a candy bar. I got back to the doctor's boat in time to sterilize all of his tooth-pulling instruments.

At about eight o'clock that night I thanked Dr. Darby for the rare privilege of accompanying him, then asked him to cast off my line so I might row down Schooner Passage (now Darby Channel), and up to Boathouse Harbour, the name given by the Wallaces to a tiny indentation just north of Addenbroke lighthouse, eight miles away. I had to go west before I could go north. It was still light, and later the full moon would rise. I'd have no trouble seeing land or floating objects and Calvert Island would keep the Pacific Ocean breakers from agitating Fitz Hugh Sound and pounding the mainland. The salt water was calm. It was a magnificent night.

I skimmed along in my unlighted boat, sliding easily over numerous gill nets. Three or four suspicious fishermen cut across my bow to be sure I wasn't pirating fish from their nets, so I sang church hymns.

Out of Schooner Channel and going north again, I rowed in shimmering moonlight straight for the flashing light at Addenbroke. For awhile I pushed the dugout. Then, singing sea chanteys, I pulled her.

Judging by the number of lights I was passing, I calculated that I should be at Addenbroke before midnight, despite the northwest wind dead against me, and I congratulated myself.

A comet blazed a path across the sky and its red streak seemed to linger among the stars for many minutes. I sat chilled, expecting sizzling meteors to drop around me and through the canoe. No sooner was I back to normal from that fright than a whale, probably a humpback, blew so uncomfortably near that I could smell its strange and unpleasant breath. I stroked double-time to get out of the way in case it should playfully slap its tail.

A painter's palette of pink and silver flushed the sky, and the faraway light at the lighthouse went out. Then I realized it was after four o'clock in the morning and I hadn't been passing lights on shore—those lights had been on gillnet boats, passing me in the opposite direction, carried on a strong adverse tide. I must have rowed all night in nearly the same spot, for I was still a mile from the lighthouse buildings and so near the centre of Fitz Hugh Sound that I might have rowed to Calvert Island as easily as to Addenbroke. I clung to my original goal of the lighthouse, and pulled wearily to the nearest fish boat.

Evidently the owner was asleep in his bunk, so I made fast to his bumper—a used tire—to rest. Groggy and disheartened, I watched the antics of sea lions lifting their whiskered faces near the gill nets as they robbed the weary fisherman. They reminded me of Fred's stories of being stirred out of solid slumber by sea lions whooshing beside his fishing dory.

CHAPTER 10

Dangerous Waters in Fitz Hugh Sound

I rowed more than 30 miles that day. There was considerable steamer traffic, and people lined up against the rails to watch me. I laughed because I knew they were thinking, "Ah! Local colour! There's an Indian girl in her dugout. Bet she doesn't know what a tall building looks like."

— Betty Lowman, *Alaska Life*, March 1940

AN ALARM CLOCK RANG, SO I WHISTLED SHRILLY until a handsome Native man poked his head out to investigate. His surprise quickly softened when he saw me. "You're the first girl canoeist I've ever caught," he said.

I told him I was aiming for Addenbroke Light, and had tied alongside when I was too tired to go on. "I hope that's all right," I said.

"Sure, you can rest here. I'm going to make a new set down by the lighthouse in a few minutes. I'll pull you along. Come aboard and get warm inside where my boy is sleeping while I empty my net."

As I climbed aboard, the fisherman introduced himself as Willie Brown from Bella Bella. He wore one of those warm and attractive brown and tan sweaters knitted with Native symbols. After a brief exchange we discovered that I had met Willie's nephew, Godfrey, at Beaver Cannery. Willie told me that he was happy to help any friend of Dr. Darby. The cabin was warm and the boat undulated gently with the water. I fell asleep standing up.

Willie hauled in his net, which contained only 17 salmon, and started the gas engine. Skillfully he threaded through the maze of nets, floating lights and boats of the other gillnetters before setting a course for Addenbroke Light. It was just after dawn when we arrived near the cliff directly below the lighthouse. Half asleep, I stumbled out of the warm cabin and onto the chill deck. Before I was fully awake Willie helped me into the canoe and pointed to a husky, dark-haired man standing at the edge of a platform above. Willie shouted greetings, explanations and introductions to his friend the keeper.

I was sitting in the dugout ready to begin rowing when loops of line were quickly slipped around *Bijaboji*. The next thing I knew we were being hoisted at the end of a strong winch cable, swinging dizzily above the kelp, rocks and waves. I really woke up when we were swung over and set gently on a wooden platform about 30 feet above the water. The keeper was laughing and before I could step out of *Bijaboji* one of his young daughters was running along the wood ramp to the square white dwelling to tell the family that the girl canoeist had arrived. I noticed right away that the keeper wore another of those brown and tan sweaters woven with Native symbols. I was fascinated with the designs on these heavy, hand-knit wool sweaters, which were the choice weather-tested attire of coastal men—almost uniforms.

Lightkeeper William Wallace, a Canadian veteran of the Great War, and Mrs. Wallace and their six children generously made me one of the family. I wanted only a place to curl up in my sleeping bag, but they sat me beside the warm wood stove while Mrs. Wallace quickly prepared a delicious and nourishing hot breakfast. We traded many questions and answers before she put me to bed in their eldest daughter's room.

By the time I awoke in mid-afternoon, the water of Fitz Hugh Sound had been excited by strong winds. William Wallace explained that normally the north and south flow of the incoming tide met within sight of the lighthouse, but sometimes the tide—flood or ebb—ran one way for a week, depending on the wind and which end of Calvert Island the ocean currents got started around. He had many years of

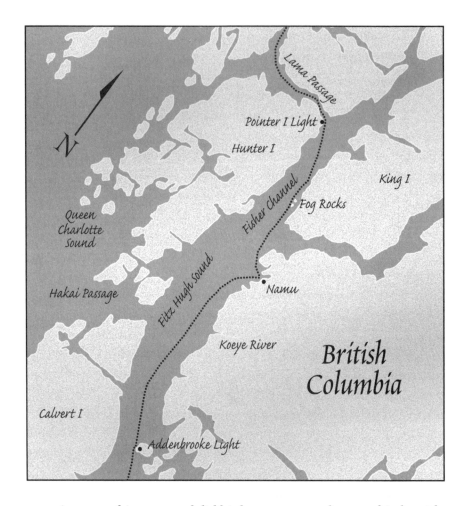

N

Lama Passage

Pointer I Light •

Hunter I

King I

Fisher Channel

Fog Rocks

Queen
Charlotte
Sound

Hakai Passage

Eltz Hugh Sound

Namu

Koeye River

British
Columbia

Calvert I

Addenbrooke Light

experience on this coast and did his best to persuade me to hitch a ride
for the rest of my trip. Mrs. Wallace, a war bride from London, was
truly concerned for my safety. I made no promises, but argued with
myself all afternoon as I worked on the ship's log and jotted down stories told by the Wallaces. One story was about Addenbroke's former
keeper, a lone man who nine years earlier had been found murdered.
He'd been ambushed, shot from behind, a bullet through his head.
The RCMP had suspects but no conclusive evidence. The murderer
had not been brought to justice.

The girls told me that the previous winter had been especially
harsh on wildlife and their father had shot a number of ravenous

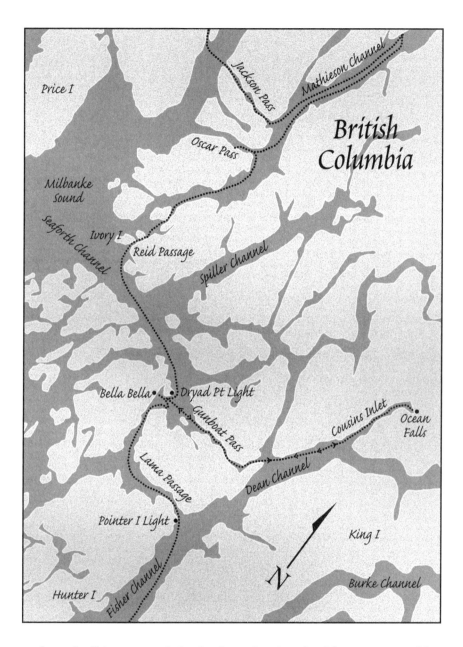

wolves skulking around the backyard—they had been attracted by the Wallaces' flock of milk goats.

Later that afternoon as we strolled through the woods the younger girls laughed as they told of the great number of fishermen who came seasonally to woo the attractive 18-year-old Margaret, the eldest daughter. Margaret wasn't yet interested in marriage and always managed to have a couple of brothers and sisters around when her admirers came to call or take her out. Our walk through the ragged woods ended north of the lighthouse at Boathouse Harbour, an anchorage for small boats in southerly winds and a place to dig clams when the tide was out.

The fretting silvered water of Fitz Hugh Sound was turning dark and dusk was cloaking the distant trees. It was time to light the signal lamp, time for the younger children to put away their toys for the night. The boys tied up their backyard gillnet fleet made of cardboard boxes, small chunks of old net, and various species of driftwood "fish," before scrambling up the steps to the light tower. I accompanied them and had a good look north, south and west while Mr. Wallace carefully trimmed the lamp wick. For miles all around there were only sky and sea and black lumps of uninhabited islands. It was Friday night, July 23, and the gillnetters and purse seiners had gone to their canneries or home for the weekend closure.

The tide was favourable on Saturday morning and, regretfully, I left Addenbroke and the wonderful, generous and thoughtful Wallace family. Mrs. Wallace insisted that I take a tin cookie box full of sandwiches that she and her delightful girls had made for me. I missed seeing the trollers and gillnetters, but I knew the men were enjoying a well-earned rest, and that the two days each week of no fishing ensured that enough salmon would enter the streams to spawn.

Just off the mouth of the Koeye River I struck the most eccentric wet acres of my entire trip. The flood tide charging into Fitz Hugh Sound was reinforced by savage, treacherous seas, direct from the open North Pacific, hurtling through Hakai Passage and across the sound to battle the river's strong outflow. That confused and tortured water leaped, popped and splashed unpredictably like hot lava in a volcanic crater. *Bijaboji* quivered and shook as I pulled or pushed on the oars, always watching each upward thrust of the wild water. I was thankful to get through that unusual stretch and to reach normally moving salt water. I was sopping wet, skirt and all. Bailing must be done, and now it was finally possible. I treated that passage as another learning experience. Although it was only 16 miles from Addenbroke Light to Namu, that impetuous water demanded extra time and effort.

Shortly before suppertime I reached Namu, the largest of the Canadian cannery establishments I had yet visited. As I came alongside the oil dock, the operator took my bowline and quickly informed me that a Vancouver news broadcaster had reported that "Betty Lowman had rowed across Queen Charlotte Sound for two days and landed at Goose Bay totally exhausted, where she was revived." Who, I wondered, were these busybodies who had nothing better to do than to spawn such wild stories?

That was bad enough, but another man at the dock stated that mail for me had been waiting so long that I'd been reported missing. Now Daddy and Mother would really be anxious—if they had heard. Won't men ever give a woman credit for doing anything that they think is strictly in their realm?

With such an exaggerated story about me going around, I dreaded tying up at the cannery dock, but it was the only thing I could do. I needed that mail and hoped that it had not been returned. Either way, I thought, all of these people will see for themselves that I'm alive and have made it this far safely.

Jack Horan, the peripatetic gill net salesman I'd last seen in Rivers Inlet, stood on the cannery's large float to meet me. I was glad to see him. Stepping forward, he quickly drew me into the circle of fishermen who relaxed on the float, discussing some of the many problems of their profession. Other fishermen were busy mending nets or bluestoning—soaking nets in a preserving solution. Jack's friends laughed as I told how the whale had scared me, and they inquired with much friendly and flattering interest about my trip. Their encouragement was just what I needed after learning that someone had reported me lost at sea. Jack's a great public relations agent for me, I thought. I hope he's doing as well selling nets.

At the post office, tucked in the well-stocked general store, I got letters galore from Mother, with grand notes and interesting magazine clippings about coastal Native people and how they live. There was also a note with the disconcerting news that my father had left orders at Alaskan-Pacific Airways for me to be clamped into jail until the first southbound steamer could take me home. I am 22 and should be free, I thought stubbornly; Daddy certainly has a strange way of expressing his concern and love for me. Somehow I would have to let my parents know that I had reached Namu and was safe as well.

Roy Bucknell, the camera aficionado at Harborview Hospital in Seattle, had sent me a tiny box camera and four rolls of film. That gave me three cameras and plenty of film to last until I reached Bella Bella, where I hoped to get more.

While I was reading my mail, a young woman from one of the nearby gillnet boats approached and introduced herself as Mrs. Hepburn, born at Avon, Washington, and married to a Canadian. We quickly discovered several mutual friends among our Skagit County acquaintances.

Early that evening Jack Horan and his friends thoughtfully included me in a small hiking party setting out for Namu Lake, a large lake above the Native village surrounded by forest and high, steep mountains. Most of our path consisted of a cedar-plank walk erected on posts and timbers because much of this forested area covered dangerous muskeg. Two rod and reel fishermen from the graceful yacht anchored in the harbour sauntered down the walk and proudly displayed a couple of beautiful speckled trout for the inspection of the tall, Irish, provincial policeman, one of the hikers.

That night I spread my sleeping bag on springs in one of the empty shacks in the village and slept wonderfully. As soon as I appeared on the walkway, the Hepburns invited me to have breakfast aboard their gillnet boat. The space under the cabin was barely large enough for the three of us, plus the boat's engine and the Primus stove in the galley. Almost miraculously, furniture was unfolded from the walls. Mrs. Hepburn quickly prepared a delicious breakfast without moving from her seat in front of the stove. Everything necessary for the meal was in the cupboard or stowed within reach, and we enjoyed sizzling bacon, fried eggs, toast with strawberry jam and coffee, while talking about Mrs. Hepburn's becoming a Canadian citizen.

The steamship *Cardena* arrived with two additional letters from Mother, each with more notes about Native Canadians. Even a vacation must be educational, seemed to be Mother's theory.

Shortly after eight o'clock I thanked Mr. Moorehouse, the cannery manager, and headed out, even though the weather was unsettled. The sombre sky was windless, the water an uninviting leaden colour. At mid-morning near Fog Rocks, a black and white steamer overtook me and passed, disturbing the sullen, calm water of Fisher Channel. It then turned westward toward the distant trees and disappeared. My chart indicated that the steamer had taken narrow Lama Passage leading to Bella Bella, my goal for the day.

Pointer Island light signalled the entrance to Lama Passage. The tide was high, enabling me to glide through the narrow stretch of water and skim over the drying ledge connecting large Hunter Island and minuscule rocky Pointer Island, site of the lighthouse. As *Bijaboji* was zigzagging between the rocks, the keepers called out, "Come up for half an hour."

The tide was with me to Bella Bella. I was making good time and sorely tempted to continue, but so many people along the way had talked about Ben and Annie Codville and their years at the light that I decided to stop. The "half an hour" stretched into a fascinating afternoon and evening.

Ben had lived with his parents across Fisher Channel, on King Island, from 1894 until 1899, when Ben's father, James Codville, worked as the first keeper at Pointer Island Light. Ben's father had died in 1917 at age 83, and Ben, then 34, took over as keeper. His mother, knowing Ben could not get away to look for a bride, gave the captain of a mission boat a picture of Ben and asked that he find a prospective bride during his trips up and down the coast. Within months, Annie came from Vancouver on the mission boat to meet him, and the missionary captain performed the marriage ceremony.

Ben saw the residents of the old Bella Bella Indian village move when sanitation demanded it. He told me that the new village, on the west side of Lama Passage, had grown rapidly during the past 20 years since the Mission Hospital had been established. Ben spoke

Ben and Annie Codville, keepers of the Pointer Island lighthouse from 1917 to 1946. Annie married Ben after seeing his photograph on a mission boat and hearing that he was looking for a wife.

Chinook jargon, the trade language, fluently and rattled off a sentence or two. That was the first time I had heard it spoken.

Annie Codville had immigrated from England. Her family had been in the employ of a British member of the world-renowned Rothschild family, so Annie could describe their system of management, schooling and generosity from an insider's viewpoint. Annie had kept busy throughout the long lonely hours at the lighthouse during the Great War by knitting socks for soldiers; for this she was awarded a medal. She also embroidered dozens of pillowcases, table runners, tablecloths and dish towels, as well as crocheting yards and yards of lacy fabric.

The Codvilles showed me pictures of the *Seattle Star* columnist H.E. Jamison and his wife, who had stopped by on their way to Alaska in their sailing yacht *Naughty Marietta*. Some time later, I met the Jamisons. I occasionally worked as a reporter for Jamie during 1940 to 1942, and was sometimes the subject of his daily column and radio program "Along The Waterfront."

The Codvilles told about a man and his small son who, while rowing to Alaska one February in a battered skiff, were blown seaward during the 19 hours it took them to cross Queen Charlotte Sound.

Thank God for the westerly that blew me ashore south of Blunden Harbour when I crossed Queen Charlotte Strait. Annie talked about four Sea Scouts from California who had stopped at the lighthouse during the summer of 1936 to make bread while on their way from Seattle to Skagway. Ben never tired of telling—with awe—about the Scouts' expensively outfitted canoes. (A book about these Scouts, *Cruise of the Blue Flujin* by Ken C. Wise, was published in 1987).

As we talked we watched a great white Northland steamer come out of Lama Passage, turn into Fisher Passage and continue southbound. From the waterline down she was painted bright green. Later I learned that some relatives of mine from Mount Vernon, Washington, had been aboard.

The Codvilles' lives and experiences centred on the lighthouse: watching the ships and boats pass, talking with the rare visitor, making infrequent 10-mile canoe trips to Bella Bella for supplies. Their connection to the rest of the world was by listening to a radio or studying their vast collection of books and old, well-worn newspapers and magazines. Ben didn't see an automobile until they retired and moved to Prince Rupert in 1946.

I could have stayed and listened to the Codvilles for days, but on Monday, at five in the morning, they helped me load the canoe and get away. The sky was clear, the sun warm and bright. There was no wind. The tide was flowing my way, a rare bit of luck. It would be a glorious day to enjoy the beauty of British Columbia. *Bijaboji* passed the scraggly cedars and spruce trees lining the shores like a speeding motorboat. I missed the high hills. Here the islands were low and gently rolling, and the air held an exhilarating salty tang.

The sun burned brighter and hotter as it lifted above me. I wanted to row without my sweater but the Vancouver radio station had given my trip so much publicity, and there were so many people who might see me. Workers in government boats, islanders, fishermen of all backgrounds went off course to greet me by name or whistle salutes. One older man, standing on a point of rock not far from several weather-beaten houses, yelled, "Are you from the States?"

"Yes."

"Want to put it in my daily log," he shouted back.

Occasionally a carved pole could be seen among the trees along the higher portions of the shoreline. I was told that each isolated pole was a memorial to a Native who had drowned. As Mother's notes had said, and the Codvilles had explained, drowning was the worst calamity that could befall a Native person if the body is not recovered. Elaborate totem poles were erected to the drowned person if, after diligent search enriched by offers of great reward, no body was found.

To my great disappointment, there was no mail for me at the Bella Bella Cannery across the channel from the Native village of Bella Bella. But I did meet Fisheries Inspector Gordon Reade, who went over my charts, marked the locations of cabins and shelters and gave me helpful advice about the tides that swirl uncertainly through these passages.

"It's just a mile across to the village," he said. "Some of the hospital people are hoping to meet you. You'll easily make it for lunch."

I counted strokes from the cannery to the dock a mile away and when I was nearly to 400 and had only a short way to go, the wind wafted a yellow balloon left over from the Vancouver Jubilee in 1936 past me. Some boys on the dock waved and yelled that they wanted it, so I chased it down. Then the boys made the canoe fast while I dashed to the hospital to greet Dr. George Darby's staff. I met Dr. Herb Banner and Miss McGee, the nurse in charge, who invited me in for lunch at their quarters. Dr. Darby must have mentioned the canoeist, for I felt much like a returned friend. After lunch, Miss Ada Morgan invited me to look over her pictures. I had admired some of her enlargements displayed at the Codvilles' home at Pointer Island, and now Miss Morgan insisted on giving me many of her prints. She was gifted with an artistic eye for subject, balance and beauty.

In mid-afternoon Mrs. Barner and Miss McGee walked with me across the bridge to the village general store and oil dock. The storekeeper and his mother asked me to carry greetings to the Jack Calvins of Sitka.

"Of course," I said, "but if I get clamped into jail in Ketchikan, I'll never see them. I'm rowing to Ocean Falls to send my father a telegram. If I phrase it right, that just might soften him up."

"Ocean Falls? Why, that's 30 miles out of the way!" Miss McGee said.

Mrs. Barner said that Dr. Barner was taking the auditor back there that afternoon, and a woman who wanted to get a permanent wave. "It is the nearest place to send a telegram, so you could go with the doctor and leave your dugout here."

Before I could answer, one of the boys ran up from the village and hollered breathlessly, "Your canoe's swamped! And everything's wet."

I sprinted to the dock. The canoe was gone, along with my few possessions. What had happened? Frantic and dejected, I went to the hospital. There I saw my things spread over the hospital's lawn, and the canoe moored safely offshore. What a relief! My clothes and food were already drying under the hot sun.

Had the boys been playing and rolled the dugout until it was full of water? I'll never know, but I will always be grateful to the hospital staff who rescued *Bijaboji*.

Dr. Barner and his passengers were nearly ready to get underway. "We'll go through Gunboat Passage," he said. "It's shorter and more scenic."

The surrounding low hillsides were a luxuriant green. Wide-spread lower branches, all trimmed level by the high tide reach of the salt water, overhung this narrow east-west passage. This was also a place where rocks and thick patches of golden kelp lurked. Dr. Darby had showed Dr. Barner the way, and he avoided all the hazards and took us safely past Georgie Point and the entrance to Johnson Channel, then into Fisher Channel. Soon we were running northward through Cousins Inlet to Ocean Falls. Verdant forests surrounded us, and occasionally I spotted the white head and tail feathers of a bald eagle perched on the bare branch of an old snag. Other eagles chose long limbs overhanging the water to sight the next meal, waiting for a fish to rise to the surface, or a sea bird to fail to stay alert.

Fishing boats, loggers' work boats and recreation boats of all shapes and sizes passed us going to and fro. After two or three hours we came to shores lined with summer cottages, then rounded a point and sighted Ocean Falls, wedged between steep hills.

"All that smoke reminds me of the pulp mill at Powell River," I said.

"That's all smoke and steam from the pulp digester," said Dr. Barner. "The mill makes Ocean Falls one of the most important towns on the north coast."

The isolated settlement appeared huge. There was even a massive hotel, reputed to be the largest in British Columbia north of Vancouver. A smooth sheet of clear water spilled across the top of a concrete dam, sparkling and splashing in the bright sun as it slid to the sea.

I could easily have believed that I was back in the city as I walked along Ocean Falls' main street. The women were well groomed and smartly dressed in the latest styles, and nearly all had professional hairdos. Forthcoming club events and meeting notices for all kinds of groups filled the bulletin boards. There were clubs for camera enthusiasts, mountain climbers, swimmers, indoor sports participants and many others.

The pulp and lumber mill at Ocean Falls.

Autos honked and tooted on the plank roads until we moved aside to let them pass. "All vehicles are brought in on barges or ships," the doctor said. "There is no road to Ocean Falls and only a few miles here."

After a malted milk, equal to any that one might get in a campus Sugar Bowl, we went to the movie *Petticoat Fever* starring Myrna Loy and Robert Montgomery. I was told that these log and pulp mills were controlled by a large American company, and that many of the employees were from the States, and I wondered whether that was why this town felt so much like home.

After the show, the doctor stopped at the company hospital to chat with old friends. The night nurse brought out tea, toast and marmalade, and cake. Others joined us in a cozy sitting room where Dr. Barner revealed himself to be a super raconteur, keeping us in gales of laughter. Later the thoughtful doctor wangled a bed for himself in the hospital so that I might have the bunk on the boat. Before bedtime I had the luxury of a relaxing hot bath at the hospital.

Early the next morning the doctor came to the float and nearly rolled me onto the deck by rocking the boat while shouting, "Breakfast at the hospital in 10 minutes."

It was a lovely breakfast — bacon, eggs, toast and marmalade. I was beginning to believe this was the *de rigueur* coastal breakfast, and I never tired of it.

While the doctor tended to some business and waited for the lady to get her permanent, I sent my telegram to Daddy and visited the logging company office. There, two of the engineers gave me blue and yellow large-scale land maps, took my picture and suggested other logging camps that might be interesting to visit. One of these was Alec Ring's camp, 12 miles out of the way in Mathieson Channel. They told me it was a large camp, with wives and children as well as the men. I realized that I'd like to see a logging camp where women and children lived.

But first, I visited a freighter from San Francisco that was loading at the dock. There, as I watched the longshoring work from the ship's bridge, I saw a great number of husky Japanese men among the dock crew, and I learned that there was a large Japanese community at Ocean Falls.

Friends of the doctor took us on a tour through the mill, where I saw great vats of mushy pulp, coloured by dyes, as at the pulp mill I'd visited at Powell River. A chemical engineer began to name off about 90 different kinds of paper made in that mill—everything from common newsprint to the delicate green tissue used by florists.

The boss of the mill's painting crew tried to persuade me to borrow one of his rifles for the rest of the trip, but I declined, saying that I couldn't hit a bear if I did see one.

He and the doctor were much concerned about the death of Chet Willard, a well-liked logger who had been burned aboard his boat when the gasoline engine caught fire and the fuel tank exploded. Fires in gasoline powerboats appeared to be fairly common occurrences, judging by the stories I heard and the dreadfully scarred fishermen I met that summer. One survivor, a salmon troller, told me he believed Dr. Darby was prescient, for he was often luckily in the vicinity when a fisherman was burned. "Doc has saved lots of us," he told me.

While we waited for the lady to get her permanent wave, I had time to relax and dry the pages of my ship's log by spreading them out on the cabin top in the glorious sun on that windless day. As I worked, an agile, self-assured woman climbed off a tugboat and walked along the float to me. "You are the coed canoeist, aren't you?" She didn't waste time waiting for a reply. "My name is Hawkins. We missed you at Namu. Come over and meet my husband."

Tugboat men know the vagaries of these coastal waters and are the best sources of information on how to take advantage of tides, eddies and currents. Captain Hawkins was no exception. He gave me helpful suggestions about every tricky bit of water from Bella Bella through Grenville Channel and into Prince Rupert. "You've done a remarkable job in getting here," he said. "Prince Rupert is only about another 180 miles from Bella Bella—unless you go sightseeing up every channel and inlet." Captain and Mrs. Hawkins were so encouraging, saying words I needed to hear.

"You aren't planning to go up Douglas Channel, are you?" Captain Hawkins said. "That's one unpredictable stretch. Always a new challenge."

"Oh, no. I won't be going up there. My one idea is to get to Ketchikan."

I said thanks and goodbye when the newly coiffed lady came back. She steered the gas boat while Dr. Barner and I enjoyed the rare treat of thick slices of still-warm apple pie, washed down with fresh chilled milk from the cold storage building.

That marvellous excursion ended late in the afternoon when we moored in front of the Bella Bella Hospital. The tide was flowing in the wrong direction for me to head north in Lama Passage. I planned to start out anyway, but the hospital staff dissuaded me—especially the engineer, who had thoughtfully refilled my kerosene lantern and dried my sleeping bag and other things. "Pack your gear in the canoe and then tie it to the gas boat," he said. "Borrow an alarm clock. Sleep on the boat, and leave at sunrise." I decided to heed his good advice.

I rested well until the alarm roused me on Wednesday, July 28, for a new day of adventure. I splashed cold water in my face, then packed

Bella Bella viewed from the water. The large building is the United Church Mission Hospital, where Dr. George Darby practised for most of the year.

and pushed off in the chill of early morning, before the sun rose above the mountains. Damp mist left globules of water on the Fabrikoid covering that protected my dry sleeping bag and clothes. Ahead, indistinct in the leaden morning haze, I could make out a steamer and a lighthouse. The steamer bore down quickly and passed, rolling *Bijaboji* in its vigorous wake. The stubby, square structure of Dryad Point light grew larger as the canoe glided nearer, then shrank as I left it behind. I turned to row westward through Seaforth Channel toward Ivory Island and into Milbanke Sound. Water, sky and forested islands were all a misty grey.

I was entertained by watching trolling boats move slowly a mile or so one way, then a mile back. Occasionally a fisherman would toss a bright salmon over the gunwale and on deck. By now I knew the routine: quickly check the shiny metal lure and needle-sharp hook and cast it out again. Then clean and wash the fish, and slide it into the hold filled with chipped ice. A few of the trollers were operated by a couple, the wife usually in the pilothouse steering and providing a plentiful supply of hot coffee or tea, while the husband, at the stern, tended the fishing gear.

I kept the bow of the canoe trained on a navigation buoy dancing sedately to the rhythm of incoming rollers from Milbanke Sound. Beyond the buoy I rowed toward trolling boats creeping back and forth around a point in the far distance. By the sun's position I guessed it was about eight o'clock when a smartly painted, southbound American cruise ship passed. Curious passengers lined the rail. Many waved or lifted their binoculars. I waved back. Then one of those men who are always ready with misinformation, said loudly: "A Bella Bella Native girl, no doubt. Yes. Yes, the Indian women all along this coast are as expert as any male in handling those little dugouts. But I marvel at how women, of such dimensions as many of them have, manage not to capsize their canoe." My joy at seeing the steamer was shattered. Then I saw my ruddy, tanned face and tousled black hair reflected in the water lying in the bottom of the canoe and I saw why they had taken me for a Native. But white or Native, why had he insulted me?

As we approached Milbanke Sound, *Bijaboji* began to lift and fall to the rhythm of ocean swells. I preferred the natural movement of the Pacific to the skewed wake created by powerful ships or fast boats. The sky darkened quickly and for a half-hour, stinging rain drove against my face. Then the sun blazed intermittently. Every time it escaped from the steel-grey clouds, it streaked the wet trees, rocks and boats with a coat of bright, twinkling silver. I got one grand photograph of a black trolling boat with its small white stabilizing sail silhouetted against the grey of the Pacific.

Following the nooks and crannies along the shore to avoid the first of the flood tide, I saw many graceful deer wading through seaweed to a wooded island barely separated from the mainland by shallow water—water too shallow to float the canoe. The shy deer disappeared before I could get a camera shot of them.

Just east of Ivory Island I had a ticklish half-hour amid low tide reefs and crashing breakers while working my way into Reid Passage to avoid the exposed waters of Milbanke Sound. Safely in the narrow passage, I discovered the flood tide was with me. A float plane flew low, just above the treetops, swimming through the foggy mist. At irregular intervals the wind carried the sound of Ivory Island's distant foghorn. Seals, crows and seagulls stayed close about the canoe. During my entire trip I don't recall a day when I didn't hear and see a flock of saucy crows cawing and fussing, or great numbers of seagulls screaming and fighting over fish entrails discarded by a troller or food scraps dumped overboard by cargo or passenger ships.

I was so happy and my appetite was so good that I ate dozens of sandwiches—dozens—and drank gallons of water dipped from many sparkling streams that danced over the rocks on their way to the ocean. Two small trolling boats passed as I steered the canoe in a favourable tidal stream running like a turgid river. "Good going!" one fisherman called out in passing. We laughed.

I passed a dandy little cabin in a serene woodland clearing and I might have made camp there if the tide hadn't been carrying me onward with remarkable speed. Eventually *Bijaboji* emerged from the narrow, broken pass into Mathieson Channel, where I saw nothing but mountains, mountains and more mountains. Great billowing silver clouds played over and around these mountains, all under a beneficent blue sky.

It was twilight and 14 hours after I had left Bella Bella when I pulled in the oars, ready to call it a day. Now there was no campsite visible through the dim, tricky twilight. I was feeling wonderfully alive and happy, and decided I might as well row on. It was only about 12 miles to Alec Ring's logging camp. For a while I was content just to drift and enjoy the solitude and the quiet, enchanting beauty of my surroundings.

Milbanke Sound was behind me and Klemtu Native village and cannery no more than 14 miles ahead. All day I had worked the tides and wind to greatest advantage. I felt as mighty and free as the eagles that soared screaming overhead in Seaforth Channel, even more carefree than the porpoise that often played around *Bijaboji*. I was as happy as I had been in my childhood summers on the islands of Puget Sound. I was alone, completely dependent on my own resources, caring for myself, creating my own schedules, thinking of and for myself and contemplating my future. I loved being close to God's sea and land, facing challenges and hardships similar to what the pioneers had survived. I had a perfect mental set-up that evening to withstand any unpleasantness—even Daddy's threat of having me clamped in jail and ignominiously taken home by a southbound steamer.

Finally I rowed on to choose a spruce "nest" on the far side of Oscar Passage for the night. I would go logging in the morning. A gas boat slowly approached, towing a large, slick larch log. I hailed the lone man aboard to ask about tides to Alec Ring's logging camp.

"The tide's changing now," he said. "You can't go any farther until after the next low water. My name's Ole. Have supper with me and I'll mark Ring's camp on your chart."

Ole made my line fast to his boat and *Bijaboji* zigzagged alongside the log until we reached his compact float camp, moored in a shallow bight on the side of Oscar Passage I'd just come from. While he tied his boat inside the boomsticks beside his small house, I took care of the dugout.

"I was a baker in Norway," Ole said while cooking us a quick but filling supper. "Worked in town for my uncle for seven years, then decided to be a hand logger." He was happy and contented with his life — a life of self-reliance and freedom in this glorious, always changing outdoors.

Ole was full of information about the tides to Alec Ring's logging camp and through Jackson Passage, an uncharted salt-water short-cut to Klemtu. After the dishes were washed and put away, I started ashore to make camp. "Sleep on the gas boat," Ole called out from the doorway. "It's going to rain hard before morning."

I pulled my bedroll into the still-warm engine room of the gas boat and wriggled in between the folds of the Indian blanket I had pinned inside the sleeping bag. Cuddled into Cocoon, I found that I was really weary. Ole was soon proven right about the hard rain.

The rain ceased sometime before dawn, and in early morning the sky was a threatening charcoal grey. I was stowing my sleeping bag and getting ready to depart when Ole emerged from the floathouse. "Breakfast's ready." It was not the standard bacon and eggs, but hotcakes. I couldn't resist.

After breakfast, he said he was going to the other side. "There's a good log I can pull off the beach at high tide," he said. "Might as well come along." We crossed Oscar Passage quickly. With a hearty "Thanks, Ole!" and a farewell wave, I rowed up Mathieson Channel. It was 12 miles of rowing, in and out of drizzling rain, but the tide was with me. One moment I was soaked with rain, the next I was getting sunburned.

CHAPTER 11

Birthday in Bijaboji

*On July 31, Betty's twenty-third birthday, she reached Butedale on
the east side of Princess Royal Island. She had been out nearly seven
weeks and had covered more than 750 miles.*

—River Magazine, 1999

ALONG MATHIESON CHANNEL, dead, fallen tree trunks stuck out from
the cliffs like cannons from a fortress. Freshly logged-off acres along
the shore and high up the hillsides stood out grey-brown against the
greens of cedar, spruce and hemlock that stood on the higher reaches,
beyond the long grasp of A-frame loggers. In this place I could see
how difficult and dangerous their work was.

Much farther up the channel than I was going were Mussel Inlet
and Poison Cove. There, in the 1790s, some of Captain George Vancouver's men became sick and one died of paralytic shellfish poison-
ing from eating mussels. Captain Vancouver is my favourite among
the great navigators and explorers and it gave me rich thrills to be
travelling up the same channel—though some 150 years later—that
he had explored.

At one o'clock, just as the men were heading back to the woods, I
landed at the logging camp floats. Alec Ring, a raw-boned, handsome
Swede, was still in camp. I introduced myself and was immediately
invited to the cookhouse for lunch. Afterward, Mr. Ring and I putt-
putted in the work boat to the big A-frame.

The A-frame rig consisted of a great log raft supporting near the
shoreward end an *A* made of two large logs, each about 100 feet long,
with their butts secured near the ends of a third log lashed to the float

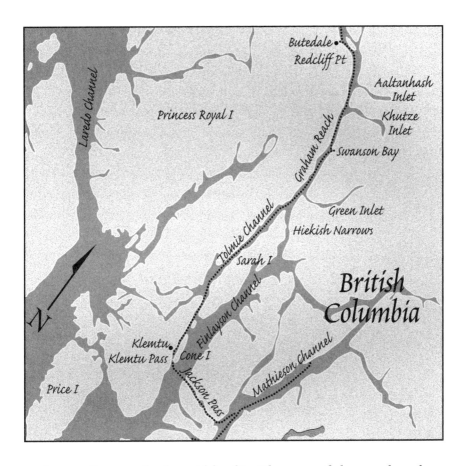

and extending nearly the width of it. The tops of the two long logs were wired together. Near the top, a smaller log was lashed across, completing the *A*, to support a large block (pulley). This massive *A* stood up, leaning slightly toward the shore and was held in position by heavy guy wires. Near the seaward end of the raft, a steam engine, or "donkey," was secured. The donkey provided power for the winch and was a counterbalancing weight on the float. Strong cables ran from the drums powered by the donkey through the block hanging in the *A* to another block anchored to a sturdy stump or spar tree hundreds of yards up the hillside. Logs felled on the hillside were "choked" by a wire, then hooked to this mainline from the A-frame. By letting wire out on one drum while taking in on the other, the workers could drag or carry the logs down the hillside to the salt chuck.

Alec Ring pointed out a safe route for me to take into the woods without being whacked galley-west by flopping, snapping cables or crushed under trees knocked down by the great logs being hauled out of the woods. By the time I reached the whistle punk (signalman) high in the woods, I was muddy from head to foot and encircled by clouds of biting no-see-ums, all ignoring my frantically waving arms. I was safe there, but my problems weren't over.

As I sat on the mossy hillside, I asked Bill Donovan, the tall blond whistle punk, about his job. He handed me an armload of electric signal wire and we moved to a higher, less dangerous spot beside a tall spruce tree. I was learning by doing! From somewhere below, the rigging-slinger yelled out signals. Bill responded by squeezing the electric gadget in his hand, causing a whistle to blow loudly on the donkey engine far below us. The steam engine hissed and rumbled. The slack mainline cable shook mightily, quivered and snapped taut. Abruptly an immense log about 60 feet long and four feet in diameter was jerked from the valley floor and came alive, swinging wildly from a choker hanging on the heavy bull hook suspended from the mainline butt rigging. Careening wildly over rocks and gullies, the log crashed into lesser trees, knocking them down or uprooting them, until it splashed into the water in front of the A-frame. The log rolled and twisted until the sure-footed chaser hustled across other floating logs and unhooked it. He waved his arm as a signal to Bill, then ran back to the A-frame, where he waited safely for the next log to be hauled out of the bush.

Bill punched in another signal, the whistle sounded, and the donkey engineer sent the mainline back with its heavy bull hook and choker clanging, snapping and swinging dangerously in a wide circle. Now and again we would indistinctly hear a faller yell "*TIM-berrr!*" soon followed by the noise of smaller trees and limbs being smashed as another centuries-old tree fell in the ravine below us.

Across the channel the dark green hillside was streaked with white where a tumbling stream bounced gracefully down a high cliff from rock shelf to rock shelf on its way into the water. "Behind it," Bill said, "there's a lake with lots of trout. And by the lake there's an old trapper's shack."

"Oh, I'd like to row over to the falls and hike around the lake, if only I weren't heading for Klemtu tonight," I said longingly. This out-of-the-way spot in Mathieson Channel appealed to me—it seemed an ideal place for the log cabin I hoped to build. Maybe that trapper's shack would be the perfect site, and need only a little fixing up.

By 10 minutes to five I was wondering if the supper whistle would ever blow, and why the no-see-ums weren't even slightly discouraged by the rain and citronella. Abruptly, Bill tooted the whistle a number of times. He'd heard something I'd missed—the dreaded yell, "Help!" Miller, the chokerman, had slipped off a spruce log onto criss-crossed tree limbs in the ravine and broken his elbow. The most accessible doctor was at Prince Rupert, a day's run away on the steamer.

Providentially, the weekly steamer was due in at Klemtu that night and the logging boat was scheduled to go there to pick up mail and fresh food. The donkey engineer saw a boat chugging by and waved for it to stop. This was Mr. Gorde and his seven-man crew from a camp farther up the channel. They were immediately ready to help.

The boss yelled at Bill and he blew the always-welcome supper whistle. Bill and I wound up the signal line before scrambling, sliding and falling over the devastation and confusion of treetops, large limbs and shattered snags as we hurried to the boat waiting alongside the A-frame. I was last aboard, being embarrassed by a generous three-corner tear in the seat of my ski trousers. I had snagged them on a broken limb during one of my spills on the way down the hillside.

At the cookhouse Mrs. Ring and the pretty schoolteacher, who was working for the summer as a flunky, did what they could to ease Miller's pain. We waited until all the loggers had eaten, then I enjoyed a fine meal with the cook, the flunky, Mrs. Ring and her little girl.

Alec Ring put my canoe aboard his boat, ready for the trip to Klemtu, but I told him I was determined to row every inch of the main course to Alaska, so would accept rides or tows only for my side trips. Riding to the entrance to Jackson Passage would bring me to the main course.

Men ceased splitting firewood, splicing wire and sharpening cross-cut saws and axes to say goodbye to Miller, who was obviously well liked and respected. I sat in the canoe, set crosswise on the stern of the boat, while Alec took a picture. The boat's engine came to life with a sputter and pop, men threw lines aboard and the boat skimmed along the edge of the float. Suddenly I froze. *Bijaboji*'s bow, extending beyond the side of the boat, was about to bash against the cross log that protruded from the float. Alec couldn't hear the men's shouts above the noise of the engine.

Horace, the log chaser, ran along the float, leaped onto the boat, pulled the canoe clear with a mighty jerk and immediately leaped back to the float. It was the quickest thinking and acting I've ever seen—so quick that by the time I found my wits to shout thanks, the boat was too far away for him to hear me. Loggers certainly have to think and act fast, and they need the sure-footed agility of cats if they are to survive in the bush.

Miller lay quietly on a bunk in the pilothouse. I took the wheel while Alec fixed packs for Miller's broken elbow and lit cigarettes for the two of them. Before me, framed by the windows, were green-blue hills with their muted reflections inverted on the smooth surface of the water. Low, threatening grey clouds covered and uncovered the sun as they rambled across a sullen sky. Miller talked about the Great War and his time in the Dardanelles. He had been through that entire campaign and was wounded four times. "You must have lied about your age to join up," I said, "for you are a young man." He didn't answer, and I realized that no matter what his years, no war veteran is young.

At the entrance to Jackson Passage, not shown on any of the charts I had seen, Alec Ring put the canoe off his boat. I'd already wished Miller a full recovery, and now with a "Thanks for everything, Mr. Ring," I let myself onto *Bijaboji*'s comfortable seat. I was setting the oars in place when we commenced rolling on the wake of the logging boat.

The sun lay below the ranks of hills that appeared to crouch over one another as I looked westward across that narrow "river" of salt water. Far ahead, beyond the gas boat's widening white wake, the sky and water were subtly turning delicate orange-pink and gold as twilight engulfed this lovely part of creation.

The current was so much help I scarcely had to row. *Bijaboji* sped along while my hearty sea chanteys echoed from the hillsides. As dusk closed in, swimming mink, handsome and inquisitive, sneaked close as I coasted along in the rushing eddies. I lifted the oars clear of the water so as not to frighten them.

Night's darkness was peaceful. I realized the passage was ending when a refreshing cool breeze from Finlayson Channel suddenly hit me in the face. The heat of the day had been pocketed in the passage during the day and held in by the trees and hills. Had there been a welcoming light at the far end of the passage, I would have visited the Japanese saltery there.

The sky was like dark velvet, set with sequins arranged in the shapes of Greek and Roman mythological figures. Tiny fish flickered phosphorescently at every dip of the oars. I couldn't see Klemtu. Certainly on steamer night the dock would be lighted. I struck many matches before one held long enough to light my lantern. Then I discovered that the dot on the map indicating Klemtu was behind long, narrow Cone Island. My problem was to determine just where among the black bumps of land ahead was the island's south end and the entrance to Klemtu Passage.

Eventually, a wide crescent moon rose behind me, distorting the great pieces of driftwood that sparkled with phosphorus, creating serpent-like creatures that disguised the indentations of the land. I made several false starts into northward trending coves before I found the correct passage. Miles to the south, a lighted freighter was heading northward from Milbanke Sound, but I lost sight of it a few hundred yards up the winding passage.

On I went, past point after point without sight of a light. The tide was wonderfully with me and the salty night air was rejuvenating. I was in the middle of the channel crossing to the shore where I thought Klemtu should appear when the noise of the freighter rounding the point behind me thundered and reverberated among the hills. It looked as though there wasn't room in that deep, narrow channel for both of us. From the opposite direction came the passenger and mail steamer. The freighter passed without sighting me, and set its searchlight stabbing at the shore until it located the pier. Suddenly I could see many fish boats and logging tenders crowded two and three abreast along the floats, all with lights showing from masts or cabins. Dogs barked. This would be a busy night in Klemtu. I approached the wharf and floats all too conscious of the canoe as a delicate mite of a thing.

But I had as great a welcoming committee as anyone else. It was the Japanese owner of the boat I had been aboard weeks earlier in Sechelt, and he also owned the saltery in Jackson Passage. "We're expecting you," he said, flashing his light on the water before me, showing the way to a landing place for the canoe.

Ring's and Gorde's logging boats were moored side by side. In the cabin of Ring's boat I found Miller as quiet as ever, but his ashtray was overflowing with half-smoked cigarettes. While Alec Ring was ashore making transportation arrangements I sat with Miller, ready to assist in any way. I also wrote to Mother and let her know I had arrived there safely.

Later I went along the cannery dock with the others to see Miller board the ship. The tide was low and *Cardena* had tied up outboard of the freighter. Alec Ring and other loggers helped Miller aboard. A few sleepy passengers stood at the steamer rail. One man looked at me intently, then shouted "Hel-lo, Annette!" and hurried across to the dock. Conscious of the tear in my ski trousers, I edged back into the deeper shadows. Then Jack Horan, the gill net salesman, was beside me. "You're cold. You need a cup of steaming coffee." Those were marvellous words.

Jack took my arm and led me to the steamer. We crossed the freighter's bridge, then Jack leaped to the rail of the *Cardena* before helping me across and into the dining saloon. The ship's steward was the man I had met in Alert Bay, and he and Jack were amused by my story of the boys and the swamping of the dugout at Bella Bella.

I went to Miller's table and said, "I'll call on you at the hospital in Prince Rupert. Don't get well and go away to another logging camp before I get there, because I won't know anyone else in that town."

As I was leaving *Cardena* after enjoying coffee and conversation, Robert Johnstone of Inverness Cannery on the Skeena River approached me. "My wife and I expect you to stop at Inverness," he said. "Don't be too many weeks getting there." He was gruff and direct and I liked him immediately.

I promised to stop there.

Finally the *Cardena* got underway and the freighter made ready to load canned salmon. Then Mr. Gorde told me that he, Alec Ring and two new loggers for the Ring camp were going to sleep on Alec Ring's boat so that I could have a bunk on Mr. Gorde's boat. His 10-year-old boy was already fast asleep there. And so another night went by without my roughing it in true campfire style.

In the morning I tried to make breakfast for the men, but Mr. Gorde wouldn't have it. "No! No!" he insisted. "We will cook for you." I don't know who cooked what, but it was another excellent and filling breakfast, made more enjoyable by interesting, fast-paced conversation about this superb salt-water and forest frontier. I was convinced that men and women who survived in this harsh and isolated coastal region could do nearly anything, and do it well.

I gave my heartfelt thanks to these kind men as the two boats shoved off, loaded with assorted quarters and halves of fresh meat, fruits and vegetables, and numerous cases of canned foods for the camps.

After a leisurely walk through town I still had to wait three hours for the tide to turn and run with me. With my back to the hot morning sun, I sat on the dock jotting notes in my book until a group of Native girls came along and sat beside me. Annie Brown, cousin of Willie Brown, who had given me a lift south of Addenbroke Light, was the most fluent talker. The girls were plainly excited about something and at last one had to tell me: a young woman in the village had delivered a baby the night before, just as *Cardena* docked. Mother and baby were doing well.

I told Annie about hunting with Billy Shields at Garden Bay and she said that he was already a widower at 19. "His wife died after they were married scarcely a year. And two of his sisters, too, from consumption."

Norman Brodhurst, captain of one of the fish packers moored to the dock, came off his vessel and sat with us, telling me about tides to Swanson Bay. "I've worked on this coast all my life and have not missed many good camera shots," he said, showing me some fine pictures. "And I've thousands more at home." He printed his Victoria address in my little blue book and told me to say hello to his friend Sheff Tompson, caretaker at the Prince Rupert yacht club.

"Happy to," I agreed. "Though I'm not sure about tying up *Bijaboji* among all the fancy yachts."

Annie soon took me to see the new baby, a tiny girl. Several middle-aged women sat in the room with the young mother and her child. I was surprised to see that she looked as exhausted as any white woman. I had read that Indian women suffered little at childbirth and went back to work a half-hour after. That writer should do a lot more research. How much other misinformation have I studied and absorbed?

The girls wanted to lead me up a stream where I might see a bear snatching fish from the water. "Bears are one of the salmon's most dangerous enemies," Annie said. "They catch salmon by the thousands in spawning streams, just for the sport of it." But the cannery manager, Mr. Chamberlain, derailed the plan by inviting me to be his guest for dinner at the mess house. "You may have a hot shower beforehand if you wish," he added.

"A hot shower! I should say so. Where is it?" These coastal people certainly knew what a traveller appreciated.

So I hurried, before any of the workers arrived, to the cannery shower in a shanty behind the cookhouse. In the changing room there were bars and bars of pink Lifebuoy soap, and it dawned on me that all along the coast I'd seen few brands other than Lifebuoy. I spent a glorious half-hour lathering under the hot water.

Tingling from a cold after-shower, I dressed and joined the cannery men for dinner at a long table in the mess hall. A middle-aged Chinese cook silently tended to our wants. I guess that I breached several rules of cookhouse etiquette when I got myself a glass of water. The meal was delicious and the rice pudding was particularly good.

Shortly after noon I said my goodbyes to the Native girls, my table companions and the boat owner/cannery man who had welcomed me. They gathered on the dock to see me off and looked properly astonished when I lifted the heavy dugout at an angle so it could slide off the float. I removed my wool ski trousers before climbing in and, clad in shorts and shirt, waved farewell and swung *Bijaboji* into the current.

Two white-painted purse seine boats whistled a salute as they headed into Klemtu Passage, between Swindle and Cone islands. I recognized friends aboard one of them, *Sidney W.*, when they stepped out on deck to wave.

Nowhere on the whole trip did I have a more helpful tide than when I rowed from Klemtu and through Tolmie Channel. My only exertion that afternoon was in steering the canoe.

On Sarah Island, across the channel, stood the handsome, glossy white, red-roofed buildings of Boat Bluff Light Station—the last sign of habitation I would see until the next morning. Swanson Bay was my goal and I was determined to see a bear before sundown, when wild animals seem to retreat far back into the woods. What sort of canoe trip would mine be without a true bear story? Forty-five days had gone by without a glimpse of a bear or even a bear track. I steered the canoe close to the mouths of streams and beached several times to poke into inlets afoot, but not a bear did I meet.

I enjoyed that beguiling afternoon in Tolmie Channel, carried by the tidal current at one to three knots between the steep wooded slopes of Princess Royal and Sarah islands. The mountains on the mainland loomed far, far ahead.

It was so easy to steer and row that I basked in the sun and guided *Bijaboji*'s progress with long, slow sweeps of the oars. Shadows of lazy, fleecy cumulus clouds played on the deep blue water and lush green mountains in magical beauty. Any sound or song from me echoed back from the steep hills as if there were loudspeakers on the peaks. I heard some of my own tones clearly—they were much like those in my mother's voice, which pleased me. I concentrated on vocalizing for many hours.

To the northwest, small white clouds gradually drifted together, forming larger and larger fluffs that hovered over the peaks, looking like great shirts turning slowly on a big round clothesline.

For a while the eddies along Princess Royal Island were helpful, then I slanted back again to the eastern shore and crossed the bow of *Andrew Foss*, a Seattle tugboat with a large barge following docilely at the end of a long towline. An unusual number of young crewmen clustered near the pilothouse door, waving. I was a little homesick and longed to joke with Americans but the tug was too fast and going in the wrong direction. Soon it was far to the south.

Ahead the mountains were showing twisty white falls. A pod of graceful porpoises played around the canoe for a few minutes. I was too slow, and moments later they were 100 yards away, turning in perfect unison, scarcely rippling the water as they rose and wheeled. The sun was especially bright just before it slid below the mountain peaks. A northbound tug towing two scows loaded with round red gasoline tanks was following the shore of Princess Royal Island, and though it was far from me, it sent small swells across the channel. The crew did not see me moving among the deceptive early evening shadows.

Between the mainland and the north end of Sarah Island, driftwood and seaweed carried swiftly on the tide into Hiekish Narrows caught on *Bijaboji*'s bow. After pulling in the oars I crawled over the Fabrikoid cover and reached underwater to push the seaweed away. The current was streaked with seaweed tangled amidst floating logs and broken limbs, and just one bit around the bow of the canoe slowed it down as if it were a square-stern boat going backward.

At last Sarah Island was astern. In Graham Reach the tide ebbed fiercely, running north–northwest from Tolmie Channel. There seemed to be no helpful back eddies along the mainland shore except across the mouth of Green Inlet, which I had not explored. I wished it were still afternoon instead of dusk. Surely one might see a bear ambling through this wild area. Several times while rowing close along that rocky shore, I caught a strong animal smell wafting seaward.

The tide was dropping fast. I couldn't buck the strong current any longer. Limbs of cedars brushed across my hair as I pulled the canoe forward by getting holds on the rocks. Except for the irregular roar of streams rushing through the woods there was no sound over that vast reach of water and black woods. Millions of bright stars shone through, pinpricks in the heavens. I felt that I'd had more real experiences during that day than in my whole life—as if there had never been any "before" in my life, no disappointments, no shyness, no misunderstanding. I had found a gentle, reassuring peace that civilization and college did not afford me.

Grabbing a cedar limb, I held the canoe with one bare foot and felt for solid rock under the water with the other. My foot slithered across a rock covered with seaweed. Stepping from rock to rock and helped by the slick seaweed, I pulled the canoe half out of the water and weighted the painter with a heavy rock. On a slight ridge beside the canoe I padded a few of my clothes into a thin pillow, zipped the sleeping bag around me and slept. In a vivid dream, grizzly bears sat in conference around the sleeping bag. I awoke with a start, but not such a start as *not* finding myself surrounded by sharp-clawed grizzlies—which, I'd been told, frequented this part of the coast. In the grey of an early summer dawn I could see a bear path just above my sleeping spot. The tide was slack. The canoe was afloat and ready to go. I departed quickly, thankful for a safe night's rest.

It wasn't until I was rowing on that I realized I hadn't had supper the night before, or breakfast this morning. I had no craving for food. Living alone in the open air does not stimulate the appetite as one might expect. But one's hunger may become agonizing as soon as there's a possibility of companionship at a meal.

It was probably a little after five when I rounded a point and thought I heard many cannons booming. Before me was the mightiest waterfall I had seen north of Powell River. It rushed and tumbled over two wide ledges from a deep cut in the green hills of Princess Royal Island. At some distance to one side were two small houses and some large gasoline storage tanks, nearly hidden by trees.

On the eastern side of Graham Reach I could see devastation and dilapidation—houses and large buildings, all sagging or fallen. Piles of brick and rusty metal nearly covered what had once been a fine wharf. Electric light posts leaned haphazardly. My 1930 edition of the *British Columbia Coast Pilot* stated: "Swanson Bay. A large saw- and pulp-mill have been established here, and the settlement is conspicuous from Graham Reach."

I realized suddenly that it was Saturday, July 31, 1937, my 23rd birthday. Here was a stop in civilization that I had eagerly anticipated, but it looked as if bombers had attacked. Not much of a birthday present.

Two gillnet boats were tied side by side behind a floating walkway. I nosed the canoe up beside them, made it fast, and wandered toward the houses. Slabs of waste wood from the mill had been piled on the beach as a seawall and covered with sod to expand the usable shore. The tide wouldn't be favourable for going on until noon, so I had six hours to poke around. I decided to start at the far end, where three two-storey white and red houses on high foundations seemed to have been spared the havoc visited on the others. Near the first one a shaggy dog chained to his little shingled kennel snarled menacingly before bursting into frenzied barking. A wondrous, deep voice from an upstairs window ordered the dog to shut up. "I'll be right down," the voice continued. "Stay right there."

Soon the voice appeared on the porch, a tall man of superb physique with a rather shy confidence. He looked me over from ski trousers to leather jacket and red-brown face. Finally he smiled. "I know who you are. I'm Roy Tapp, caretaker and postmaster here. Have you had breakfast?"

"No."

"Come along."

I ascended the 10 or so worn wooden steps. He showed me the kitchen and we set about getting breakfast. Roy Tapp was strangely flustered. "You'll have to excuse me," he said. "The last steamer from Vancouver brought news that I'm the father of a healthy son. I haven't been normal since. My wife—and son—will be back from town in a few more weeks."

I had to laugh at Roy Tapp speaking of Vancouver—more than 400 miles distant—as "town," just as a farmer does of the village a few miles away. The order in which he served breakfast was also strange: eggs, followed by hot porridge, and then, when we were nearly through, an orange. After that he offered home-grown "icicle" radishes, shaped like big white carrots, for appetizers.

While I waited for the tide, Roy pointed out the giant smokestack set well back from the bay and guided me around the deserted mill town. "Eight years of disuse has done all this," he said of the wreckage. "Only last week the hotel dropped four feet on one side. The aviators on the Fisheries patrol plane that are headquartered here rushed out of their house to rescue me. Luckily I had just come away from the building. The company has my life insured." With a wry smile, he added, "They missed out again."

Roy showed me his garden. "Very poor this summer except for the icicle radishes, on account of all the rain." We hurried back to the house so he could hear a radio report from the steamer *Cardena*. "It stops here once a week. They report their approximate time of arrival. It helps a lot to get their estimate and know within a few hours when the steamer will be here. She's coming down from Prince Rupert."

Though disappointed in Swanson Bay, which was far from being the bustling mill town that I had anticipated, I was glad to have stopped here, for Roy had given me a tour of a coastal town that was rapidly becoming history. Shortly before noon I said farewell and shoved off into Graham Reach, helped by a favourable tide.

A few miles north was the wide entrance to Khutze Inlet. I had not heard of any activity or habitation there so passed it by. Two miles farther north was a slash in the coast called Aaltanhash Inlet. I was making good time so I looked in while crossing the entrance, figuring that I could reach Butedale well before dusk. My small world was all green and blue and white. *Cardena* and another southbound steamer passed. Several purse seine boats with Native crews waved and hailed me as they chugged by. *Bijaboji* took the swells of their wakes beautifully. The Fisheries inspector's boat saluted me with a blast on its whistle as it overtook me on its way to Butedale. I enjoyed all of this activity.

Five years earlier, Daddy had given me *Bijaboji* on my birthday. My Sunday school class had been wide-eyed when I told them about it. "And how I've loved you ever since!" I told the dugout. "You are a real thing to me. I'd rather have harm come to me than you. I could recover, but you might not."

Around Redcliff Point I rowed into the sun, now sliding behind the hills beyond the Butedale Cannery. With the sun's brilliance hidden by the trees I drifted a short distance outside the bay in mute appreciation of the wide white melodious falls slipping over the cliff just north of the cannery and pounding into the salt water below.

CHAPTER 12

Exploring Gardner Canal

To row along the entire length of British Columbia's rugged coastline is no small achievement. Such a feat demands strength, stamina, determination and the will to see it through. Miss Lowman has plenty of each.
—*Evening Empire* (Prince Rupert), August 1937

THE BUTEDALE CANNERY FLOATS WERE CROWDED with red-cabined fishing boats of assorted type and size. The grey Fisheries patrol vessel and a white and black Forestry boat lay alongside the fuel dock. More than anything in the world I wanted a swim, but my suit was long gone on *Tyee Scout*.

"Just swim in what you've got on," Mr. Moore suggested when I greeted the Fisheries officers. I jackknifed off the oil dock in my shorts and sweater and nearly caused a stampede of cannery workers and fishermen from the bunkhouses and store. The American girl must have been a shocking novelty, although many workers and children swam off the cannery dock or up the hill at the lake. I hurried into the Fisheries boat to dress after a good swim.

Two letters awaited me at the post office in the cannery store. One was from Mother, the other from Getty Stonjalsky. Butedale was the last telegraph station before Prince Rupert, so I sent a collect telegram to Mother: "Having glorious time..."

Some Native fishermen and a handsome young provincial policeman stood on the dock with Lloyd Stuart, the cannery manager. I

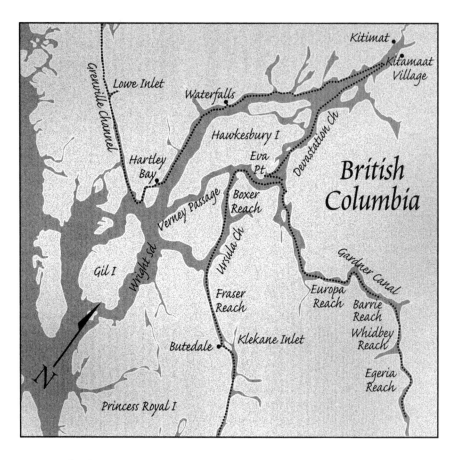

approached him, asking if there was a shack or shed where I might sleep that night.

He thought for a moment and decided I might use the watchman's room, since he would be making rounds all night. Later, as I sat on the dock beside *Bijaboji* reading my mail, Margaret and Dorothy, two Alpha Phi's from UBC, invited me to spend the night in their summer quarters. Both women had svelte figures and wore tailored slacks and light sweaters, and I felt large and awkward when I was near them. But they were charming and interesting, and I gladly accepted their gracious invitation and happily followed them up the wooden walk to a modest hillside cottage.

The Stuart living quarters were exquisitely furnished. Mrs. Stuart was resting, so Margaret brought me warm woolly house slippers and set up a card table so that I could write in my ship's log. Three other friends came in, and while I wrote, they eagerly exchanged observations about the many interesting young men who had summer jobs in the cannery. The provincial policeman was frequently and favourably mentioned. Not long after the three girls went off, two young men called on Margaret and Dorothy. The taller one, who worked in the cannery's cold storage plant, told us that a Chinese labourer had died recently, and that his body had been frozen for transport on the weekly steamer. This was the custom for deaths in isolated spots.

As we chatted over Ovaltine and cookies I was told of a hot spring in Klekane Inlet, on the mainland side, across Fraser Reach. "The water's wonderful," Margaret said, "but it's risky if there is just one person. A bather is liable to enjoy the hot water so much that he becomes too enervated to get out."

The girls made plans for all of us to go swimming next day in the lake hundreds of feet above the falls. Large, curving pipes made of wood and bound with iron hoops carried water from the lake to the cannery, the homes and the generator that supplied electricity for Butedale. "This year several hundred steps were put in to replace the trail through the woods to the lake," Dorothy said. "That makes the hike much easier."

Our swimming plans were disrupted by Mr. Stuart, who delivered the thrilling news that I could go up Gardner Canal early next morning behind a fish packer. "Mr. Moore tells me you haven't seen a bear yet," said Mr. Stuart. "Certainly you ought to see one back in Gardner Canal. It is said to be the wildest part of BC accessible by waterway."

Before bedtime I hurried to the canoe to get my pajamas and found two young fishermen looking the dugout over. They watched as I dug through my few possessions. "What! Pajamas on a trip like this!" one said.

I explained that I had to be civilized when I stayed overnight in people's homes. "Maybe this scarlet pajama top will come in handy sometime for a distress signal, too."

The Cardena, *docked at the Butedale Cannery. Betty rowed into Butedale the night of her 23rd birthday.*

At the house the girls were entertaining four young men with stories of how they had crammed for their university exams, studying for 24 hours at a time and staying awake with gallons of coffee and tea.

I was astonished. "I had no idea Canadian students ever crammed as we Americans do!" I said. "I have grown up with an idea that your study habits and discipline were irreproachable."

After a refreshing hot bath, I slept between cool cotton sheets with an alarm clock at my side. Tomorrow *Bijaboji* and I would go on a long side trip eastward, into the wilds of Gardner Canal, and I would see its many bays and inlets. There would likely be bears, maybe even big grizzlies. Anything might happen up there. A day or so late, but what a birthday present! I didn't dream about bears that night.

The alarm clock snapped me awake and sitting up. Outside it was dark and misty, and Mr. Stuart was fussing with a fire. I had tea and toast before hurrying to the float where the packer waited. About 20 Natives, young and old, were aboard, ready to be taken back to their dories and nets in the canal after the weekend fishing closure.

The Japanese deckhand knotted my line to one from the packer, allowing *Bijaboji* to trail farther astern, where she rode easier. The sun peeked over the hills. After a farewell wave from Mr. Stuart, the packer set off up Fraser Reach with me aquaplaning behind in *Bijaboji* to keep her from swamping.

The Natives standing on the stern looked down at me and grinned. I grinned back at them. They'd talk together and look back at me, then we'd grin some more. I didn't know what they were saying. The Japanese skipper spoke barely a word of English but he frequently looked aft and smiled understandingly, even when *Bijaboji* was sideswiped alarmingly by the boat's wake. Ahead were a bewildering array of reaches and channels through which the sea's fingers ran blue and white-capped. The land rose steep and mountainous. Graceful falls were always within sight. Tons of fresh water tumbled wantonly from sheer cliffs. These uncounted attractions varied from misty "maidenhair" to violent, thundering falls. One formidable stream dashed over a series of giant rock steps before crashing into the salt chuck. We headed inland through Ursula Channel. Some of the steep mountain slopes were bare and slate-like. Here and there in the green wooded areas were brown logged-off acres. Far up the channels, on all sides, were hazy ranges, the farthest ones dimming into the blue-grey of the sky. We passed Bishop Bay, where there is a logging camp, a store and a hot spring. A relaxing hot bath every night—those were lucky loggers.

Farther through Boxer Reach, to the junction of Verney Passage and Devastation Channel, a big yacht—an elaborate display of the latest in pleasure craft and comfort, like the one that had been at Namu—plowed out of Gardner Canal. Smartly dressed men and women relaxed in deck chairs on the sundeck. Some of the ladies had colourful blankets draped across their laps. No sunsuits today. The yacht looked incongruous as it moved swiftly out of that isolated waterway. I was glad it was moving out, not in. How fortunate I was, seeing all of this, getting ashore anytime I wanted, and meeting so many of the interesting, hard-working men and women who were developing this vast and wild country.

Just then the sharp-topped swells left by the yacht rushed at *Bijaboji*'s five inches of freeboard. The fish packer stopped—that considerate Japanese skipper was a real seaman. Without forward motion the canoe rose and fell gently on the yacht's wake, dissipating shoreward, where it rolled under and gently lifted a small float camp.

Two handsome young Native men, Ralph and Moses, pulled the canoe close to the tender and we chatted until the mouth of Devastation Channel was calm again. They told me about Coqualeetza Indian Institute, the three-storey brick residential school for Natives on the Fraser River. I told them about Pomona College. The older Native men looked over my dugout appraisingly. With approval, I wondered? As the packer resumed its speed, Ralph let out the line and *Bijaboji* again skimmed along on the end of her rope.

We pulled alongside a seasonal fish camp moored in a bight at Crab River, on the east side of Devastation Channel. This 60-by 30-foot log float supported a small shack, gillnet drying racks and bluestone tanks. Ten or more red dories, each with canvas stretched over a ridgepole slanting to the bow from a pole amidships, were tied alongside the float.

A Scot named Crichton operated the camp. Two Japanese men were on a smaller fish packer. The smell of fish permeated the air and there were hundreds—yes, thousands—of great stinging flies. So far as I knew I was the only woman or girl within miles and miles. Just one girl, four Japanese men, an Irishman, a Scot and 20 or more Natives. But at the time, there was no thought in my mind of any awkwardness or danger. Mr. Stuart wouldn't have arranged this junket if my safety were at risk.

With help I hauled *Bijaboji* onto the float, where the grey-headed Natives clustered about, touching her with expert hands, discussing her in their native tongue. Ralph and Moses translated for me. "They like your canoe. They like it very much." Nothing makes me take to people faster than to hear praise of *Bijaboji*. I liked those Natives from

Kitimat Village (now Kitamaat Village), and one of the men, Albert Starr, offered to show me a cedar dugout he was making in the woods nearby.

Standing in the stern of his sturdy dory, he rowed past two rotting pilings before beaching on the seaweed-littered shore. He walked to the edge of the woods, then proudly uncovered a dugout about the length of mine. He had started cutting it during the first of the fishing season and had nearly finished before seriously gashing his leg with the special axe that was used to shape dugouts. The bottom of that boat was much flatter than *Bijaboji*'s—it was a river canoe.

"Will you use this canoe for eulachon fishing?" I asked, indicating the flat bottom and bellying sides.

"No," Mr. Starr said with a twinkle in his eye. "When I haven't anything else to do, I'll row it down to Seattle."

I shook my head and laughed. Never again would I believe anyone who said that Natives didn't have a keen sense of humour. We covered the canoe and returned to the float.

Mr. Crichton had prepared a luncheon of sausages, eggs and lettuce sandwiches. We ate on a table covered with oilcloth and set between the stove and his bunk. On the wall was a watercolour painting that became our topic of conversation. Mr. Crichton offered me one of his flower paintings, but I had to refuse, explaining that things got wet in the dugout despite my waterproof cases, and that I couldn't accept a gift so likely to be damaged. I had no inkling of the sad end that painting would come to.

Before the packers could go farther into Gardner Canal with their tow of fishing dories, Mr. Crichton had to finish mending some nets. I occupied the time reading, and swatting flies that had a definite taste for my bare ankles. The magazines were the usual pulps I'd come to expect on boats and in logging and fishing camps: *True Confessions, Adventure Stories* and *Murder Mysteries*.

Paddy, a grizzled Irish gillnetter with a beloved sleek black cat, showed me a story in his week-old *Daily Province*. "This girl's name is Annette," he said. "She sounds like you, but you call yourself Betty. Do you know her?"

Betty hitched a ride with some fishing dories.

"Yes, rather," I laughed. "My name is Beatrice Annette. Betty for short."

Paddy soon set off in his little gas boat while the Natives were making their dories fast in a string behind the packers. I manoeuvred my red dugout behind the last dory in line. Mr. Crichton stood on the end of the float watching the preparations.

"You can leave your boat here," he offered. "The packer will take you clear to the end of the canal and back. You'll see it without rowing."

"I hate not to ride in this string of boats," I said, smiling at Ralph from the opening of his dory's canvas shelter. "May I ride with you, Ralph, if I leave my canoe behind?"

"Sure," he grinned.

I put my sleeping bag aboard the fish packer and scrambled into Ralph's dory. He was second behind two Japanese boats, tied side by side, ready to be towed to the fishing grounds. Slowly the tender pulled away from the float, gaining speed when the last boat was clear of the float. The boats trailed sinuously as we headed east through

Europa and Barrie reaches before turning southeast into Whidbey and Egeria reaches. We travelled through 40 miles or more of the narrow, ice-blue Gardner Canal, slashed between steep, rugged, glacier-fringed ranges. I sat on Ralph's pile of net snapping pictures of the pastel majesty surrounding us, of the boats winding behind us, of Ralph pointing upward to mountain goats, of the Japanese fishermen crouching over supper preparations in their small boats.

Then pictures of something more startling to me than if I had caught sight of Cleopatra's barge—a mammoth passenger steamer gliding slowly and silently out of that wilderness where there was no dwelling. A wilderness where no house had ever clung to a towering mass of rock, and no cabin had been built alongside a dancing stream. A wilderness with trees overhanging the lapping, cold blue water. Passengers clustered along the rail gazing down at us. A raw, penetrating breeze swept down from the glaciers. Shivering, I pulled on my leather jacket while wondering how many sets of binoculars had picked me out and what speculations were being made about the sunburned girl in the ski suit.

"It comes up here every week in the summer," Ralph said. "Just excursion people from Vancouver. They pay lots of money for the trip."

I felt so lucky to be seeing all of that magnificence for free, and meeting people like Ralph who lived and worked here and told me so much about life on the coast. At the moment, though, he appeared discouraged and weary.

"How many fish did you get last night?" I asked.

"Twelve sockeyes and cohoes and as many fish heads left by the seals," he muttered, sounding as though ready to chuck the whole fishing business right then.

I commented that seals seemed a worse menace to the salmon than fishermen. I had even seen seals swimming right into the spawning streams. Why wasn't something being done?

I counted seven seals peering at us from a safe distance. Fishermen often shot seals or sea lions that approached their nets, but it did little good.

"Some of us aren't going to fish after today," Ralph said.

The large packer was going to stay and then tow the boats out many hours later. I thanked Ralph as he cast off, then boarded the small packer that came alongside to pick me up for the return trip. The Japanese Canadian deckhand, who was also an interpreter, told me that the young captain had designed and built this staunch boat himself. The pilothouse was clean and thoughtfully designed, and like many Japanese boats it was decorated with fresh flowers—a canning jar was filled with artistically arranged white yarrow blooms and ripe crimson elderberries.

Sitting outside I dozed with my head on the sleeping bag until the deckhand patted my shoulder. "Go below. Use bunk." I was tired and happily climbed down behind the engine to sleep soundly on a comfortable and neatly blanketed bunk.

It was late the following morning when the gentle jolt of our landing at the fish camp woke me. Outside, the sky, water and land were so vastly different from the day before that for a moment I thought I had slept for a week and this murky grey place was somewhere far away from sunny Gardner Canal. But there was the scarlet *Bijaboji*, safe on the float, and I curbed my impatience to be on the way north.

Mr. Crichton and Moses, who hadn't gone to the fishing grounds, helped me load the canoe—reluctantly. They tried all the while to persuade me not to set out, but I had no alternative if I was ever to reach Alaska. My course ahead lay across Devastation Channel, down Verney Passage into Wright Sound and northward up Grenville Channel. By rowing all that stretch I should more than make up in mileage for the rides in Johnstone Strait and from Butedale into the canal.

I put on my black sou'wester against the sprinkles of rain and Mr. Crichton helped me into the half-length oilskin coat. I pulled away from the camp, exultantly facing a logged-off splotch across the canal. How good it was to curl my tanned fingers around the oars, and to feel the familiar response of my sturdy dugout to each stroke. I had no money, I was 50 miles from a telegraph station and more than seven days from the next mail stop, and I was perfectly content.

By quick degrees the weather grew less encouraging, however — colder, windier, bleaker, drizzlier. Out of sight of the camp I rowed onto a small point covered with seaweed and rummaged among my things for everything I'd need to ride out the storm with some comfort and without having to lift the Fabrikoid covering during a deluge. Then I had to slither about on the jags of rock to free the dugout, caught firmly by the rapidly dropping tide, and we were again underway.

The outbound packer towing Moses' dory soon overtook me. Moses grabbed my bowline and pulled me almost two miles across choppy Devastation Channel. Set free, I pulled for an A-frame logging outfit beyond Eva Point, on Hawkesbury Island. There a large, fine-looking man in tin coat and pants (water-repellent gear) was tying a boomstick to the A-frame float. The wood-fired donkey engine was steaming. Greeting me with a pleasant smile, he called out: "Stop at the floathouse ahead and say hello to my wife." His voice was genuinely friendly.

"Yes. Thanks." Which one was it? Would she be pleased to see me, all damp, dishevelled and alone? I was shy about presenting myself to her.

The massive log floats, all chained together, supported several cottages, bunkhouses, and work and tool shacks. After tying up my dugout I sat hesitantly on a step for a moment, watching a logger split wood. Another huge fellow emerged from a house where curtains and flower boxes bespoke the presence of a woman. He stared at the canoe, at me and at my bare feet.

"Where are you going?"

"Just here this minute, and on to Alaska almost immediately," I said, as unsensationally as I could.

His face lighted with interest, as did that of the wood-splitter. "We read about two girls from California paddling up here early this summer. Do you know them?"

"In a way," I said. "We were from Washington and my friend had to turn back. And I don't paddle, I row."

"Come over and talk to my wife," the big one urged. "Women are scarce up here. My name's Vilen." I followed him over a caulk-chewed plank to a small cabin where window boxes overflowed with blooming flowers. A slim woman in a fluffy apron with a cute, flaxen-haired little girl at her skirts began to set out food almost as soon as I said, "How do you do, Mrs. Vilen."

While eating a third slice of Finnish rye bread and a huge helping of creamed cauliflower, I told her about my night in the steam bath at Sointula. "We have a steam bath too, right here over the water," she said.

A small, bright-eyed man with standout ears arrived at the house and introduced himself as Lex Johnson, a forest ranger. "And I know who you are," he said, laughing at my surprise. "We're on the way to Kitimat Village as soon as I've finished my business here. Would you like to accompany us?"

I certainly did. I'd been wanting to meet the missionaries there after hearing so much about them. It was yet another lucky break! Everyone was so good to me and I was seeing so much. But all of these side trips were delaying my voyage to Alaska.

After lunch Mrs. Vilen carefully dressed her little girl for the 25-yard walk across the float to call on the boss's wife. They had a few minutes to gaze at *Bijaboji* before the forester signalled to me. I made another quick farewell and rowed out to their boat in a light drizzle.

Our combined strength wasn't enough to get the loaded canoe over the rail of the *Alpine Fir*, so the engineer, Ole Urseth, decided to tow it by running *Bijaboji*'s shortened bowline through a hole in *Alpine Fir*'s low stern. That way my dugout lost her crankiness and followed along nicely despite blustering, rain-filled winds and complaining seas. I enjoyed sitting on a high stool in the dry, warm cabin, studying Forestry land maps and learning a little about the duties of the British Columbia Forestry ministry. They were going to cruise the timber near Kitimat Village. Captain Johnson marked my marine charts with the location of every logging camp and handlogger's shack or shelter on the north shore of Douglas Channel, where I expected to row the next day. We noted the time and direction of the tides for each day. Captain Lex Johnson assured me that the tide ceased to flood north and began to ebb in that direction near the midpoint of

Grenville Channel. "By timing the tide within an hour you can have fair help for 40 miles," he said.

I was perturbed that in 50 miles of coast along Douglas Channel there was only one deserted cabin, which lay near the entrance to Foch Lagoon at the head of Drumlummon Bay. Two handlogging couples, one Native and the other Swedish, worked more than 30 miles from each other. I would certainly be alone with my thoughts when I stopped at Drumlummon Bay the following night.

Below decks, a few steps from the helm of the *Alpine Fir*, was a compact cabin arranged with a bunk on either side, set-in drawers and bookshelves crowded with official records and publications. At about three o'clock Ole Urseth unfolded the wide sides of a permanent table located between the bunks and we sat down to enjoy tea and cakes. With the table expanded to full size, the bunks served nicely as seats.

During the afternoon I washed a few clothes, caught up on the ship's log, and napped. Outside, nothing but Scotch mist. Knowing how poorly surveyed these waters are, I was glad to be with someone who had navigated them numerous times. Nevertheless, I knew moments of apprehension as lusty waves tossed us broadside and the *Alpine Fir* rolled sickeningly.

Toward evening, shortly after we entered Kitimat Arm, Ole served tasty Boston baked beans, brown bread and tea. We ate ravenously, except Lex, who had been dreadfully ill since the day before. Still, he was ever alert to the sea conditions, and ready with answers to my many questions.

Finally *Alpine Fir* was brought smoothly alongside the well-made dock, built by the Natives of Kitimat. Lex and I pulled the canoe over a large log beached beside the dock, and then hurried through the driving rain to the missionaries' home to ask permission for me to sleep in the dock warehouse.

Rev. F. McConnell, the missionary, drew us around his living room stove, where he had been jawing with the fish warden. Mrs. McConnell was at Bella Bella Hospital, and the warden's young son was patiently entertaining the McConnell youngster, who obviously missed his mother. Rev. McConnell insisted that I carry my sleeping bag into the warmth of the mission house. He also invited the warden's son to stay the night.

Lex Johnson, still looking ill, excused himself early and returned to the boat. My thanks to Lex could never be enough for all of his assistance. Without his generous offer I wouldn't have gotten to Kitimat.

For a while the warden, the missionary and I sat in the dimness of a rainy twilight speculating about Amelia Earhart's sensational flight and dramatic disappearance, and talking of Lord Tweedsmuir's memorable journey through the Canadian interior earlier that year. Before it was completely dark, Rev. McConnell showed me around the Native village with its generous assortment of wood homes. Some were painted in bright colours, as varied as the stained glass in their doors and windows, while others were unpainted. Cardboard had replaced broken panes in numerous windows. A few homes had fancy wood trimmings and pinnacles. White marble tombstones occupied a place of prominence in many front yards and a few graves were decorated with fresh flowers. Weather-worn totems stood tall and beautiful along the shore. I had read that they told a story, but couldn't identify many of the stylized figures. Between the two short rows of houses was a stout plank roadway, built by the residents and paid for with money they had raised together. They had also constructed a simple but welcoming wooden church.

The Elizabeth Long Memorial School stood on a cleared hillside slope above the village. "We must call on Mrs. Durnin, the matron," said Rev. McConnell. "There are more children here than usual because those with measles couldn't go to the salmon canneries with the rest of the villagers. They are well now."

Light shone like beacons from the school dormitory windows. As we climbed the wooden stairs to the wide front door, I noticed the fine playground. The matron saw us approaching, flung the door open and invited us into a room where two chubby young boys and four teenage girls in blue aprons played a game matching coloured sticks. All of them were much stockier and broader of face than other Natives I had met, and this quality gave us a common bond so far as I was concerned. I was delighted when the matron asked Rev. McConnell if I might spend the night at the school.

Before the children's bedtime we sang and played the piano and organ. And how those children could sing and carry harmony parts! Those little fellows had more self-assurance than I did at singing alto, so most of the time I sat back to listen to them sing hymns and folk songs. Two of the girls took great delight in playing organ duets, and I respected Matron Durnin more and more for her skill and understanding. She was doing worthwhile work and I admired her.

After the children were in bed, the matron and I sipped tea before the cheery fireplace and talked about San Francisco, a city we both liked, and of mutual acquaintances along the Pacific coast.

"Lately the girls have been afraid at night and call me persistently," Mrs. Durnin said, before showing me to my room. "They claim to hear steps and see shadows."

"Is that because of Seymour, the kidnapper?" I asked, little shivers going down my spine. *He might take my canoe to make a getaway. What if Seymour is occupying the deserted cabin at Drumlummon Bay where I expect to stay tomorrow night? How much protection would my hunting knife be against a desperate criminal?*

I couldn't dispel the thought of the fugitive Seymour taking my canoe. It was horrible—I just couldn't be stranded here without a penny, no clothes, and no mail for a month. I was all for hauling *Bijaboji* up the hillside to the school, but was too shy to suggest it.

Tired, and lying in a room by myself on the second floor, I tried to sleep between the cool white sheets. Rain lashed the windowpanes in noisy fury. A corner of the railing on the upper veranda was visible through the window, and my imagination followed the movements of a man drawing himself over the rail. The window blind rattled and solid darkness loomed. "Matron! Matron!" I screamed in sudden panic.

No one came. The wind shrieked and moaned intermittently from off the deep, cold channel. Scornful waves roared along the treeless shore below. I steeled myself, threw off the covers and felt over every square inch of that room in the dark. Of course I was completely alone, and ashamed to have let fear get hold of me for even those few minutes. I hoped the matron had not heard my call. I climbed back into bed and slept peacefully until a lazy hour in the morning.

I would have enough time to dress, eat breakfast, load the canoe and get away on the ebb tide. The storm was less frightful by daylight. I hurried downstairs, where Rev. McConnell, neatly attired, sipped steaming coffee. He told me about his mission work while Mrs. Durnin and I enjoyed a hearty several-course breakfast, beautifully served by Native girls. During breakfast the matron and Rev. McConnell, both familiar with the vagaries of local weather, implored me to stay until the storm was over. But I insisted upon setting forth in the wind and rain. The reverend helped put the canoe in the water and I set out, dressed to fend off rain.

CHAPTER 13

Swamped in Douglas Channel

Betty Lowman, the Anacortes girl making a canoe trip alone, is presumed to be somewhere along the BC coast, on her trip to Alaska. The last heard from her was when she sent a wire from Butedale, BC.
    —Evening Empire (Prince Rupert), August 1937

ALPINE FIR BOUNCED IN THE MEAN CHOP as she circled me when I was halfway across to the north side of Douglas Channel. Ole Urseth clung to the rail and shouted, "Wait until we finish our timber cruising. We'll take you down to Grenville Channel this afternoon."

Through the vicious wind-driving rain, he and his voice were far from distinct, but I heard enough. "I like this weather for a change," I yelled back, "but if I haven't reached Drumlummon cabin when you and Lex come along, give me a lift that far, will you, please?"

He waved, and the Forestry boat disappeared toward the river. It rained ceaselessly, cold and dismal. The canoe was never in quiet water. I rowed or bailed, or both, all day. Several times I considered making camp under a tree, but the entire shoreline was a babbling freshet, or worse. I had counted on help from the ebbing tide, but a strong wind blew up-channel, setting waves and surface water against the canoe.

In the inadequate protection of jutting rocks I let the oars drag and bailed gallons of rainwater. To make sure I had something warm and partly dry when I could make camp, I took off my ski trousers with

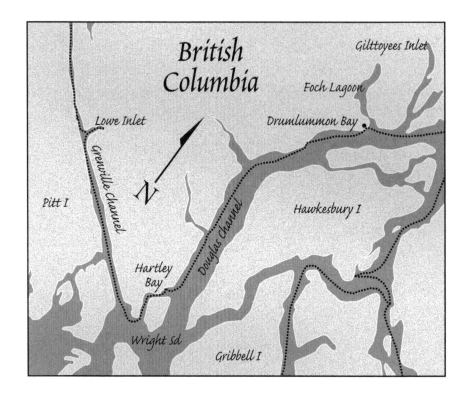

the hunting knife attached to the belt and waterproof container of matches in the pocket and folded them carefully under the Fabrikoid covering.

In the deep bay west of Markland Point a gillnetter was anchored. A small cabin crouched under dripping trees. I rowed by, then turned back. I did not know that I would see no other shelter and no other people until the next day—if then. I circled the boat, saw no one, and went on. The *Alpine Fir* would soon be along to pick me up.

Visibility was poor and the wind was singing its unpleasant tune, but I saw and heard the wild Jesse Falls, where extravagant volumes of rainwater, collected in the steep, funnelled valley around Jesse Lake, tumbled violently into the salt chuck.

On I went, bailing, rowing and singing. Frequently I fell silent, listening intently, hopefully, for the chug of the boat engine. The wind whipped the water and trees more violently as a rain-dimmed sun descended. The shore sheered off more abruptly. My soggy chart showed me still to be several miles from the deserted cabin at the mouth of Foch Lagoon. Darkness was rapidly concealing all landmarks. I rowed west, parallel to the solid stone wall of the channel, against which white-crested waves slammed, only to bounce back, rolling and pitching the dugout dangerously. Finally I reached the mile-wide mouth of Gilttoyees Inlet. Rain and salt water lay heavy in the canoe, sloshing from side to side and sometimes rolling the gunwale right to the water. The backwash from the cliffs soon drove me out into the channel. I was guided in my directions by the wind blasting hard in my face and by the sound of warring waves battering the cliff to my right. Why didn't the Forestry boat come? Was I lost in one of British Columbia's remote inlets? Was this the end of all vacations for me?

There was no relief even when I did get into open Drumlummon Bay. At last I made out the entrance to Foch Lagoon. The water was berserk. Weariness deadened my relief, and I pulled with lead-filled arms toward the blackness where the old cabin might be, if it was still standing. Or where Seymour the kidnapper might be hiding. In the black night I headed *Bijaboji* into the mouth of Foch Lagoon.

Then it happened. The outflowing tidal river, swelled by the downpour rushing from the broad catchment of the high surrounding mountains, hit and careened off a precipitous point before ripping across the agitated currents of the main channel. That, and the jostling backwash waves from the cliff, were our Waterloo—*Bijaboji*'s and mine. She wallowed under wild, wave-tossed waters and I sat unsteadily, spluttering as the churning tide rip washed over my sou'wester and up the sleeves of my oilskin jacket. Stunned, I tried to row with oars now floating free of their oarlocks. In desperation I braced my knees against *Bijaboji*'s sides and paddled with heavy arms until a heaving, high-rolling wave flung me clear of the dugout. Automatically I shifted from paddling to swimming—swimming to the water-filled canoe. Both oars washed away into the darkness.

There was nothing to do but swim and tow the canoe. The Fabrikoid covering bulged with water. Floating grub box, camera container, clothes, lantern, ski pants and cooking kit jerked about inside.

Cross-currents made the heavy, swamped dugout twist and jerk at the rope in my hand as I swam toward the nearest solid ground, a rough, wave-whacked rock cliff. The oilskin jacket was tearing and gravely cumbersome but I couldn't let up for even a second to free myself. I had to hang on to the bow rope for my life.

Now I know I should have thrown it off, but at the time, how awfully I had to fight, physically and mentally, not to let everything go, not to let the slicker drag me under! What would the heavy ski pants have done to me if I had not taken them off earlier? Could anything be worse?

Then the canoe seat tore away, releasing the covering that held in all of my possessions. Off floated food, matches, candid camera shots, copious notes—notes I needed if I were to have any chance of writing articles and selling them to pay my college debts. Cameras, hatchet, knives, lantern, cooking gear—everything was washed or swept out of the rolling, wave-tormented dugout and sank. But the canoe seemed to tow more easily, and the rocks were closer. I thrust any worry about cramps from my mind since I hadn't eaten all day. The force of an impetuous wave threw the canoe cruelly against me as I clutched at smooth, bare rock for a handhold. It was no fairy tap, and the sound of my own cry in the dark, stormy night, with no one to hear for over 15 miles, nearly undid me. Abruptly I realized that if rescuers didn't find me, I'd have to find them.

I clung for a second longer and one fumbling hand scratched into a crevice on the sloping rock ledge. Hang onto the bowline, I told myself. I found a toehold. Then another. Solid, narrow, flat rock. The dugout slammed into the rock alongside me, carried on the last high wave of the flood tide, and we were on solid rock.

I held on and gradually the waves retreated. Yanking the sleeping bag out from under the crossbar, where most providentially it had caught, I pulled out my scarlet and blue pajamas, which had kept dry inside. I got out of my cold wet shorts and sweater and put on the pajamas. Where was the *Alpine Fir*? Had they, too, been caught somewhere? There was a chance of rescue if they had decided to wait out the storm at Kitimat. That was my one flickering hope as, totally exhausted in mind and body, I curled myself along the ledge and slept. Sometimes my head dangled over the edge, sometimes my feet hung over the lower end, and more than once I squirmed away from the edge.

In a grey, rainless, windy dawn I looked out from the ledge, assessing my situation. The tide was out. *Bijaboji* and I were trapped on narrow ledges, now well above the restless salt water.

Fortuitously I had landed at the height of the tide. Low, dark, menacing clouds raced toward me over the freshly washed forest. Where was the water? Where were the angry waves? I rose carefully, the dugout's bowline still gripped in my hand, and found myself on an overhanging ledge 15 feet above the water. *Bijaboji* was caught on a rocky projection slightly below me, the stern hanging over the water.

Across the inlet and 500 yards back from the main channel, between a stream and a roaring skookumchuck flowing from Foch Lagoon, was the weather-beaten cabin.

Ironical, that! Me, perched on a ledge with the hulk of a canoe, useless without oars or paddles, and there to the west, within sight, was a windowed cabin. "Yah! Yah!" I bellowed against the wind. Then I wept. That was the tonic I needed. The Forestry boat hadn't passed yesterday, so surely it would today. "They'll be along at noon," I said to reassure myself, "at high tide, and won't they laugh to see me stuck up here?"

Hunger set me to looking for handholds and footholds on the cliff. In the woods above I ought to be able to find berries. Bracing myself against the sides of the crevice, I worked my way up, caught the limb of a spruce tree, climbed up through other limbs and found nothing but rock moss and dense, damp undergrowth. Then I thought I heard a motor. I climbed down, slipped and caught a spruce limb. I laughed ruefully at what the *Alpine Fir* crew might have found if it hadn't been for that limb: a battered red dugout, a sleeping bag and a few clothes spread on a rock ledge to dry, and maybe a splotch of gore where my head had been bashed on the way down. There would be no more climbing cliffs if I expected to be alive when a rescue vessel arrived.

Damp and chilled from my exploration foray, I crawled into the sleeping bag for warmth, and dozed. The tide had risen nearly to the ledge again when a droning sound awakened me. Surely it was the *Alpine Fir*. "Oh, God, please!"

To sit still and alert, cramped on a narrow ledge, waiting for a boat to appear from Kitimat while I looked the only way I could, westward, down the channel, took more nervous energy than a day's hard rowing. At last the drone became a chug-chug-chug and *Alpine Fir* sped from behind the cliffs and on across the mouth of Foch Lagoon. I cupped my hands and screamed, "Lex! Lex! Ole! Ole! Oh, please! I'm up here!" I flapped the pink sweater frantically. I prayed for the wind to cease blowing the screams back into my face. To cease blowing just for a moment. But no head appeared at the windows of the warm pilothouse. It might as well have been a pilotless ship sent down the channel to tantalize me.

No torture has been worse in my life than that next hour of sitting with my chin on my knees, my heart bounding and flopping as I watched the silhouette of the westward speeding *Alpine Fir*. Sometimes it seemed to be turning around, but it never did. Of course they were looking for me. Why else had they followed the shoreline so closely? Why didn't boatmen ever look back? Why didn't they walk outside, where there was a chance that they would see *Bijaboji*'s bright red sides against the dark granite wall? But I knew they wouldn't come back. They were going to Prince Rupert. They probably thought I had gone exploring up one of the inlets.

May I never again know the low spirits I knew when the tip of the mast disappeared beyond the horizon and again I was alone—more alone than ever.

It was after lunchtime, judging by the tide. Waves were again battering *Bijaboji* and there were no footholds, no handholds. I had to stay put until the tide changed to the ebb. Seagulls bickered and scolded over a choice morsel. I would have fought them for it if I weren't a prisoner of the elements.

"We've got to make plans," I chattered to the canoe. "Got to find a paddle. Got to get out in the channel where a boat, if there is another in these waters, can see us. Got to work fast when the tide is out again. Get away before dawn, before that surly ocean wind blows up the channel."

To pass the hours I recited Kipling's "If," and thought of Mother in Washington and Daddy in Alaska. Mother should be getting the letter from Klemtu today. She wouldn't be worrying. Daddy had the telegram from Ocean Falls. He wouldn't worry now that I had survived all the dangerous places. No one would worry. No one would imagine that I was here.

The Inside Passage in the 1990s. The vessels travelling it may have changed, but its sheer majesty has not. Courtesy BC Ferries

With the khaki sleeping bag as a backdrop I gave a concert of sacred songs with a reverence and dignity befitting that great sky-domed cathedral. Then I sang through the program of a recital I had once given in Anacortes. I liked tones in Burleigh's "The Sailor's Wife" that I had never liked before. I crooned with the lapping waves for rhythmic accompaniment. Seagulls noisily gave my best efforts the "raspberry."

I wondered if it might be a good idea for me to swim across to the cabin at the north end of the inlet, to risk the skookumchuck before I got too weak from lack of food. But then I wouldn't be able to get back up there until another high tide, and there was likely nothing at the cabin anyway. Les had said it had been unoccupied for years.

For another hour or so, while my eyes were fixed on a white splotch against the distant green forest to the west, I told myself stories—stories about the trapper who had crawled 20 miles after being mangled by a grizzly, about Amelia Earhart, who had not been found yet. Why, I am in luxury, I told myself—a warm sleeping bag, a breakfast only five meals back, and enough education—or lack of it—to keep me from going crazy. But I feared I would go crazy if that white splotch didn't change, if I had to sit there for another hour.

The hours passed and the tide fell again. I inched around the cliff to a crevice where a trickle of water slid silently down the stone, threading through the millions of barnacles and mussels stuck there. On hands and knees, animal-like, I bent over and drank. Cold, fresh water washing into me was a tonic that set mind and muscles astir with impatience to get away. Above me a shattered cedar tree had been uprooted and knocked down by some forgotten storm, and was now held fast in the rock's jagged crevice. I worked my way up to the log and wrenched off a splintered outer strip to use for a paddle. The problem of getting back to the ledge with it was a real one until I secured it to the belt of my pajamas. Finally I was safe again on the narrow ledge, and its few square feet seemed as vast as any ballroom.

The steady wind rippled the water, filling the canoe. I spent the next few hours bailing by slapping the water over the gunwale with cupped hands, and making all possible preparations to get away at dawn. These preparations consisted of placing the cedar slab in the canoe.

The tumultuous storm was spent, except for the persistent, chilling southwest wind. I calculated that I could reach the nearest help, the Swedish handloggers, 20 miles west and toward the main channel, in one day of steady effort. The forest ranger had said they were nice fellows.

Weary from boredom and uncertainty, I lay in the Cocoon counting stars like silver drops on the tallest spruce tips and longed for sleep to put the hours behind me. But I counted the stars until my eyes blurred with tears of exasperation. Sleep wouldn't come. Wouldn't come.

When it did come, it was ragged sleep. Nightmarish flashes flooded me with terror at the various ends I could meet if I left the solid safety of the ledge. Scudding charcoal grey clouds delayed the dawn, and I woke hours after I had planned to leave the ledge. Rain spotted the sleeping bag. The tide was falling fast. Every minute's delay was leaving the canoe and myself farther from the water; higher and higher on our bare perch. Could I take another 12 hours until the tide was right again? Was I afraid to leave?

I tried to be patient and somehow managed to wait, half stupefied with crushed hopes, for another two hours. Then clouds of hungry gnats found me. Bad as they were, they were only the advance guard of uncounted legions of more nasty noiseless insects. Somehow they managed to get inside the sleeping bag, even when I pulled the top tight over my head. They bit and chewed me mercilessly, even on the soles of my feet. My nerves were in tatters.

"I'll start babbling if I have to see the tide rise or fall one more minute, if I don't find something to eat, if I don't hear a voice other than my own," I screamed. "I won't stand it another instant. I won't! I won't!"

And I didn't. Quickly I pushed the sleeping bag into its Fabrikoid covering and stowed it under the dugout's crossbar. Grabbing the strong rope in *Bijaboji*'s bow, I hesitated only a second before releasing the dugout from its pinnacle, praying and reassuring myself that I had sufficient strength to let the canoe down 15 feet.

But I hadn't nearly the strength of a few days before. *Bijaboji* zoomed down 15 feet and so did I, at about 60 per, in a sitting position, dragged over barnacles and mussels into the salt chuck. A fall of such distance, at such speed, drove me far under water. At last I came up under the water-filled dugout, desperately clutching the rope. A fast glance around and I spotted my makeshift paddle. I retrieved the cedar slab and pulled the canoe to a rock. Climbing out of the water I realized that the barnacles had scraped the seat out of my pajamas — and considerable extra off me.

Even that was bearable in my joy at being free of the ledge. I tipped the water out of the dugout and sat in the stern to paddle across Foch Lagoon. There I tied the dugout to a rusty chunk of iron on the tidal flats, a remnant of bygone mining activities, and set off to the cabin barefoot over 500 yards of barnacle-covered rocks. I hoped to find food, a bailing can and a better paddle. But after a horrible time of falling off logs, slithering through seaweed and wading the rust-coloured stream, I found only a can suitable for bailing, which nearly got lost a dozen times on my return trip, banging into tree limbs, slipping on those miserable rocks and watching out for someone's old trapline. That would have been a last straw — putting my foot in a mink trap, or worse, a bear trap.

At the canoe I found something else to cope with. My trip to the cabin had taken longer than I expected and the incoming tide had floated *Bijaboji*. She bobbed several yards offshore with the painter stretched straight downward. I swam out, put the can in the canoe, squirmed out of the torn rain jacket, took deep breaths and, after several dives, managed to untie the knot. Then we were on the way toward that white splotch with the green forest in the background, far ahead to the west.

The sun rose and so did the wind. All that day I bucked wind and tide, plus strong currents from the thundering falls that poured out of the virgin forest. Sometimes I leaned over the stern and pushed forward from rocks near the surface. Too often the wind caught *Bijaboji*'s lifted bow and turned us completely around. Logs floated off the beaches by this high tide now drifted in mid-channel and moved in the opposite direction at twice our speed. The makeshift paddle wore the skin off the palm of my left hand. It seemed impossible even to hope to reach the Swedish handloggers that day. The sole of a boot floated by. Shuddering, I reached to pull it into the dugout, praying that there was no leg or body attached. It was a hip boot, in good condition, probably worked loose from some ill-fated fisherman. I didn't want to touch it and I didn't want to throw it away. Into my head rushed many stories of fishermen drowning.

It was late afternoon. I had to stop. My heart was thumping from the exertion and my throat was dry. The tide was falling, but it hadn't changed direction in the channel. *Bijaboji* nosed ashore. I sprawled on the rough white rock after making myself toss the boot away. A mink, sleek and rat-like, ran within reach of my outstretched hand. Crows complained loudly at my intrusion. Ravens circled, eagerly appraising the possibility of a meal.

An inner something drove me on after a bit, on beyond the white splotch I'd seen from afar and hoped was a building or ship. Disappointment—it was only a wide and noisy waterfall. That had taken several hours more of fighting tide and wind, in utter physical fatigue. Beyond the falls I couldn't force my makeshift paddle one more stroke through the water. I had exhausted heart, nerve and sinew.

In the shelter of a boulder I flopped, chanting monotonously, "Send a boat. Send a boat. Send a boat." My simple words were a desperate prayer. The canoe was safe from the falling tide and I felt that I had earned a rescue. "Send a boat," I chanted on and on, so loud and single-minded that I didn't hear the engine of an approaching purse seiner until it was near enough to blanket the sound of wind, birds and waterfalls. I listened as though to phantom noises and took my hands away from my eyes very, very slowly. One more disappointment and, well…

I stood up as quickly as my exhausted and battered body permitted, then rushed wildly over the rocks waving my arms and sobbing. Unconscious of my scanty attire or of the sharp barnacles, knowing only that I had been seen, I raised my right arm, closed my fingers in a fist, stuck out my thumb and waved the international hitchhike signal.

A strong curly-haired Native fellow rowed ashore, flashing a broad friendly smile at my tear-streaked sunburned face. When I felt myself really safe in the sturdy flat dory with that kind young man, who introduced himself as Chuck Howard, I shook with sobs. I was embarrassed. I apologized. "My brothers wouldn't let me go on like this."

"I know what you've been through," he said. "We were wind-bound a week last winter. You are lucky a boat came here—we only did because we couldn't find fish anywhere at all."

The skipper, Sam Hall, helped me aboard his black and copper painted seine boat. "We saw you in Butedale. Thought you'd be in Prince Rupert by now. Where do you want to go?"

"Hartley Bay, I guess, or wherever I can get oars."

The boat was the *Kitgore*, with a crew of Natives from Kitimat Village and Kemano.

Chuck made tea in the galley and offered me food. The cupboards looked pretty bare and he explained, "We eat more when fish are scarce. Tomorrow we have to get supplies."

With food before me I had an appetite only for tea and the thick mug felt enormously heavy. Chuck wanted to hear my story, but tears flowed whenever I started to talk. He guided me to the pilothouse, calling attention to thousands of Arctic terns wheeling in the sunset. He put me in the skipper's bunk, brought several copies of *Maclean's* magazine and left me. Physically and emotionally exhausted, I fell asleep before I got to the middle of the first story.

It was deep dusk when they roused me at Hartley Bay. One man had gone ashore to find Pete Long, a Michigander who worked as caretaker of this Native village while all the residents were away fishing or working in the canneries. I stood on the afterdeck talking to one of the men who plays in the Kitimat band until Pete appeared.

Being hard of hearing he couldn't patch together the explanation about me, but he could see that I needed rest and food. He opened his house to the coed canoeist, and when the compassionate men of *Kitgore's*

Betty was marooned for three days after being caught by one of the fierce storms that lash the West Coast. Julia Moe

crew had seen me established with kindly old Pete, they chugged away. I prayed they would have the best fishing of their lives.

Pete showed me to a narrow, brown leather-covered couch, raised at the head, beside the wood heater in his living room. "That's just like the one Daddy has in his study," I said happily, laying out the sleeping bag. From it rolled a can of milk and a loaf of bread — generous surprise gifts from *Kitgore*'s slim supplies. A lump rose in my throat. Pete polished a kerosene lamp, lit it, and then sat and rocked contentedly near the heater. He recounted an adventure he'd had rowing his heavily loaded boat in Douglas Channel while taking a schoolteacher to the Mission at Kitimat Village after she had missed the monthly boat. He described the mining settlement at Surf Inlet, now abandoned. He told of a woman found wandering on a nearby beach who had fallen off a passenger steamer in Grenville Channel. He painted a verbal picture of the sawmill that had once stood here. Then Pete took his lamp upstairs and I had 10 hours of fitful, though uninterrupted, rest. All night I was back on that narrow rocky ledge, hungry and cold and exhausted.

In the morning, wearing a pair of Pete's heavy rubber shoes, I tagged along with him across the bridge from his house to the Native village, where we gathered eggs for the Natives, picked loganberries for canning, and fed numerous cats. After a breakfast of Roman Meal and Pete's homemade bread we returned to the village. Pete took me through every house, even the missionary's, and each one was astonishingly clean and comfortably furnished. I think there was not one home without Congoleum, a piano or organ, a battery-powered radio and a polished wood-burning kitchen range. Above the houses stood a church, recently built by the Natives to replace the church that had burned. On one side of the boardwalk was a community hall where youngsters could play ping-pong and basketball. A notice of reward for anyone finding the body of a boy drowned many months before was posted on a bulletin board.

"Yesterday, about two hours before *Kitgore* rescued me, I found a large hip boot drifting in the channel," I told Pete.

"Not the boy's. He wasn't wearing boots when he went overboard."

Along the beach were many sheds for boats and firewood. Pete searched them all for oars small enough for my dugout, and ultimately found a long pair that could be shortened and shaped to fit my hands.

Before commencing work on the oars, he had to mow the lawn surrounding one of the finest homes. While he pushed the lawn mower, I enjoyed three happy hours playing hymns and sheet music on a properly tuned piano. After a filling lunch of brown rice, bread, fresh loganberries—my favourite—and mountain ash jelly, he started work on the oars.

When the oars were ready, I put the *Canadian Home Journal* aside and shouted in Pete's ear, "As soon as I can put a seat in the canoe I'll be heading up Grenville Channel to Lowe Inlet."

"Just a minute." He gripped my arm and pointed to *Sherman*, a purse seiner entering the harbour and preparing to anchor. Two men leaped easily into a seine skiff and quickly rowed ashore. "That's Jack Pahl, a chief here, and his son. You can get a ride with them to Lowe Inlet."

Silently, Mr. Pahl and his son Henry walked across the bridge to where I stood. The chief was about 30 years old, heavy-set, strong and dark. He was the man who had designed the new church. He greeted Pete, asked whether I was the girl who wanted a ride to Lowe Inlet, and said, "The *Kitgore* told us about you yesterday."

I told him I was the girl, and that I would rather row, but that I was handicapped without charts and a seat in my dugout. Arrangements were made for *Sherman* to take *Bijaboji* and me to Lowe Inlet, where there were women and clothes. Pete gave young Henry all the eggs collected from the village chickens. I said goodbye to Pete and *Bijaboji* was pulled aboard and stowed over the fish hold.

As I climbed aboard *Sherman*, Pete called out: "Be careful, and God bless you, young lady."

CHAPTER 14

North to the Skeena

*I had no money after the first two weeks, no compass, no gun, no
mirror, no watch, and in the last two weeks I had only the hulk of the
canoe and the sleeping bag, but I wasn't out for a stunt.*
        —Betty Lowman, *Daily Colonist* (Victoria), December 19, 1937

THE SEINER *SHERMAN* GOT UNDERWAY, turning southwest for the run
through the dark water of Stewart Narrows and Coghlan Anchorage
before entering Grenville Channel. The forest grew lush and nearly
impenetrable to the water's edge, with pine and cedar trees that were
just slightly greener than the quiet water sparkling under the bright
afternoon sun. Near shore an eagle struggled with a large salmon. It
had sunk its sharp talons into the fish near the water's surface, then
tried to fly away with it, but the fish fought back. The eagle could
neither fly away with the salmon nor release it, only frantically flap
its wings, trying to drag its prey toward shore. In the canoe I could
have observed the fight to the finish. On the faster boat we were too
soon by. Who won? Or did both perish? I'd read of such struggles
but never before seen one.

Chief Jack Pahl was steering when I climbed to the top of the
pilothouse to express my appreciation for the lift. He identified our
route and told me we had just entered Wright Sound at Camp Point
and turned northwest into the long, narrow and straight Grenville
Channel. That much-used channel runs between rugged, timbered
mountain ranges rising one behind the other as terraced steps on Pitt
Island and the mainland.

I asked him about his name, and he said it was German—his father
was a Prussian seaman and he was proud of it. "He gave me lots of

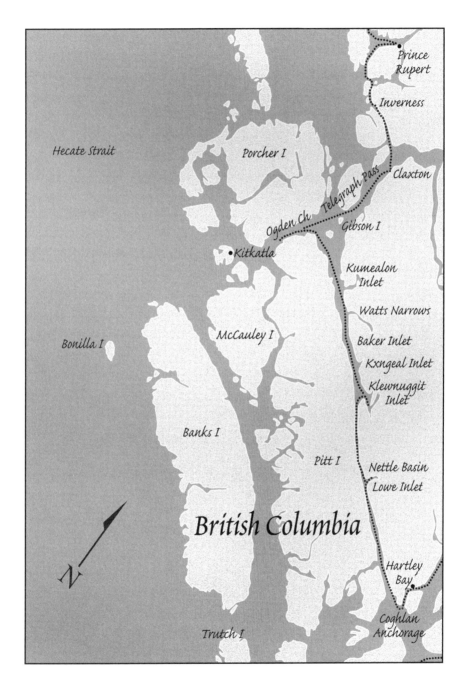

sense and taught me a lot. I build my own boats and fix my engines
when they need it."

His mother, a Native woman, had died, but he remembered her stories. "The Indians have a legend about a flood," he said. "It's like the Bible story, with adaptations to these lands and these people."

Grenville Channel extended for miles and miles before us, a ribbon of untroubled blue water separating high, green wooded hills with folded ranges rising behind their bare peaks speckled with snow. *Sherman* rose and fell easily on swells left in the wake of a fast northbound steamer. Puffs of clouds drifted lazily from one rocky peak to the next as though searching for a place to rest. In the canoe I might have feasted on the scenery for a day's rowing to Lowe Inlet. I should have been a glutton for any change from the panorama that had spread before me on the ledge. But in the canoe I'd not have met *Sherman*'s crew or heard aboriginal legends interpreted by a German-Indian man. Nor would I have heard the Natives' side of the controversy about Japanese people getting into the commercial fishing industry as buyers and cannery workers, competing for jobs that had long been held by Natives.

About three hours after departing Hartley Bay and 15 miles north of Wright Sound we turned east, passing through the bottleneck entrance of Lowe Inlet—less than 500 feet wide—behind a fish packer from Claxton Cannery. Skipper Pahl pulled the whistle three times

A label from the salmon cannery in Lowe Inlet. Harbour Publishing archives

and the packer slowed. *Sherman* turned and eased alongside. Few words were spoken—this was obviously a routine occurrence. Covers were lifted off fish holds and Alfred Anderson, *Sherman*'s deckhand, nimbly stepped over the combing, dropped into the hold and began pitching up the day's catch, about 500 salmon. The Japanese workers separated, weighed and counted sockeyes, pinks and cohoes before sliding them into the hold of the packer, where they were chilled with chipped ice. After unloading we moved to the dock at a disused cannery on the northwest shore of the circular Nettle Basin.

"Come with me," Jack Pahl said, and we leaped onto the dock— hot under my bare feet—and walked to a long, narrow cabin ashore. A grey-haired Scot sat inside reading.

"Hello," he growled.

"Meet my stepfather, Bill McMillan," Jack Pahl said.

Mr. McMillan looked at me with a bit of interest. "I suppose you're that crazy girl paddler the forest ranger told us to look out for. What took you so long getting here?"

"Lost my oars and most everything else in Douglas Channel," I replied. "Couldn't get off a ledge for two nights and three days. The *Kitgore* rescued me. If it's all right, I want to stay here awhile to put a new seat in the canoe—after I find some clothes."

"You're not going on!" Bill growled. When I nodded, his voice boomed through the room. "Rats!"

I felt jittery, gooey and furious all at once. I rushed out of the cabin to get hold of myself, saying over and over in my mind that I would rather drown than arrive in Ketchikan aboard a powerboat. I'd drown myself before I'd let anybody say, "I told you a girl couldn't do it."

But Jack and Bill were talking and finally Bill said, "We'll get you everything you need to make a seat for your coffin. Come along."

Stepping carefully over the splintery dock, I followed them into the cannery. Bill found nails, hammer and saw, and Jack cut a short length off a wide board. In single file we trudged down the board-walk to the float where the boys had put the dugout. The two men stood over me, silent, judging overseers, as I set about measuring with string and sawing the board to size. After all my measuring and sawing, nothing fit. Neither man offered a word of advice as I scratched my head in greatest perplexity. Surely I'd done everything just as I learned in junior high manual training—before the teacher banned girls from his classes.

Finally Jack couldn't stand it any longer. "I brought another board just in case this happened." He picked up the saw. And I, feeling completely and helplessly feminine, stood by for the few minutes it took him to put in a jim-dandy canoe seat.

"You'll have to wait until tomorrow morning for the tide to Klewnuggit," Bill said as he inspected the new seat and nodded his approval. "And I'll find you supplies to go on, and shelter for the night."

Returning to *Sherman* to get my sleeping bag and oars, I discovered Alfred Anderson examining one oar with a look of surprise on his face. "I had an oar just like that," he grinned, "in my shed."

"It…it is yours, I guess. Pete and I borrowed it."

"And you can have it," Alfred said, still grinning. "Just have a safe trip."

The engine banged and ka-chugged. Alfred threw off the lines and leaped aboard. Smells of supper, fish and engine exhaust wafted to me.

"Thanks again, Jack, Alfred and all of you," I shouted, though only Jack stood on deck. A broom waved up through the hatch, a handkerchief flapped from a porthole, a hand gesticulated below the broom and Captain Pahl saluted.

At Bill's cabin he ordered, "Sit here," pointing to a chair on one side of a wooden table with an oil lamp on it. He sat down on the other side. "Now, what do you absolutely need to finish the trip?"

"I can't think of a thing," I stammered, thinking of the cameras, notebooks, ski trousers and other clothes, food, hatchet, knives, oil-skins and cooking equipment that I'd lost.

"Well, if you can't, I can," Bill said gruffly, and went out. He returned with a frying pan, a hatchet, two tin cookie boxes, a tide table booklet, tin plate and eating tools.

Someone tapped on the door behind him. "Come in," Bill boomed. Bright sunshine flooded into the room. At the open door stood a young woman in white beach togs, so slim and comely under the floppy brim of a white beach hat that I caught my breath. I had heard many mentions of the lovely and talented Gwen Weaver on my way up the coast. Could this be Gwen? Would anyone so beautiful and rather glamorous stay in such a place, without even a weekly mail boat to break the monotony? Behind her were two boys and their young white-haired mother.

"You are Miss Lowman?" Gwen queried in a voice as smooth and clear as the blue sky. "Tell us what has happened to you?... But wait, have supper with me. Then we'll all get together. We've just come from swimming," and she gestured gracefully, indicating her companions, "Mrs. Lisa Edwards, the boys and I. Bill will show you to my house in an hour."

When they had gone, I sank into the chair in a daze, feeling awfully freckled, tousled, ragged and sunburned.

"It's just the jitters," I told myself half an hour later, while walking the few yards to Mrs. Weaver's cottage. We entered through the neat, cheery, well-designed kitchen, which opened into an attractive bedroom–living room and a bathroom with a big bathtub. I sat in a spacious wicker chair comfortably cushioned by a pillow. I appreciated that for my numerous barnacle scratches acquired during the last two days of rough treatment.

Gwen had been busy. The subtle aroma of salmon stew and steaming soda biscuits was almost too much after my days on the ledge without food. A square of butter and a jar of raspberry jam completed the first course. Her attentive interest in my trip kept me talking between bites. Hot tea and a thick slice of chocolate cake completed our delicious and filling meal.

The Edwardses came in after supper, bringing me soap, matches, cans of food and a warm blouse. How could I ever repay such generosity and kindness? These people knew exactly what a person needed to survive along this colourful, weather-beaten, sometimes dangerous coast, and they gladly offered it to me. The women told about their husbands' work as Fisheries inspectors. This included checking the fishing boats for licences and legal fishing gear, plus hiking along the streams and rivers in their area to count the various species of salmon working their way upstream to spawn—and even shooting the occasional bear. Mrs. Edwards was clear and decisive in expressing herself about salmon conservation. I listened with great interest to her stories about their winter home in Bella Coola, where Lord Tweedsmuir had visited during his trip across Canada earlier that summer.

She told of summertime, when Native boys, dressed with gypsy-like flair and riding spirited horses, rode down the steep hills from interior ranches and camps, some as far inland as Williams Lake. I learned about another settlement—Hagensborg, a few miles east of Bella Coola—which is like a transplanted Norway. For some reason these fine ladies had determined that my reason for rowing up the coast was to write about the local people and what they do.

"No, I'm not. Writers who want material about coast Canadians visit them in yachts and ply them with liquor," I said, explaining that I was out to realize a selfish personal ambition, with the incidental hope of writing articles about camp craft and canoeing to pay off my college debts.

When the Edwardses were departing I noticed that they carried strong sticks—obviously not walking sticks—and asked about them. "To knock the porcupines out of our way," Mrs. Edwards replied.

I lingered for some time in the luxury of a hot tub, then Gwen painted my barnacle scratches, many of which were already infected, with stinging iodine. Soon after, I crawled between cool, soothing sheets for a much-needed rest. Not even the torrents of rain that pounded the roof and poured off the eves during the night, or the threatening roar of the turgid stream rushing between the houses from the mountain behind, awakened me. Only when I had slept myself out did I awaken. Then I dressed and ate in great haste, telling Gwen, "I mustn't miss this tide."

When I went for my things at Bill's, he was adamant in discouraging me. "You don't leave in a rain like this without a raincoat, and nobody here's got one to loan you. Just make up your mind to stay this day." It sounded far too much like something Daddy would say.

"Yes, you must," Gwen Weaver agreed immediately.

That was a restful day of gaiety and fun. We visited back and forth among the three small cottages, Bill's, the Weavers', and the Edwardses'. Mrs. Edwards made lemon pies for a big supper. Bill gave me dozens of bits of advice about catching tides and back eddies in Grenville Channel. Gwen got out her large photograph album and told me the story of each of the interesting pictures as she knitted.

There was one photo of Len Weaver. He hadn't got a job with the Fisheries department when he first applied, so the two of them went handlogging. "That's work that sharpens one's tongue and temper," Gwen said, laughing at my wide-eyed astonishment that this delicate, feminine lady had been a real outdoors helpmate to her logger husband. She had helped snake big logs out of the woods and into the salt chuck, then pushed them into booms, all with endurance and skill equal to any man's. She also had photos of the motion picture actor John Barrymore and his fancy yacht, and of the actress Dolores Costello in hiking breeches. "They stayed here one summer to go sport fishing," Gwen said. "And the handsome young men in the yacht crew were presumptuous about us non-Natives here. I had to lock the screen in one man's face. They expected the girls to kneel before them just because they come from Hollywood. Such soft, lazy loungers didn't impress any of us. Here, summer jobs are important for survival."

She had many stories of adventure about winter fur-buying trips for the Hudson's Bay Company. She and Len had run their boat to the Native villages and wherever the trappers worked. "Len has had lots of experience in grading furs," she said. "That's a real art. And he's fair with all the trappers. We carried both cash and supplies to pay for the furs. Sometimes we had thousands of dollars' worth of furs on the boat. We had to be well armed."

I stood by a window looking at the dismally heavy rain and wondered at the prodigious capacity of the clouds. The Edwardses arrived, their rain gear dripping. They unloaded knitting, pictures and other things from under their coats—even scissors and clippers. Whoops! Only the traditional bowl was missing for a haircut.

Gwen placed a stool in the middle of the kitchen, transforming it into a barbershop but definitely not a beauty parlour. With her and the two boys giving advice and voicing judgement, Mrs. Edwards slashed away at the bush standing out all over my head. Each spectator pointed out a rough spot that needed shearing and by the time they were satisfied and I was handed a mirror, there remained only a circular crop of hair above my ears. I was a little sad about it, not relishing the mannish look, but at that moment Mrs. Edwards showed me a picture of herself, completely bald. "It all fell out after my operation, and came in white. Now it's black on top. You have fine thick hair, not like a boy's."

After supper and a piece of both Edwards and Weaver lemon pie, we co-operated at dishes, then played cards until time for bed. I fell asleep to the sound of the pitiless rain rattling on the cedar shake roof.

The next morning was misty but rainless, with no wind. Bill helped me load the dugout. I thanked him for all of his help and good advice before he gave me a shove-off. Gwen Weaver got into her clinker-built skiff to row out of Nettle Basin with me. At sunrise the Edwardses had gone crabbing. They hailed us near Whiting Bank and rowed out to put their autographs on the dugout. Then we pulled apart, with Gwen taking pictures and all of us shouting hopes of seeing each other again. Little did any of us know how soon that would be.

The water in Grenville Channel between Lowe Inlet and Klewnuggit Inlet is squeezed into a narrow passage, creating a lively tide that rushed me along at more than four miles an hour. I did not get far offshore, but clung along the outer edge of the kelp beds. In the middle of the channel, drift logs and wreckage from derelict boats and canneries moved as swiftly as in a river current; all washed out from overflowing riverbanks by the tremendous rainfall of the past 48 hours. Huge delimbed logs and a red-painted section of fish elevator moved in a curving course, revealing the conflicting surface currents. A path of riffles broke across the currents from shore to shore, and along its edges kelp and small drift bobbed and twisted without purpose. At the change of the tide, all of this would wander in the opposite direction, eventually drifting ashore—or, if caught by combined wind and tide, it could escape to roam the ocean. On the far shore was the cause of the riffle: tons of falling, tumbling white water, rushing crosswise into the tidal current. It was not easy to follow the waterfall by eye from base to sheer mountain cliff at least 2,000 feet above. Wide and steep was its gorge and outfall. Above, hidden behind ancient wide-branched spruce trees and twice concealed by jutting cliffs, the water appeared again, only to disappear over a rock shelf in front of a snow-striped hollow, probably an overflowing mountain lake.

Boats came down the channel from the north. One swerved dangerously close to me, leaning against the powerful tide. It was Captain Jack Pahl's *Sherman*, and the crew was shouting. The words I picked up and patched together were: "You were reported lost. We cleared that up. Good luck." And with a friendly wave they quickly disappeared astern of me.

So on I went, revelling in the current that pushed the canoe forward. Alaska, here I come! I counted streams of various widths roaring out of the woods and spreading through the boulders on the shore. Some I only located by their roar and the black seaweed growing under dense, low-branched cedar trees. Above the cedars, great spruce and hemlocks grew. Several times I banged into drift that had been caught in the kelp and held there, just below the water's surface. These abrupt stops nearly snapped my head off.

Reaching Klewnuggit Light—only a steel column poking up high atop a rock of Morning Reef—I slanted across Grenville Channel to the shore of Pitt Island, there rowing as close to shore as on the mainland side. Now I could look far into the several arms of Klewnuggit Inlet, but not far enough to see the logging camp I'd been told about, run by a man named Harry Scott. I counted eight levels of mountains east from the channel inland. Zigzags of snowslide devastation slashed downward in ever widening gashes from nearly all the highlands. The sharp, naked summits were so steep that only speckles of snow could cling. The basins of high, scalloped hills held unseen lakes where frolicking water pushed over the rims to become falls and streams, and again falls and streams until debouching into the salt water.

North of Klewnuggit was Kxngeal Inlet, then Watts Narrows, the entrance to Baker Inlet, and beyond was Kumealon Inlet. I could only see the mouths of these uncharted waterways as I drew even and passed on the Pitt Island shore. If only I had proper oars, I thought, and more time to enjoy these magnificent channels and inlets. I had had no idea there would be so much to see on this vacation, or so many splendid people.

Freighters, passenger ships and fish boats frequently passed going north or south in Grenville Channel's sheltered waterway. Each generated series of waves that sent me scurrying toward shore like a frightened duck. There were many constricted stretches where I couldn't do that, and to get beyond the steep, merging, confused wakes I rowed frantically and as close to shore as possible. The black hull of a three-stack steamship loomed as I pulled through a passage, trapped between high, vertical rock walls. The hull grew and grew. It became gigantic. Was there enough room for me? Then the ship seemed to barely squeeze past before diminishing rapidly behind me, leaving great, uncomfortable swells and dangerous backwash.

Intent on meeting those monster swells, I rowed over the submerged end of a log balanced on a jag of rock. A swell lifted the log under the canoe and neatly flipped us over.

My rage knew no limits as I swam around collecting floating gear while trying to hold the heavy, water-filled canoe. It took many minutes to gather everything and swim ashore. "You're as clumsy as a crippled monkey trying to climb a ladder," I muttered, dragging myself onto the steep rock. By yanking, hauling, grunting and groaning, I managed to upend the canoe far enough to tip out the water.

Everything was wet, even the top end of the sleeping bag. Fortunately the hatchet, frying pan and eating utensils had been held under the oilcloth cover. An airplane flew north and I didn't bother to hide—it is warmer to have no clothes on than wet ones. A fire was impossible because every match head had been rubbed off. I shivered and shook. The sleeping bag afforded little comfort, though I huddled in it while calling myself all kinds of a stupid lummox and wishing Daddy might suddenly appear to scoff at my predicament. He'd not call me Buddy until I'd got myself out of this fix. Then he'd hug me tight and say, "Nice work, Bud." At this rate it would be another month before we'd be together and there was no use shivering myself into a spasm.

I wrung out my tennis shorts and sweater, pulled them on, loaded the canoe and pushed out into the middle of the channel to flag down the first boat along, whether headed north or south.

The first was *Yanagi*, a grey Japanese fish packer headed south — back to Lowe Inlet. It was a step back but I was so exasperated I would have gone to Timbuktu. Captain Tanaka swore profusely when he saw my wet gear and scanty clothing. If only I'd had all those same words on the tip of my tongue, I might not have worn myself out in prolonged silent rages. He got the canoe aboard and spread my gear on the hatch cover to dry. Then he bustled into the fo'c'sle and beckoned me after him. He quickly brought out a pair of trousers, a shirt, socks and boots, and enormous woollen drawers. I managed to get into everything except the woollen drawers, which I refused to wear.

It wasn't long before five Alaska-bound halibut boats met and passed us. Now I was sorry to have got impatient and taken a south-bound ride. The only other person on the *Yanagi* was a dignified grey-haired Japanese man who sat on a stool in the pilothouse, spoke not a word of English, and seemed marvellously uninterested in me. He was indisputably not a labourer, for he wore a luxuriant silk brocade robe and Captain Tanaka treated him with deference. Late in the afternoon the Captain brewed sweet tea and cooked supper, Skeena River abalone and a peculiar green vegetable in a watery sauce, with rice that had already been boiled and cooled in a wooden bucket. We crouched on the clean floor of the pilothouse to eat, scooping food off the lip of the bowl and into our mouths with chopsticks. A fork would have been much clumsier. Our meal was enjoyably tasty. After our tea, the old man had a drink of something stronger after pulling a dark bottle from under the bunk.

At Lowe Inlet the slanting sun was shining and the Fisheries inspectors' wives stood on the cannery wharf watching the aviators moor their plane. From the pilothouse I could see they were puzzled by the arrival of this unfamiliar boat. I waited for the opportune moment, then spring-danced onto the deck in my miscellaneous getup. It created some sensation. Gwen and Mrs. Edwards recognized me right away and stepped aboard to gather up my wet things. I quickly got into my own clothes and lent a hand. Captain Tanaka cast off and headed out while the ladies and I prepared for our parade to their kitchens. My friendliest smile and most vigorous waving got no response from the old man, although he did poke his head out of the wheelhouse.

That night I had one mighty hard time of it bluffing that the "third try at Grenville Channel will be a charm." But I insisted on it when the Fisheries department aviators, Gordon Hazlett and Dick Arnett, suggested I'd do well to hitch a ride to the Skeena River and avoid my jinx. I was so furious I nearly stamped my feet when Mr. Edwards began flinging around remarks that Amelia Earhart and the crazy girl canoeist were doomed by their egotistical one-track minds. Vainly I tried to switch the subject by fairly thrusting myself at Dick Arnett with offers to help with his bookkeeping. Dick politely declined and quietly continued recording times of takeoffs and landings, adding mileage and computing gallons of fuel used and passenger pounds.

Gordon and Dick were heartthrobbers and I wished I were at least meeting them in choicer clothes and far from the conspicuous contrast of Gwen Weaver's charming femininity. They were reticent, matter-of-fact and handsome enough to be devastating, had there been anyone around to devastate but a couple of married women and a wrecked girl canoeist. Len Weaver's patrol boat came in before dark and Gwen ran to the float to greet him. So I was left with the Edwardses, the aviators and a copious supply of cookies and tea.

When I rowed out the next day, I intended to hitch a ride with the first northbound boat to the place where I had swamped the day before and to continue from there. I was so confident of a lift that I headed out even with the tide strong against me. I had seen numerous halibut boats going north the day before. Now, only three ships went by in the whole afternoon—all southbound.

The natural beauty of Grenville Channel is worth seeing many times, so I didn't mind rowing that 15 miles again. But I have never bucked such an adverse tide, and may I never work the heart out of myself that way again. It may be that all things worthwhile are difficult, but by nightfall my temper was in shreds again and I was mad for the sight of another human being. I had not realized it, but those three days on the ledge had left their mark—I had a new horror of being alone. In Klewnuggit I steered into one of the arms of orange water, painted by reflections from a vivid polychrome sunset, determined to meet the logger Harry Scott or any yachting party before I pushed on a mile farther north.

Finally I saw a southbound purse seiner snaking along near shore. The flash of the sun on its windows was visible long before the slogan painted across the pilothouse: "Here We Are Again." It was the *Sidney W.*, which I had met in Klemtu. Captain Dave eased the boat alongside the dugout and the five friendly young Natives took me aboard. I decided to return to Lowe Inlet with them rather than spend a night away from people, although I could anticipate the expressions on the faces of the people there when they saw me and "Here We Are Again." But I was in luck—the crew of *Sidney W.* decided they would do just as well going north to fish in Ogden Channel, so they took me north the same distance as I had re-rowed.

These fishermen were jolly and we had a happy time in the pilothouse, singing popular songs as the skipper accompanied us on his instrument, the first cornet of the Kitkatla band. *Sidney W.* was not a fast boat and we must have performed 50 songs, marches, drags, waltzes and whatnot before it was time for a mug-up of tea and toast. All but the helmsman gathered around the foldout table in the fo'c'sle to eat and talk. It occurred to me to take notes, but I did not. The loss of all my notes and paper in Douglas Channel had considerably disheartened me in the taking of more.

When the *Sidney W.* anchored in Ogden Channel, off the northern extremity of Pitt Island, I went out on deck. The seine net loomed black on the boat's wide stern. It was dark and there was no moon. The boat rocked sleepily in a bright pool of phosphorescence, and more phosphorescence outlined the ever-changing watermark on the rocks along the shore. Trees rose ominously still beside the water, mute, tall and black. Looking northeastward, past Gibson Island along the miles of Telegraph Passage, I could see the lights of dozens of gillnet boats working at the mouth of the great Skeena River.

"Where is the likeliest camping spot around here?" I asked Skipper Dave.

"We've stopped in a unlikely section of the channel for you, but it has the best anchorage. You may have my bunk in the cabin and I'll sleep below."

"Oh, I couldn't do that. Isn't there a logging camp within rowing distance or an old cannery site where I could find shelter? I've put you out enough."

But without charts and in the dark I was almost as helpless as though I had no boat. I accepted the skipper's kind, sincere offer.

I unrolled the sleeping bag on his bunk and when the boys had gone below, I turned off the light and crawled into my Cocoon fully dressed. Salt water had so corroded the zipper that it now took me fully 10 minutes to squirm in, and once in I was definitely encased. Neither the peculiarity of the situation nor the voices of the young men in their berths in the engine room below me, rising and falling as they conversed in their own language, could keep me from falling sound asleep. There is no muscle weariness quite like that from half a day's row against a strong tide in Grenville Channel.

An alarm clock woke me momentarily at six o'clock and I heard Cecil Robinson, the cook, hit the deck from his bunk in the engine room. An hour later someone jogged my shoulder. "Breakfast," Cecil said. He stood beside me and hesitated, ready to say something. "Weren't you afraid?" he finally asked, quietly.

"Not a bit, Cecil," I answered as quietly. "There wasn't anything to be afraid of."

"That's right," he said, and he turned and went down the ladder.

It was a struggle to get out of the Cocoon and all the crew were crowded around the table when I joined them. They had set out boiled eggs, toast and jam and tea—a double portion at my place. As the boat swayed, tea splashed out of our mugs and Cecil mopped it up. I helped him with the dishes while a dozen plans flocked through my head. Outside, a rising wind roughened the channel and chilling rain slanted across the light bluish-grey water. I had lost a lot of my daring—or was it confidence?—and didn't want to head into the broad Skeena River. My new narrow-bladed handmade oars got only about half the response from my canoe and the thought of a day in the rain without a windbreaker didn't make me gleeful. But there was no alternative, unless I squelched my conscience and hitched a ride to the nearest shelter.

The boys were fastening on rubber coats and pants ready to fish. I thought it was a cue for me to bid them adieu. But the wise and considerate Skipper Dave had read my thoughts. He told me that they had fish in the hold to deliver to the packer, which would be going across to Claxton Cannery on the Skeena River, and that the skipper of that vessel would be glad to take me there.

The engine was started and Dave climbed atop the pilothouse to steer and watch for leaping salmon. I sat at the cabin window, watching the scenery as *Sidney W.* cruised through Ogden Channel southwest toward the Kitkatla Islands, away from the heavily fished Skeena River. A few salmon leaped exuberantly a hundred yards or so off the port bow. Dave rang the bell vigorously, alerting the crew to prepare to make a set. Then he decided against it. We passed a white man's seiner making a haul on the Pitt Island side. Nearer the shore was an anchored halibut boat with tall bamboo poles, each with a bright red flag lashed to its top. Large red floats were piled on the stern. We sighted the Claxton packer and tied alongside.

When I stepped outside I don't know which startled me more, the penetrating chill dampness or the sheer size of the wooded mountain heights around. From the cabin my eyes had registered only a narrow band of shore and the leafy lower ends of dense stands of trees.

I pulled the thick wool Hudson's Bay blanket tight around me and huddled on a pile of rope while the young men pitched fish onto the packer.

The packer's captain came aboard *Sidney W.* and Dave introduced us. Captain Rudge invited me to bring *Bijaboji* aboard the packer and said that they would be shoving off for Claxton shortly. The canoe was slid from one boat to the other and Cecil helped me roll the sleeping bag. The crew of *Sidney W.* joked and autographed my dugout as we shook hands all around in parting. I certainly appreciated what they had done for me. "Maybe now that I'm off your boat you'll catch a lot of salmon," I said, although Natives do not subscribe to the superstition that a woman on board is bad luck.

The Japanese deckhand-cook on the packer offered me another breakfast. I ate a piece of toast while reading a McFadden *Liberty* magazine. I think I saw that magazine in more places on the coast than any other publication. The deckhand showed me a clipping from the *Prince Rupert Daily Province* about a canoeist and asked if it was me. I admitted it. He seemed pleased that I was aboard.

In the packer's warm galley I read all the way to Claxton Cannery. I know those few miles only by the colour of the water, as pelting rain obscured all landmarks. (A month later, while coming south with Daddy, skipper of the tender *Una Mae*, I proved my competence in piloting. At any time of day or dusk, even when the landscape was concealed by thick fog, I never missed giving our near position just by seeing the colour of the water.)

Before noon the packer tied alongside the Claxton Cannery fish elevator and the crew helped me launch *Bijaboji*. During those few minutes in the pitiless rain I was completely soaked. Sweater and skirt clung in wet folds, dripping hair lay plastered to my skull, water trickled along my face and arms. Everyone else about wore gleaming slickers and dripping sou'westers. A bit of a crowd collected on the dock to watch me row to the float and haul up the canoe.

Captain Rudge brought the cannery manager, Angus Currie, to meet me. "It looks as though you are short a few things," Mr. Currie remarked.

"Yes, I lost everything in Douglas Channel," I said. "Will the fireman let me get dry in the furnace room? I want to make it to the Robert Johnstones at Inverness Cannery today."

"Before anything else you shall have a hot lunch. Please come with me." Mr. Currie guided me up the stilted walk to his cottage and introduced me to his young wife. By the time I had scrubbed my face, cleaned my nails and dried out a bit by the kitchen range, she had a full lunch steaming on the table. The main dish was a savoury vegetable stew. Never in my life have I had such a hot and tasty stew. But it was no match for her homemade bread and pastry. Mr. Currie was indeed to be envied for his pretty, sweet, capable wife and two healthy little wide-eyed boys.

During that wonderful meal we listened to music from the Prince Rupert radio station. That was the only daytime radio reception that I'd heard for a month. "You'll have a good tide to Inverness starting about two o'clock and I'll get you a raincoat at the company store," Mr. Currie said.

The long, narrow wharf at the Inverness Cannery, where Betty stopped briefly.
Harbour Publishing archives

At the store, situated between the manager's cottage and the cannery, the office man and storekeeper found many of the charts I needed to reach Ketchikan, and they fitted me with a raincoat.

With the 12 or so miles to Inverness Cannery well pictured in my mind and a half-length raincoat fastened high under my chin, I set off before mid-afternoon into the silt grey-brown waters of the Skeena River. Many gillnet boats bobbed in the muddy chop and *Bijaboji* galumphed higher and lower than any of the larger boats, steadied by their long tails of net. In Rivers Inlet the majority of the fishermen were white, and here they were stocky, bronze Native men.

Across the passage that heads at right angles from Claxton, I followed the tracks of the Canadian Pacific Railway, rowing more than a few yards from shore only when grass warned of shallow water, or a cannery and its associated floats thrust seaward as obstacles to go around. Wood smoke angled skyward from a few cabins in the Native villages. A gillnet boat or two whipped by, leaving light streaks on the silt-laden river. Sky and misted woods blended with the water. A good wind behind the canoe and a tide with it got us to the red buildings of Inverness Cannery by late afternoon. The float walk was wide enough to let only two people pass, but I put the canoe on it anyway and went ashore to find Robert Johnstone.

A big man pointed the way through the cannery. Operations had ceased for the day and two men were doing maintenance. The Johnstones' summer home was probably the best looking home I had seen on my trip. It was well painted, fenced, and surrounded by a great variety of flowers of many colours, shapes and heights. The appealing residence and garden suddenly made me realize just how far from home I had been for the last two months.

A smiling young man flung open the gate, saying, "They're expecting you."

Up the steps I went to meet Mr. and Mrs. Johnstone and Mrs. King. It was a strange but pleasant feeling to again enter a home with the luxury of a hallway, a living room complete with a telephone, photographs on the piano, and a kitchen, bedrooms, bathroom and back porch. Mrs. Johnstone said she was glad to see I wasn't quite so crazy as she had been calling me. I liked her. She is my favourite kind of people—no gushing, no frills, and a heart of gold that she tries to hide. She got out a suit, stockings and shoes, and made me change before leaving me with Mrs. King and the family dog while she prepared supper. We went through all of Mr. Johnstone's Irish songs, with me accompanying at the piano. An eastbound train with passenger coaches passed and I ran out to wave. I felt a little sick when the last car passed and I turned away. It reminded me that in just a few more days my vacation would come to an end. I'd be back in an urban setting. I missed home, but I loved the beauty and quiet of the wilderness.

In the evening the Johnstones' two sons-in-law came to call and I recounted details of my shipwreck, trying not to reflect too sadly on my seamanship. Mr. Johnstone delighted us, especially me, with stories of his first years on this British Columbia coast, when the Haida were still apt to go on the warpath, and of a trip to the Queen Charlotte Islands. He described early cannery operations and showed me a framed fishing treaty between Mr. Windsor and the Natives in the 19th century. "Mr. Windsor's son is now manager of Wales Island Cannery, north of Port Simpson."

That night I had a hot bath and slept on a Beautyrest mattress with a silk coverlet. Though the Johnstones had planned to give me the thrill of breakfast with the cannery men in the mess hall, Mr. Johnstone hadn't the heart to disturb my slumbers until 10 o'clock the next morning. By then the tide was just right to row on to Prince Rupert.

Walking down to the float with Bob Johnstone, I nodded goodbye to the whites, Natives and Japanese working in the cannery. He said hello to a teenaged Japanese girl, then turned to me, saying, "Yesterday she timidly asked me if you were an Indian. I told her you were white when you started out this summer but I wouldn't vouch for what you are now."

I laughed and repeated what some Native girls along the way had said about my trip—that no Native girl would do it, unless she was under such emotional pressure as the devoted sister commemorated by the totem pole in Pioneer Square in Seattle. That girl lost her life in an attempt to reach her dying sister on the Nass River.

"Yes, the Native girls are too busy in the summer to be taking trips," he agreed. "They wouldn't be nearly so safe along the way as an American girl." Two men carried my package of food from the Johnstone house and helped to load the little luggage I had. They pointed the way to go. When I was dipping for the third stroke, Bob Johnstone shouted, "Follow the railway tracks, Indian, and put your dugout up at the Prince Rupert Yacht Club."

CHAPTER 15

Prince Rupert by Land, by Sea, by Air

Betty Annette Lowman is an Anacortes lass who has packed more adventure into a few short years than most of us experience in a lifetime.
— H.E. Jamison, *Seattle Star*, January 1941

WITHOUT A LARGE-SCALE CHART OF PRINCE RUPERT and the Skeena River I had no way of knowing what islands and points I was passing. The Canadian coast is remarkably devoid of signposts. I checked my course by the shoreline cut for the railway. My memories of the 12 miles to Prince Rupert are not of one point and another, but of the railway tracks and a bright sapphire sky where great, lazy silver clouds drifted. Far across Chatham Sound were dusky lines of low islands with green trees and dark mountains far behind. Playful waves washed over a nearby reef to surge among the seaweed-covered rocks.

Nearly to Prince Rupert, along the shore of Kaien Island, I beached in front of a lighthouse built beside the tracks. The keeper came down a set of stairs chipped out of the native rock. As he helped tie the canoe, I told him, "I'm looking for a place to change my clothes."

"Go right up to the house," he urged. "My wife is upstairs."

I climbed to the lighthouse, greeted the keeper's wife and put on a white blouse Mrs. Edwards had given me. Just as I was starting off, they called me back. "We're making tea. We've heard about you on the radio and been wanting to meet you."

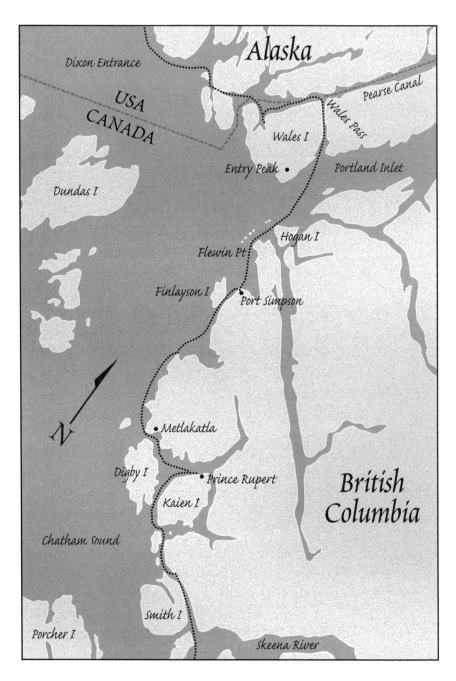

While we enjoyed meat sandwiches and tea, they talked about their lighthouse—likely the dream of all lonely keepers. "Here we are, right alongside a railway and only a few miles from town. The foghorn is important, but the only rescue work we do is of parties hiking along the tracks who get caught in the rain." The keeper's wife laughed and added, "You're the first seagoing person we've helped."

I made good time riding the flood tide to Prince Rupert. The first structures I saw were the cold storage building and grain elevator. Soon the public buildings of the city proper on Kaien Island came into view. An excursion steamer with a blaring jazz orchestra was moored to a long dock. Bored-looking, well-dressed ladies and men lined the ship's rail and stared glumly at the brown girl in the shabby red canoe while flicking cigarette ashes down on her.

Three boys were fishing from the end of one of the docks. I said hello and asked them where the yacht club was. They pointed east and preceded me on their bicycles to help pull up the canoe.

"What is this? What is this?" the manager called out as he hurried along the float.

Though Mr. Johnstone had told me it was all right, I felt guilty about putting the battered, autographed *Bijaboji* among those shiny white sail and motor boats with all of their polished brasswork. I started to push her off, apologizing. "Bob Johnstone told me it would be all right to stay here," I said, "but I'll just go to the city float until I clear at customs."

"Oh, you're the coed canoeist!" The manager now smiled broadly. "Welcome to Prince Rupert! Welcome! I'm Sheff Thomson. Now don't worry about the canoe. You get along to the customs and I'll take care of everything."

What a difference it makes to drop a name.

Three things were troubling me as I walked along the railway tracks with the boys. One was how to clear customs since all my papers had gone down in Douglas Channel, another was money, and the third was: how could I word a telegram to Mother to let her know that I'd lost everything and still not cause her worry?

The customs officers asked for a complete explanation of how I'd lost my clearance papers. While I was recounting the disaster in detail, a man wearing a light coat came in and immediately commenced taking notes. The officers asked a couple more questions, said I was lucky to be alive, and told me to return sometime later to pick up new clearance papers. Their kindness and courtesy brightened my feelings and my outlook on Prince Rupert.

As I was leaving, the note jotter said, "I'm Alec Hunter from the *Daily News*. I want a story for Associated Press."

"I need to see if I have any mail before I can talk."

Alec Hunter offered to walk with me to the post office. Along the way he saw a Provincial Police officer and introduced us. At the post office, Alec stood by while I waited in line at the general delivery window. My hopes were dashed—there was no mail for me. Then the thought came sneaking into my head that I hadn't left Prince Rupert on the list of mail stops since it was so near my destination. What a plight! Here I was, almost 700 miles from home, without even a toothbrush. I was definitely blue. I'd wanted to buy new wide-blade oars for the canoe—and also paint, because I couldn't bear to think of Daddy seeing his birthday gift to me in such battered condition.

"I'll have to send a telegram," I said, feeling pretty ragged and out in the cold. Alec escorted me to the telegraph office. Of course we were talking about my trip all this time, and he was getting his story. At the office I chewed on the pencil before deciding the words most likely to assure Mother of my health and happiness would be "rowing on." My 10 words—sent collect—were: "Lost everything but canoe. Indian rescuers third day. Rowing on."

While we waited for the telegram to be sent, Alec asked more questions and scribbled down my answers. "What would you like more than anything else?" he asked as we left the telegraph office.

"Fresh, cold milk," I replied instantly.

He bought a quart of milk as we walked to the hotel to say hello to the proprietress, a friend of Gwen Weaver of Lowe Inlet. She gave me a comfortable room facing onto the street. Alec said he would call at six o'clock to take me to supper at the home of the secretary of the yacht club.

I made the milk last as long as possible while contemplating the coverlet and curtains as possibilities for a dinner gown. What a sight I should be to go out for dinner. Yellow running shoes with just strands of canvas holding them to my feet, a thin, ragged skirt and a white blouse covered by a sweater with many holes. My red, freckled face was shiny. My black hair was dirty, sticky and still not long enough to show its natural wave.

Finally I decided to go visiting. I might possibly have one friend in town, Albert Miller, the logger who had been injured at Alec Ring's camp in Mathieson Channel. I strode along the streets of Prince Rupert. Everybody seemed to stare and snicker so I barged clear through town and up the high, steep hill to the hospital. The nurses were crisp and clean and nice to look at. They checked the records and found that Miller had been discharged two days previously, but a friendly young nurse named the boarding house where Miller was staying.

I still had *Bijaboji* to care for, so I trekked to the yacht club by as many out-of-the-way paths as I could find. *Bijaboji* was the centre of attention, being ogled and discussed by residents of Prince Rupert from all walks of life. No one noticed me. I felt I had lost a good friend.

Slinking back to the hotel, I passed Miller's boarding house. He wasn't in, so I left a note of good wishes for him.

Promptly at six, Alec Hunter called for me in a taxi and we rode to a commodious home on a hill where Mr. and Mrs. Alex McRae welcomed me warmly. The delightful meal was beautifully served in a spacious dining room and the conversation was sparkling. But no one could answer my questions about the waters just beyond the British Columbia–Alaska boundary. In fact, no Canadian I ever approached, even at the boundary itself, was able to give me any real information about Alaskan waters. That was the most profound evidence I could have of the separation that an invisible national boundary can effect.

The reporter and Mr. McRae decided that we should walk to the yacht club and look over the best large-scale chart aboard one of the yachts. Along the way we met four men climbing the hill. They had been to see *Bijaboji*. The tallest of them, Mr. Alder, was the port commissioner. The other men were from Vancouver and represented a group proposing to build a pulp mill in Prince Rupert. The commissioner drew me aside and said very quietly, "You have had hard luck. You have nearly completed a remarkable voyage. We will help you in every way possible, and you mustn't be too proud to let us."

"I can't thank you enough, Mr. Alder. You and Alec Hunter, Sheff Thomson, the McRaes and many other people of Prince Rupert have been thoughtful, generous and welcoming. I shall hate leaving tomorrow morning."

"Then you mustn't," he insisted. "You must accept the hospitality of our city for another day, and do not worry about your hotel bill." Not being the sort of man who wanted thanks, Mr. Alder quickly walked off with his friends while Mr. McRae, Alec Hunter and I went on to study charts. I memorized my route. Sheff offered to find proper oars among the strays left on the floats, and to put in a seat as nearly like the original as possible. Now I was beyond trying to thank the kind people of Prince Rupert.

Back at the McRaes' I sank into a corner of the overstuffed lounge. Mrs. McRae got out her knitting and we talked about shooting parties. Mr. McRae told of a party back in 1913 that really hadn't been a shooting party. One hunter's boat was apprehended and found to be equipped with a wireless radio, supposedly to communicate with German warships. The man and his family had been sent to wartime internment camp, and I suspected it was a family I had met.

The next forenoon I stopped at the customs office and received my clearance papers. The officers were most courteous and kind. One of them gave me a card with a phone number on it and offered the use of his telephone. I dialled and soon heard a sweet, lilting voice saying, "I am Mrs. Mandy, an American too. Dr. Mandy and I want you to have lunch with us. We camp in the out-of-doors a great deal ourselves. We'll have much to talk about."

I was almost speechless. To be put in touch with such a congenial person, with common interests, was more like a storybook than reality. I stammered acceptance and told her I would be at the yacht club all morning.

"Then Dr. Mandy will call for you there."

With the clearance papers in my hand I was walking happily along the waterfront when my eyes nearly bulged out. There alongside a float was the *Alpine Fir*. I ran down the wooden stairs and nearly bowled over Ole Urseth and Lex Johnson beside their ship. "You went right by when I was wrecked on a ledge at Foch Inlet!" I said accusingly.

Lex apologized, saying they'd been looking for me. They invited me aboard for a cup of coffee. Ole presented me with a notebook and a map of the local land. We were still discussing my troubles at Foch Inlet when a man from a nearby boat approached, saying, "Do you remember me, Miss Lowman?"

I did remember him. "But just where did we meet?"

"Down at Rivers Inlet. I'm the travelling photographer with the two magazine girls." We shook hands vigorously and chatted about our various adventures on the way north as we walked to the yacht club.

With shirt sleeves rolled up and cap set on the float, Sheff was hard at work shaping and fitting a new canoe seat. "Found a set of oars for you," he said. "Take a look at them."

I picked one up, admiring its strong, wide blade, and checked its length against my height. "Oh, Sheff, they're perfect! They're so much lighter and broader. I'll make great speed with these. Thanks so much." I sat down with Sheff and asked him about his various tattoos and about his life belt and seaman's cap, until Dr. Mandy came for me.

Dr. Mandy, large, broad-shouldered and with a handsome, weather-tanned face, was a doctor not of medicine but of geology—a mining engineer. On the way to the cottage we stopped to select two potted plants from a Chinese gardener and when we reached the Mandy cottage I wondered at his buying more plants. Where could they be set out? The cottage was breathtakingly beautiful, with trellises covered in bright climbing plants, window boxes aglow with blossoms, flower beds painstakingly filled with blooming plants of all sizes and colours. Vines crept up and across the house, flowers bordered the trim walkways and all was surrounded by a light green fence. Down the steps came Mrs. Mandy, a small brunette with a joyous and welcoming smile. She wore khaki breeches and a shirt open at the throat, a wonderful outdoor outfit.

Despite working in the garden all morning, she had prepared a substantial lunch of halibut rolled and cooked in crisp cornflakes, and generous slices of fresh melon. With eyes alight she described some of their trips in the outdoors, up seldom-travelled rivers, into the wild interior and over remote glaciers, even to the Queen Charlotte Islands. She spoke of interesting people they met on their trips, people whose diverse achievements were so exciting and worthwhile that I felt good just hearing about them.

I wandered about the Mandy home almost in a trance, lingering before colour photographs of unbelievable beautiful northern scenery, and hesitating to touch Native artifacts such as white beaded moccasins, decorated paddles and argillite carvings made by Haida people in the Queen Charlottes. Everything had been selected with great care by the discriminating Mandys, to whom each article had much more than superficial meaning.

Mrs. Mandy presented me with a checkered wool shirt and coloured handkerchiefs. With extreme reluctance I left the Mandys' lovely residence to answer a call telling me to get in touch with Sheff Thomson. Dr. Mandy drove me to the yacht club, where a smiling Lex Johnson met us with a pair of shoes for me, and the question, "Ever been up in an airplane?"

"No, why?"

"See Sheff," was all he would say.

The walk creaked and bounced as I ran to the yacht club float.

"Call these two numbers," Sheff said, delighting in my excitement.

The first number was answered by the US customs official who asked me to see him about a telegram. The second got me Ted Dobbins, one of the Dominion's aviator heroes, the pilot chosen to fly Lord Tweedsmuir around the region. Ted invited me to go flying that afternoon, "over the channel you will navigate in the next few days." It was just too much. My sanity sent a-winging and I ran pell-mell to the customs office.

The official smiled as he handed me a typed yellow paper. "I received this telegram from Don Wright in Ketchikan," he said, "acting for your father."

The gist of it was: "We're back of you. We'll send you anything you need to get over the finish line, even steamer passage. Love, Dad."

"Gosh! Gosh!" was all I could say; then: "Could you wire Don that everything is under control and that I've been rowing on for days since the disaster. And thank you millions for contacting me."

Dashing to the aircraft mooring, I met Ted Dobbins and his wife, an assured aviatrix in a blue and yellow slacks outfit. She showed me how to climb into the airship. I sat in the front seat, dithery with excitement while the plane warmed up. At last we were moving over the water, bouncing, splashing, lifting, flying. Then water, islands and Prince Rupert gradually receded below us. We climbed up and up before circling out over Chatham Sound. Far below were many boats and ships, each followed by widening and diminishing white wakes. Shiny dark puddles—lakes—decorated Dundas and many of the other islands. All the islands, islets and rocks were adorned with sparkling white necklaces created by lively water smashed in from the ocean. Breakers, white with foam spread over brown reefs lurking just below the surface. There were so many dangerous reefs, all the way from Prince Rupert to Port Simpson, every one of them a hazard to the unwary seaman. I scanned the rugged shore for camping spots and decided I'd have to make it all the way to Port Simpson the next day.

Beyond Port Simpson was the wide, waving blue ribbon of Portland Canal, the middle of which marked the BC–Alaska boundary. To the northwest was Dixon Entrance and Ketchikan, and beyond lay Skowl Arm and Daddy. In half an hour we flew over or within sight of all the waters I would spend the next five and a half days rowing to cross. This was modern travel—lightning fast compared with my Indian dugout. But with the dugout, I consoled myself, I got to see everything close up, and to meet so many interesting people.

My first flight was a never-to-be-forgotten experience. Now I knew why Amelia Earhart had been totally captivated by flying. We

landed and, with water spraying high from both big pontoons, tax-
ied back to the airplane float. After heartily thanking Ted and Mrs.
Dobbins, I hurried to the yacht club. There I met Dr. and Mrs. R.G.
Large and friends, who asked me to join them in a jaunt in their yacht.
They were off to Salt Lake on the Tsimpsean Peninsula for a swim
and supper. What fun! We met a number of other yachting parties at
Salt Lake, among them the Dobbins, the three pulp mill consultants
and the head of the Forestry ministry. Dr. Large's oldest boy dove off
the top of the tower and in following him I splashed everybody and
lost a borrowed bathing cap. It was time to get dressed.

All the light of a long northern summer day had been used by the
time we returned to the yacht club. Sheff was waiting there, to show
me that he had the dugout and my things in readiness for an early
morning start. Also, he tried to persuade me to accept a lift from
Wales Island to Ketchikan, and to write a book about my travels.

"I'll be down for breakfast in the morning," I told him. "I won't
take a lift, but I may try writing—someday."

Sheff gave me a substantial breakfast and friendly send-off in the
early dawn of Friday the 13th. It was good to be pulling across quiet
waters to old Metlakatla and into Chatham Sound. High-rolling
swells charging in from Dixon Entrance pounded the jagged coast.
Riding over them, I wished *Bijaboji* had more weight in the bow.
Sometimes she would bounce in a swell without forward motion for
several minutes, despite all my efforts at the oars. I landed on a tiny
sheltered beach where rocks were plentiful. I wanted just one—one
with a specific shape and size to fit firmly in *Bijaboji*'s bow. Failing to
locate anything suitable, I went on without extra ballast. Of all the
Pacific coast I know, there is no 25-mile stretch with more treacherous reefs than that one from Prince Rupert to Port Simpson. Often I
shuddered as a breaker suddenly curled over a hidden rock that the
canoe had missed by inches. Occasionally I had to make a few hard
tugs on the oars to get us off a rock left dry by a receding wave and
out of the way of the next lifting curler.

Far across the sound, steamers appeared distorted by the rolling
Pacific. Humpbacked salmon leaped around me gleefully and slapped

back down on their sides. It was a temptation to go into Big Bay and visit the local mill, but I rowed on inside a string of small islands. The sun burned me mercilessly all morning. Then the wind rose, and in late afternoon low-hanging rain clouds blew in from the southwest. It began to rain shortly after I reached flat-topped Finlayson Island and sighted the section of Port Simpson that is on Village Island. One must look closely to be sure that it is an island. I would have rowed around it if I hadn't poked close along shore in hopes of finding a narrow pass. The tide was high enough that I could get through over the rocks and into Port Simpson harbour where there is a long pier and a small float.

It was raining in torrents when I sloshed the length of the pier and up the winding path to the hospital to keep my promise to Alec Hunter of the *Daily News*, that I would telephone him and report my safe arrival. The head nurse answered my knock and told me the Hudson's Bay store in the village had a public telephone. There, Mr. Houston, the manager, left his merchandise sorting to get the number for me. After a short talk with Alec, I asked Mr. Houston for permission to sleep in his storeroom or a shed.

"Just a minute," he said smiling, and went upstairs. He returned with his young wife. Taking me by the elbow, she said, "We have rooms and rooms upstairs and you are most welcome to one tonight."

The upstairs was neat and cheery. Soft, lulling music played above the clattering of the rain. "You are wet and weary and you shall have a hot bath to warm and relax you," Mrs. Houston said, "and then supper."

When I emerged from the refreshing tub I found a complete outfit of clothing laid out on a big bed resplendent with bright-coloured Hudson's Bay blankets. The clothes fit nicely. I sat down to a sumptuous supper feeling quite presentable. I marvelled again that nearly everyone I had met in small or isolated places along the coast understood what a sea traveller needed. And they had a generosity of spirit to help and share. I thought it must be a real pioneer quality, one that had been, and still was, required for survival.

We relaxed after supper by playing the piano and singing, while Mr. Houston read. Mrs. Houston told me the Hudson's Bay Company had established a trading post there in 1834 and named the port after Aemelius Simpson, an employee who died in 1831.

The monotonous rain gave no indication of letting up, so Mrs. Houston and I tramped through it to the hospital to visit with the nurses and Dr. Gibson. We had a jolly hour and a half, though I thought I did too much of the talking.

The next morning was bright. The air had that special fresh-washed smell as we wandered around the predominantly Native fishing village of about 600 people, reading the inscriptions on family tombstones in many of the front yards. Then we climbed aboard the Hudson's Bay delivery truck for a hair-raising ride to the end of the pier, where Mr. Houston turned with a great flourish and let us out at the top of the slip.

The Houstons, off-duty nurses and some of the Natives put their names on the canoe. Just before I slid *Bijaboji* into the water, the hospital staff presented me with a large sack lunch. It was a glorious pleasure to row across the quiet water of Port Simpson's spacious harbour, then through a passage choked by islets, rocks and shoals just north of Flewin Point and Hogan Island. Dozens of trollers were slowly working this salmon-rich area while I rowed happily and finally crossed the mouth of Portland Inlet. There is something terribly big and uncivilized about the great mountains and expanse of water up the inlet and out into Chatham Sound. The lazy ocean swells rolling into the inlet were broad and rounded. I liked the ease with which *Bijaboji* boldly rode up one side and slid gently and slowly down the other. I enjoyed each minute of the several hours it took me to get from Port Simpson to Wales Island. When well away from the trollers, I discarded my shirt and got almost full benefit of the bright, warm sun. Entry Peak, with its sharp, conspicuous summit, was always before me until I got into Wales Passage in the afternoon.

A couple hours later and still in the passage, I was disturbed by a loud throbbing noise for some time before one of the largest of the cannery tenders bore down on me and stopped right in my path. From the bridge a man called out that a "brass band" was waiting for me at Wales Island Cannery, and he invited me to come aboard and look over the ship. All I can remember of the vessel is that there was a large bathtub—yes, a bathtub—and in the galley oodles of sharp knives. And I cannot forget that the men offered me all possible assistance in getting to Ketchikan. They had stopped just to tell me that. Is it any wonder I love Canadians as I do?

Pearse Canal was calm as I rowed southwestward, looking for the cannery located somewhere along the Wales Island side of the channel. The sun was setting when I squeezed in between the multitude of fish boats in the cove to one side of Wales Island Cannery and pulled the dugout onto a float and between vacant net racks. The Native fishermen smiled and nodded, or gave me friendly hellos as I moved among them while walking ashore to their village.

I knocked at a door to ask the way to the Windsors' and a stout, pleasant Native woman came out. "Adya will show you," she said, then paused. "Are you from the States in a canoe?"

"Yes," I nodded.

"I shake your hand. I am first. It is good luck!" she shouted in her excitement, wringing my hand.

Adya showed me to the home of the Windsors, who had saved a thick T-bone steak for the canoeist's supper. Mr. Windsor had many tales to tell about my grandfather, Will Lowman, a pioneer cannery man. These stories were new family history to me. In between talking we listened to the short-wave radio, as Alaskan tenders notified their canneries of their estimated time of arrival and types and tonnage of salmon. Late in the evening the bookkeeper and Ed Jean, the foreman, called. I was leaning on the porch rail getting my first look at Alaska, just beyond that invisible watery boundary running across the front of the cannery. "Tomorrow I will be on American soil," I exulted, "after two months in the Dominion of Canada."

Ed remembered Will Lowman too. He had been a young kid in Seattle when Will was a legislator and big-time cannery man, but Ed was deported from the States after working there for many years.

Of all the fine, lovely cannery men's wives I met, I believe Mrs. George Windsor was most nearly ideal for her role. There was not an employee, fisherman or cannery worker—white, Native or Japanese—whom she couldn't address by name and recall something about, something showing the kindliest interest in the problems and joys of each family. She was strong, she loved the outdoors and she always preserved a dignity befitting her position.

As Ed, Harry, the Windsors and I were talking, a delegation from Indian Town arrived. There was Mary, the woman who had called me good luck; her husband Steve, a fine, hunched chief who remembered long-ago trading trips to Victoria in 10-man dugout canoes, and Adya. They carried a cedar chest carved with the symbols of the Wolf and Bear clans and embellished with inlays of abalone shell, "a prize to you from all the Bartons of Kincolith on the Nass River for rowing from the States to Wales Island."

The thrill and pride I knew when these Native people presented me with an award for doing what their older relatives and ancestors had done as a matter of course was overpayment for any hardship I had endured in making the trip with limited funds and equipment. I don't recall what I said to express my thanks and appreciation to the Bartons, but surely it was inadequate.

On Sunday morning I ate in the cookhouse with the men. No sooner did I stow away one tasty item than the silent, slim Chinese cook set something else even more delicious before me. After the fourth platter full, I began to wonder how much longer it must go on. Ed Jean rescued me when I was so overloaded with food I couldn't have set out on the morning tide for love or money. So I attended the Native church service that had been advertised for days on posters hung around the cannery. This was the final Sunday the Natives and Japanese would be in the cannery, and the service was to last all day.

Mrs. Windsor and I walked to the village and stood to one side for the fine Salvation Army service. Wearing red-trimmed uniforms, the leaders circled and planted the flag. One of them called the number of a hymn and everyone joined in singing. The Native women in dress-up clothes sat on the front steps, while Native men not taking part in the service occupied their hands with small tasks. To me the outstanding part of the service was the oratorical fire of the young speaker. He spoke only in his native tongue, except for the word *wickedness*, a concept that had not been part of their culture until the missionaries arrived. The sincerity and fire of his delivery was eloquent and inspiring.

The service was still going strong at noon when we returned to the cannery. Again I ate in the cookhouse, with the over-eager Chinese cook anticipating every possible bare spot on my plate. Mrs. Windsor made up a box of food and clothes for me and I tied everything securely into the canoe with yards of cord. John Peters, an American fisherman who was docked at the float, agreed to take my precious cedar chest to Ketchikan on Thursday, the end of the fishing season. Aboard his boat it would be safe and dry—I wasn't so sure about what might happen in my dugout. He was also able to provide me with much-needed local information about the American side of Dixon Entrance and Tongass Passage and Cape Fox.

While Ed Jean held the canoe I stepped out of my skirt, ready for rowing. "Glad you did that," Ed said with a teasing grin, looking at a streak of white skin that had been revealed. "That's the only conclusive proof that you aren't Native."

Somewhere before I reached the Canada–US border, men in a speedboat stopped me. They were obviously not fishermen and it quickly became clear that they were not on any official duty. The leader told me they were patrolling the border and demanded that I come aboard. He asked what I was doing alone in a dugout in those waters, but none of my answers appeared to satisfy him. I was being treated as I'd heard some men treat Native girls, and I began to be afraid. One of the men had dropped into my dugout and was going through my few personal things. Suddenly he climbed aboard and showed a newspaper clipping to the leader, who looked at me, then back at the newspaper picture. He cursed and said a few words to his men. Their demeanour changed abruptly.

"Looks like you're innocent. So we'll let you go, instead of taking you into town."

No apology. No explanation. No help in getting me into my dugout. They just departed at full speed. I suspect they were the rotten type who prey on lone women, especially Native girls. I don't know their nationality. I do know that it was the worst experience on my entire trip, including the shipwreck. Thank God for those Prince Rupert newspaper clippings and photo!

CHAPTER 16

Reunion with Captain Lowman

The water was shiny, the islands black and spotted with yellow fish trap
lights. As she rowed, schools of fish and phosphorescent crawling creatures
scattered from beneath her canoe. She passed fish traps and floating
canneries. In 66 days, she had rowed nearly a thousand miles on her own.
—River Magazine, 1999

THAT AFTERNOON I CROSSED THE BC–ALASKA BOUNDARY with the
expectation of reaching Tree Point lighthouse by dark. This far north,
summer days are long. Softening dusk occurs around 10 p.m., with
darkness enshrouding everything some half or three-quarters of an
hour later. I planned to stop at Tongass Island to inquire if Charlie
Lowman, a long-time resident, might be a relative. His name had
been mentioned a few times on my way north.

The afternoon was young when I rounded the westernmost point
of the mainland and headed into Port Tongass, a small harbour about
400 yards wide formed by the passage between low Tongass Island
and the mainland. A yacht shot out of a cove, dead for me. About 25
yards from *Bijaboji* the engine stopped and *Lazy Lou* drifted quietly
alongside. An attractive curly-haired woman attired in a flattering
blue and white nautical outfit stood on deck near the pilothouse and
waved. "Are you Annette Lowman?"

I nodded and knew immediately she was a Californian. Annette
was the name I had gone by while attending Pomona College.

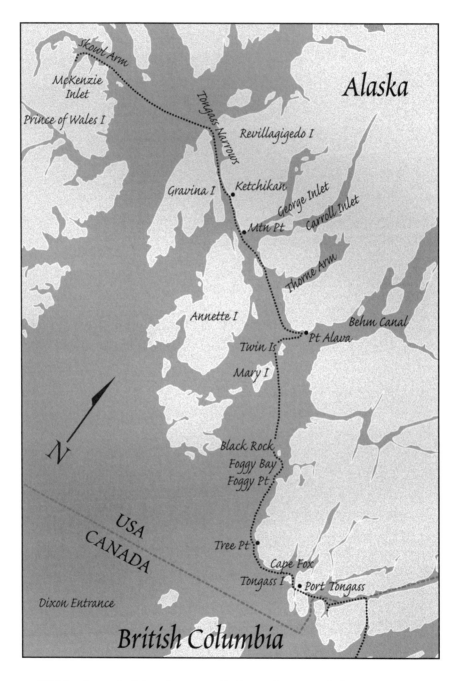

"We've been looking for you all along the coast," she continued, as her husband filmed me in the canoe, amid our spectacular surroundings.

"We had Kathleen Cassady, one of your glee club friends, with us as we came up the coast to Vancouver." She introduced herself as Mrs. Preston, and said that they would be glad to have me ride with them to Ketchikan.

I was too near my goal to accept a lift, and I was eager to have the crossing of Dixon Entrance in my résumé. "Thanks for the offer," I called, "but I'm almost there and I'm going to finish under my own power. We'll meet in Ketchikan."

The Prestons waved, water churned around *Lazy Lou*'s stern and the yacht swung onto a northward course.

I rowed on amidst the ledges and sunken rocks fringing Tongass Island, and drifted awhile, gazing at the weathered totems. What did they represent? Was this part of the record of a civilization without a written history? After a half-hour or so of rowing I saw a floating fish trap silhouetted against the clear blue sky over the vast open Pacific. Fish traps I understood thoroughly. There were two types of these efficient, seasonal salmon traps. Stationary traps were constructed by driving piles the size of telephone poles into the seabed from the shore to seaward some 200 yards. Horizontal braces were added from above the high-tide line to the seabed, and wire net was hung from the frame. When salmon returning from the ocean encountered this obstruction, they swam along it toward deeper water and were led into a maze of nets until they were trapped in the spiller. There they swam until they were brailed into a scow and taken to the cannery. Floating traps, similar in design but without driven pilings, were built by suspending wire net from floating logs, then anchored. The end of the lead was secured to the shore. Both types of traps had watchmen's shacks at the seaward end, and some had a second shack ashore. The watchmen's job was to maintain the traps and prevent fish pirates from stealing the trapped salmon. (Washington state outlawed salmon traps in 1934, and they were used in Alaska until 1958.)

I ran the dugout ashore in a sand and rocky-bottomed cove. I pulled on my ragged skirt before picking my way through tall grass and weeds to a lone log lodge set in a modest clearing. There is some-thing strangely exciting about finding a heretofore unknown relative in an out-of-the-way place. It's like discovering treasure. I'd never heard of a Lowman who was not a relative, so Charlie Lowman and I must be cousins by some disowned great uncle of whom I had not been told. When I was almost at the door, two fat white terriers dashed from around the corner, barking and snapping at my ankles. I froze to the step, not daring to proceed or retreat.

"Maggie! Jiggs! Quiet!" The commanding baritone voice came from inside the cabin. The thick door opened wide and the dogs went quietly to a husky man with silky white hair who nearly filled the doorway.

"I am Betty Lowman. I just came by to learn if we are related."

"Come in," he said, with an easy smile.

The room was surprisingly large. A broad set of elk antlers held four well-oiled guns. Deer antlers and conveniently placed hooks for fishing gear, clothes and kitchen utensils hung from the walls. This was my idea of a frontier bachelor's castle. After much questioning, however, I gave up the cousin idea, even distant cousin. His family branched from Ireland, mine from the German province of Hesse in the 1770s.

I invited Charlie Lowman to partake of my picnic supper, and it took a great deal of urging. Throughout my trip I'd come to believe that all northern people want to do is give, give, give to a stranger stopping by—it's almost a day's job to get one of them to accept any-thing—and Charlie was no exception. Finally he agreed, and put on the coffee pot. I brought in the heavy box of lunch Mrs. Windsor had prepared and we enjoyed every bite of that delicious and ample meal.

"How far is it from here to Cape Fox and Tree Point lighthouse?" I asked between bites of a juicy tomato.

"Five miles to Cape Fox. Three from there to the lighthouse."

"I should easily make it by 10 o'clock tonight. Unless I get into a bad tide like the one down by Addenbroke and make only eight miles all night."

"You won't make even that much if you leave here before the next change of tide." He stepped outside and gazed about for a moment. "It's foggy out there, and Tree Point foghorn won't help you on this side of Cape Fox. And farther along is aptly named Foggy Point."

"That means a night on Tongass Island. Do you have a good hayloft around here?"

"No. No hayloft for you, but a big guest room."

I spent the evening reading, washing clothes and watching the terriers' many tricks. They responded to Charlie with almost human intelligence, seeming to understand every word of his conversation. The dogs were jealous of anyone dividing his attention, and his cow was jealous of strangers.

Charlie set his alarm clock for five o'clock and put it beside the gun rack over his cot. He sent the dogs to their beds before showing me to the guest room, handing me matches at the door to light the lamp for my first sleep in Alaska.

At six o'clock in the morning he rapped on the door. I hustled into my clothes. The lovely aroma of fresh-brewed coffee led me to the kitchen. Charlie was buttering sourdough hotcakes for his dogs. "They eat first, so won't beg at the table." The golden brown hotcakes he flipped off his griddle really did melt in my mouth. Fog still lay thick over the water, so we lingered over breakfast and steaming coffee. Two hours later I was pacing along the shore, watching impatiently for any sign of the fog clearing. Near mid-morning the first green of trees across the passage became discernible through the opalescent fog. I lost no time in putting the canoe in the water and loading it, ready to set out.

"I'll start out with you, get you on the right course," Charlie said. "Looks like the fog may hang around the cape." I thanked him and we exchanged a few more words before he and his two loving dogs climbed into his small powerboat and putt-putted ahead of me toward Cape Fox. Too soon he was swallowed by the relentless fog pocketed between the mainland and Fox Island. The cape was still a few miles ahead. There was no discernible life at the two floating fish traps I passed. On I went into the dense low-lying fog embracing Cape Fox and the waterway along the inhospitable shores of Revillagigedo

Channel and Dixon Entrance. Although I had almost nothing to judge by, I felt that I was making good speed.

I am a poor one to describe the natural beauties of Cape Fox and the coast to Tree Point lighthouse. All I remember is fog so dense that at times I had to look twice to be sure the bow of the canoe hadn't dropped off. The sound and direction of the waves kept me heading up-channel until two anchored boats and a scow loomed suddenly. I was happily surprised to see Charlie in one of the boats.

"You are heading right," he said. "You'll find floating fish traps every few miles along here and a standing trap at Foggy Bay. The fog should lift by noon." After a cheerful wave and a loud "Good luck!" Charlie yanked the starter cord on his outboard and turned his boat toward home. My hearty thanks were drowned out by the noise, and Charlie disappeared into the fog almost immediately.

By noon the fog had thinned a little and I pulled the canoe up on a floating trap. The shack was empty, so I took temporary possession, prepared a lunch and read magazines as I ate. I was startled when a broad-shouldered, bronzed Scandinavian appeared suddenly out of the fog.

"My gawd!" he growled. "Where did you come from?"

"I'm a fish pirate," I said, displaying my sardine sandwich. "I've been lifting your trap. This fog's a great help."

"You'd better come ashore and have some hot coffee with your lunch," he said.

Coffee? Of course — I was back in American territory. No more tea. He introduced himself as Peter Weie and rowed us ashore. There his trap mate, Ed Schlais, an engineering student from Fairbanks, helped me up the rocks and along the bouncy plank walkway to their shack. I'd been fending for myself so long that I hardly knew how to accept his helpful attention. They served coffee and peaches while showing me half a dozen rope doormats they'd made just to pass the time. We talked about the big storm that had swamped me in Douglas Channel. It had also given them two wild and memorable days on the lively floating trap.

Ed gave three cheers because the season would be over in two more days and they could go to town. "I'll take you to the dance in Ketchikan on Saturday night," he offered.

A Saturday night dance — how remote that seemed! I agreed to go, even though I was no dancer.

Peter and Ed rowed beside me to Tree Point lighthouse, though there was no trouble finding it even in the fog, for every three seconds blasts of the diaphone nearly lifted the top off my head. But had I seen anything ahead, I would not have stopped at Tree Point. It looked impossible to land through the boisterous waves leaping and breaking over treacherous rocks. The trap men and I held our boats off the rocks with difficulty while discussing the situation. A keeper saw us and clambered down the slippery rocks to a point where he could leap into Peter's boat. He guided us into a cove where a concrete landing had been built. The helpful trap men said goodbye, and the lighthouse keeper held the dugout while I stepped out.

"We've been on the lookout for you for weeks, and now that I see you, I'm sure I've seen you or your double before." He peered at me. "Are you a Californian?"

"Not by a long ways. But I was there for three years of college."

"Not Pomona, by any chance?"

"Yes, that's right." I looked closely at him but couldn't recall his face.

"Then I *have* seen you. I'm an interior decorator and I did some work there in Bridges Auditorium, about two years ago. I had some military wounds and got into lighthouse work, and I'm liking it well enough." We exchanged reminiscences of Pomona and southern California as we walked to the lighthouse.

We entered the octagonal main floor. The diaphone continued to blare as he explained the machinery, pointing out the notches on revolving wheels that determined the duration of sound and silence of the foghorn. We climbed the square white tower to the light. "We're 86 feet above the sea now," the assistant keeper said. He showed me a special lens that focused and concentrated the light so it could be seen for 15 miles.

"And on a clear day I'll bet the view is great from here."

The head keeper, a kind and quiet Norwegian, was oiling the fog-horn machinery when we descended. He took me to meet his family in one of three large, well-heated, red and white homes. A lush and recently trimmed lawn surrounded the homes and lighthouse. The keepers invited me to stay for cake and coffee. That was tempting, but I wanted to push on. All of them accompanied me to the landing and wrote their names on *Bijaboji*. As I prepared to shove off, the assistant keeper gave me a jar of jelly he had put up.

The fog had thinned just enough to grudgingly yield a mile of visibility all around when I pulled away from the lighthouse. All afternoon I rowed onward, stopping at fish trap after fish trap, accumulating signatures on the canoe. At each stop I asked the distance to Foggy Bay. According to some of the estimates, I was racing backwards. My most dependable, though vague, information came from two fish trap men living ashore in a tent. "Foggy Bay? Oh, that's up ahead."

Several young men and Mr. Rowe, the Fisheries officer, were chatting aboard a Fisheries patrol boat that came near me. They appreciated my lack of charts and were more explicit. "We'd be glad to tow you into Ketchikan," Mr. Rowe said. I declined, with thanks, and he readily understood my determination to finish the trip unaided. "Besides, it'll probably be calm for another day or so."

Calm! All day long *Bijaboji* had been rising and falling, slapping and bounding on the fog-ridden waves. I had tried putting ashore only once because that ride in on the back of a foaming breaker had landed *Bijaboji* too roughly. I was sure it would have cracked and split if it had not been for the oak ribs Bill had fitted shortly after Daddy gave me the dugout. I had decided to be more careful.

As I bounced beside the patrol boat, Mr. Rowe told me that fish pirates in a large boat had tried to run him down the night before. "The fog was so dense I couldn't identify their vessel. But I'm sure they recognized mine."

A few miles farther along another patrol boat approached and the captain shouted, "That's a fine boat you've got!" No one could have said kinder words. The wind wasn't right for my answer to be heard, so I just smiled and waved.

When I reached the standing trap in Foggy Bay, Harold Stephenson and Ben Goodland helped me tie up to the pot scow. I delivered Fishermen's Union cards from Ed Schlais and asked Ben if I might use his cabin farther back in the bay for the night.

"You bet!" Ben said. "We would go along to show you how to get in and build the fire for you if *Eskimo* weren't due here soon to brail salmon."

"May I stay long enough to see the trap brailed?" I was eager to watch that operation, and I might get some first-hand word of my father from *Eskimo*'s captain.

It was dark when *Eskimo*, the bulky cannery tender, arrived from Ketchikan, and nearly midnight when the fascinating work of

Brailing fish from a floating trap into a packer, Alaska, 1937. Betty (at centre, near jumping salmon) helps to pull the net.

transferring thousands of lively silver-sided salmon from the trap to the boat's fish hold was completed. Members of the crew repeatedly tried to persuade me to ride to town on their big boat but I stubbornly refused. John, the excellent cook, put up a big lunch for me and said, "This will be enough to keep you rowing all day." The loaded tender shoved off into the dark.

Harold, Ben and I had not taken time for supper while we waited around for the cannery tender, so Harold set about fixing a midnight snack. Ben put a lump of sugar on his dog's nose and made him hold it there a long time before nodding permission to eat it. I can still remember the expression on the dog's face.

"Dawn is only a few hours off. The wind has died down and I can see the light on the next trap," I chattered as we ate. "I'm just working up enough ambition to row the night out."

"You'll row yourself out," Ben warned. "You'd better have a few hours' sleep here before you go on."

I accepted gratefully and headed for the canoe to get my sleeping bag, planning to unroll it on the platform before the shack. "If I roll off of here in the night, I'll just float down there with any new-caught fish until morning."

But as things worked out, Ben slept on the hard floor of the shack and insisted that I, protesting, occupy the narrow upper bunk. Harold slept on the lower bunk. The men stayed as far away as they could on the trap while I made up my bed of Native blankets and crawled into them. Then Ben and Harold returned, groping in the dark. I felt terrible that their kindness would put Ben on the hard floor. For me, sleeping on boards would have been luxurious comfort after some of the rock piles I had used for mattresses.

I began to laugh, and I laughed uncontrollably. No one could sleep because of my laughing. I couldn't stop thinking of the eyebrows that would go up among all my family and friends at the mere suggestion of a girl spending a night in an eight- by 10-foot fish trap shack with two men and a dog. They wouldn't believe how much safer I was here than some of my college friends were while sitting in parked automobiles with a smooth "date" approved by Mamma and Papa.

Early the next morning Harold rowed beside me to the nearest trap. No smoke. All quiet. The door was shut. Harold told me that a dental student and a schoolteacher were on that trap and I was bound to see what sort of watchmen they might be. We made our boats fast and walked across a sagging plank to the door. Our knock brought forth three groans of sleepy annoyance. Someone pulled the door open and growled. "What do you want?"

Inside, one man slept on the floor and two others in bunks. The faces of the two in the bunks were bushy with black beard. Ah, I thought, grizzlies at last.

As they awoke and sat up, their bare chests were exposed and I was a little worried that they had mistaken me for a boy and were going to dash out for a morning dip. Instead, they said together, "Hello there, Betty. We'd just about given up on seeing you."

From the bunks, one introduced himself as Walter French, the other as Jim Whaley, and the man on the floor as "just another dugout canoeist." He had all his clothes on so he came outside to show off his green-painted dugout while Jim and Walt dressed. He was a Virginian and had bought the dugout for two dollars. In one day he had rowed from Ketchikan to Foggy Bay. I'd say that was a feat, for it took me two and a half days from Foggy Bay to Ketchikan. Of course it was his first lap, and for me it had been the last.

Once I had thought of a morning dip, I had to have one. The day looked fair and warm. Shorts and sweater would dry on me. I took off my skirt and dove in among the trapped fish. The grizzlies Walt and Jim barged out. "What's a da mat? A seal play weeth da feesh and eat wan. Shoot heem!"

I splashed water on them and went on swimming with my head submerged to watch the fish. They swam deeper and deeper and soon I had to resort to diving off the low trap for my fun. Jackknives ended in flops and sprawls so Walt helped me get atop the shack. From there I could dive rather decently. When the swim was over, Walt treated me to a first-rate shampoo with lemon rinse. Jim traded me his rubber-soled sport shoes for my smaller canvas affairs, whose soles had almost completely separated from the tops.

Harold decided it was time to return to Ben and their trap. The Virginian and I checked the visibility and sea conditions and prepared our dugouts for departure in opposite directions.

There were light scattered clouds in the sky but the sun was bright. Revillagigedo Channel was still "calm," but there were threats of fog. "Fog petrifies me," I told Jim. "I guess I'll take a couple of extra days and follow around the mainland to Revillagigedo Island and Ketchikan instead of taking the 14-mile shortcut across open water to Mary Island."

"Why? " Jim said. "Why are you on this trip anyway?"

He seemed truly interested to know and, unlike many others I had met on the way, didn't have a preconceived idea of what had inspired me to it. The other men were holding the boats to keep them from being thrown on the trap by waves, so I didn't have time to give Jim a proper answer. I hinted at love problems.

"Hey, what is this?" Jim said, realizing I was kidding him. "When I have love troubles, I just eat more."

For the first two miles from the trap I rowed from point to point debating whether to take the long or the short way. The Mary Island lighthouse didn't look so far. If a fog did settle down I could get the direction from the foghorn. So I headed away from shore to pass westward of Black Rock and kept on as straight a line as possible between Foggy Bay and Mary Island. Wind and waves were not against me, so when I felt like resting I'd pull in the oars and eat a ham sandwich from the generous lunch given me by John, the cook on *Eskimo*.

No boats passed near. Without a chart, the channel ahead and hills and island were just wooded lumps to me, none so tall or so impressive as those I had seen in Canada. The hours passed in singing and rowing, eating and watching the white structure on Mary Island grow and materialize into a square tower. The keepers' dwellings and other buildings were on the northeast side of the island. By the time I drew even with the tower, the sky was clouded over.

"Are you from the States?" a man hollered.

"That I am."

"There's a landing around the point."

Carpenter MacDonald and another man met me there and lifted the canoe onto a small rail car. It was easily pulled to a shed.

"I was told to say hello to the O'Connors here. Are they around?"

"Yes, they're over at the hog shooting," MacDonald said. "I'll lead the way."

We headed toward the edge of the woods, but we had missed the shooting, and thousands of gnats made it too unpleasant to stay long watching the butchering process. Mrs. O'Connor took me to their large house for a hearty supper. After that she showed me through the new light tower, almost completed, and introduced me to the workmen. Returning to the house, I met Mr. Harris, who was responsible for much of the excellent Alaskan lighthouse construction. Mrs. O'Connor was an outstanding hostess who wasn't content just to arrange fine meals. She saw to it that I had a hot bath and a lovely bed. She also wanted to load me up with supplies of all sorts, but I was too near the end of my trip to accept more of her generosity.

I wished I could linger at Mary Island, but with only another day of rowing separating me from my goal, excitement urged me on. How would Daddy greet me? Would he chide the life out of me about my disaster in Douglas Channel?

Those were some of the thoughts that played around in my head as I pulled away from Mary Island under the chill, unpleasant drizzle on Wednesday morning, August 18, 1937. I was confident of reaching Annette Island by noon, and Ketchikan before dark. I could barely believe that this was the last full day of my vacation. I didn't want the trip to end. There could never be anything like it again in my life. I was sure of that.

My wish to prolong the trip was granted in the most logical way a mile or so west of Twin Islands. In that wide channel between the small Twin Islands and Annette Island I was suddenly enveloped in as soupy a Scotch mist as anyone has ever got lost in. All around was whiteness—whiteness and dull, lazy, confused waves holding no particular direction. I rowed on and on. The waves gradually relaxed. It was only when I passed an easily identifiable piece of driftwood for the third time in what I guessed was an hour that I realized I'd lost all sense of direction—and gave up.

No sensible person wastes energy rowing in a fog. In a small boat without a reliable compass, one hasn't a chance. I now realized that I had been exceedingly lucky while crossing Queen Charlotte Strait.

I pulled in the oars and selected a box of cheese snacks from the bounteous supplies Mrs. Windsor had given me. I wished I had a good book, for it might be hours or days before the fog lifted or help could reach me. Exhaustion and the lulling roll of the dugout finally put me to sleep.

I awoke damp, chilled and stiff from sleeping in the cramped canoe. A wave broke into the canoe, quickly followed by another. The tide was changing. The flood was charging in from Dixon Entrance and through Revillagigedo Channel. Where was I? At least the incoming tide was carrying me shoreward.

The bailing can served its purpose until my situation was under control. I visualized myself—all too vividly, as the water roughened quickly—again towing a swamped canoe that wouldn't rise on the waves. Then I was embarrassed by the thought that if anything should happen here in this home stretch, Jim Whaley would remember my little story and think I was the least bit serious.

I choked and shivered and wished the waves wouldn't jostle me so. There was only one thing to do: row with the tide and wind. In that direction the canoe moved with least effort. And I was warmer when rowing than just sitting. After what seemed an eternity, I nearly smashed into the fog-wrapped Kasaan trap near Point Alava, on the north side of the entrance to Behm Canal. I had rowed and drifted about six miles northeast from Mary Island, instead of going northwest to Annette Island, my destination.

The two young men at the trap made the canoe fast, ordered me into dry clothes and shared their noon breakfast of French toast. One was Jim Chevalier, tall, lean and curly-haired. The other was Lee Steadman from Utah, handsome, purposeful and tanned. Lee was a philosopher, a scholar, a romantic, yet hard and practical about the things at hand. He told me that during one sunny day on the college campus in Utah he had been overwhelmed by the sensation that "my destiny lies in the far north." Never one to have a feeling like that and not act upon it, Lee sold his car and bought a one-way ticket to Alaska. Since then, he'd been a trapper, a logger and a commercial fisherman, he'd worked on pile drivers and now on a fish trap.

I asked him about fish pirates and he said that pirates must have some encouragement from trap watchmen before they would steal the fish. "None of them like this trap," he explained crisply. "Also, rough water makes this one too dangerous. Even our own tenders won't come alongside and brail half the time."

Later in the afternoon, while the fog still hung heavy, I was lying on Lee's bunk reading, Jim was reading in the bunk above and Lee sat on the coal box poking at a sizzling roast. Over the stove hung my Native blanket, sou'wester and wettest clothes tied with cord in grotesque shapes to dry most effectively.

"Maybe you can help Jim and me with something we've tried to figure out all the time we've been here," Lee said. "What is love?"

What a question to ask me! "That bowls me over, Lee. My heart has never really been touched. I wouldn't begin to define love."

"The only idea we've got is that love is psychic harmony."

"I would like love to be that. It suggests that a greater being fashions each of us to harmonize with another and somehow the two must get together by predestination."

Lee said, "A woman is a success when she has been loved, envied and hated."

"That puts me on the failure rack. Few men or women would bother to hate me because the things I enjoy and do are not explicitly feminine. None would envy me because I do not excel at the things a girl is expected to excel at, and so far as love goes I am two weeks over 23 years old and have never been kissed in the moonlight."

The topic died from lack of knowledgeable participants.

Our early supper was something to remember. Lee loaded my plate with a thick slice of roast beef, sweet potatoes, string beans and other vegetables. "You need something that will stick to your bones," he said. "And if you intend to reach Ketchikan tonight you'll need money for a hotel room. Here's two dollars and some dry socks."

"Thanks, Lee. I'll pay you back—sometime. Right now I don't know when."

The fog was clearing gradually. Purse seiners passed, heading full speed for Ketchikan. The two men helped me load up and I rowed on, moving from trap to trap. It was almost a dead calm around the point from Lee and Jim. I crossed the mile-wide entrance to Thorne Arm. The islands ahead were well-defined and I had the feelings of six holidays rolled into one, for only 15 miles ahead lay Ketchikan, and beyond that Daddy, on the cannery tender *Una Mae*.

At the next Kasaan Canning Company salmon trap I stopped to get more signatures on the canoe. The lone watchman and I were chatting when a patrol boat came alongside with the other watchman. A man and his wife were also on the boat and they gave me a huge piece of fresh cake slathered with thick chocolate frosting.

"Everyone along here will be in town by tomorrow," the lady said. "All trap fishing is over tonight." The boat was slowly pulling away when she called, "They're expecting you in town."

What was she talking about? Few people in Ketchikan even knew me and no one knew where I was.

I rowed on and on and on. The islands were black and the water was polished ebony, spotted only by a few yellow kerosene trap lanterns. Schools of fish scattered under the canoe like myriad speeding phosphorescent creatures. The lights of Ketchikan did not appear. I sang lustily and rowed as quietly as possible, just to puzzle trap watchmen, who might think I was one of the legendary Sirens. Or a mermaid.

At one trap with brightly lit windows, I decided to give the men a real start. With long, quiet strokes I propelled the canoe toward the light, and as I came alongside I sang a lusty round of "Bow Down to Washington." I was crushed when the two watchmen casually greeted me, "We feel that way too. We're from Bellingham."

Because it was 10 o'clock and Ketchikan was still about four hours away, I asked to sleep inside a shed at the back of that Libby, McNeil

& Libby fish trap and go on when I could see my way. The men readily gave permission so I hauled the Cocoon to the shed and slept.

The sky was coming alive with a new day when I awoke on Thursday, August 19. A light fog lay over the water. All fish trap operations had ceased for the season. This was the last day that packers and other boats would be busy working in these waters, and the watchmen would be going to town. After a hearty breakfast I got an early start for Ketchikan. The dugout seemed to move slowly. Around me, broad-beamed wooden scows, loaded with the season's final catch of silvery salmon, pushed aside water and foam as they were towed to the various canneries by sturdy diesel-powered cannery tenders. On many fish traps, men were busy cutting down the wire leads, releasing the salmon to continue their one-way swim to the spawning rivers and streams. I didn't stop and bother any of these active men. *Bijaboji* was now making good time. This is like a racer, I thought, getting his second wind when approaching the finish line. We crossed the entrance to George and Carroll inlets and left Mountain Point behind. Purse seiners overtook *Bijaboji* quickly then disappeared in the East Channel of Tongass Narrows.

Swarms of biting, stinging gnats clustered on my bare legs and I frequently had to stop rowing to flail my arms and a damp towel at them. Soon we were in Tongass Narrows. Ketchikan's mile of wharfs, hillside of residences and radio towers were before me. At Thomas Basin, a small boat harbour lying off the mouth of Ketchikan Creek, I found *Lazy Lou* and the Prestons. After a few words with them I rowed on past the sawmill and canneries to the Forestry float. There, my hometown Anacortes neighbours Don Wright and Bonce McCallum, now of the *Ketchikan Chronicle*, plus Emery Tobin of the *Alaska Sportsman* magazine, met me. Daddy was not among them.

"Your father is in Skowl Arm," Don Wright said. "He was here with the *Una Mae* a few days ago, and probably won't return for a couple of weeks."

There was no hiding my disappointment. It had been a wonderful vacation, but it wouldn't be complete until I was with Daddy. Skowl Arm is 30 miles from Ketchikan and the skipper of a cannery

The proud and happy canoeist pulls into Ketchikan, Alaska, after 66 days and some 1,300 miles.

tender comes to town only when his boat or the cannery needs fuel and supplies.

"We will be happy if you stay with us," Don said. "And we've got your good clothes sent by your mother."

I had no idea that my vacation trip had been so well publicized until Don Wright told me that the theatre manager had called asking permission to put *Bijaboji* on display in front of the theatre and offered to pay me for speaking to his audiences on Friday and Saturday. This was a wonderful and welcome surprise. My financial situation was such that I could not say no. With the clothes Mother had sent, I would be presentable. Each night I gave a speech about a half-hour long and then took questions from the audience. I was flattered by the good turnout at each speech, and the theatre manager was well pleased.

The four days that I stayed with the Wrights were bursting with action. On Saturday the manager of the local radio station asked me to speak about my trip and gave me an opportunity to broadcast my thanks to the Canadians for their outstanding hospitality, kindness and generosity during my marvellous two months along the extraordinary coast and inlets of British Columbia.

On Saturday night I went to the dance with Ed Schlais. The stag line looked like an Anacortes reunion. Lee Steadman was there, and although he protested, I repaid the two dollars he had given me a few days earlier.

The mayor and his family invited me to go on a picnic. We got back to town just in time to meet my brothers Jack and Bob, homeward bound from Yakutat on Captain Wright's *Retriever*, a floating cannery.

Then I simply had to see Daddy.

There was always my trusty and seaworthy canoe. I prepared to go out Tongass Narrows, cross Clarence Strait, then cross the south end of Kasaan Bay and enter Skowl Arm. Even late summer storms were not going to deter me. But a Pacific American Fisheries cannery tender gave me a lift and I reached Skowl Arm at midnight. The *Una Mae* happened to be in that night. Daddy was asleep, but Chet Blackinton, one of the crew, was awake and told me which cabin Daddy was in.

I poked my head in the window. "Hello, Daddy."

"Who's there?"

"It is I."

"Oh, Buddy! Hello! How did you get here?"

"In my little red canoe on a big boat."

By then Daddy was dressed and outside. Our hug lasted for a long time. Many lights were on at the home of the Buschmanns, owners of the salmon cannery, so we walked to their home. The women of the

Betty and her father pose in front of the Una Mae. *Although she defied him, he was proud of his willful and adventurous daughter.*

family were making candy, and Lorraine Buschmann invited me to stay with her for a while.

For the next month I visited back and forth between Skowl Arm and Ketchikan while the *Una Mae* towed fish traps and scows and other equipment into McKenzie Inlet from distant locations on Prince of Wales Island. I tried to reconstruct the notes I had lost in Douglas Channel and write letters to the many Canadian friends I wished to thank for their generous hospitality and kind help.

Then, on one of those rare, clear and sunny days in the middle of September, the *Una Mae* pulled away from Skowl Arm cannery. Her whistle blew lustily three times in farewell salute. A whistle from the cannery blared three times in return, and as the echoes ricocheted between the wooded hills, a great glad-sadness overwhelmed me. Home and Mother were ahead. The most glorious vacation I could ever have was behind me. And along the coast from Pomona College in California to Kasaan, Alaska, I had added links in a chain of friends who gave so generously of their wisdom, fellowship and fun, and to whom I can never give enough. Each of those persons helped me to row the length of the British Columbia coast plus numerous excursions into glorious inlets, passages and bays. I calculated that my delightful trip had covered at least 1,300 miles, twice my planned distance.

Such a unique vacation is not to be valued with silver or gold.

EPILOGUE

Bijaboji— The Next Sixty Years

MY TRIP TO ALASKA WITH *BIJABOJI* changed the course of my life more than I could ever have dreamed.

Due to unanticipated newspaper and radio publicity, I was frequently invited to be the featured speaker at service clubs and other organizations. In 1938 I visited Alaska again, this time as a representative of the Seattle Chamber of Commerce. In 1939 when I went back, I met General Wood, advisor to President Roosevelt, and Colonel William "Wild Bill" Donovan, later the first head of the OSS.

My interest in writing about the commercial fishing industry led me to work as a reef net fisherman in Puget Sound in 1938. I was elected a delegate to the convention of the United Fishermen's Union of the Pacific, in San Pedro, California. In July 1937 I fished aboard a halibut schooner in the Gulf of Alaska.

After resuming my job as a waterfront reporter for the *Anacortes Mercury*, I met officers and crew members of numerous foreign ships docking at Anacortes. Many of these men and ships could not return to their home ports in European countries after war started in September 1939. I encountered some of them again in Halifax, the great Allied outpost, during the summer of 1940. Other ships and merchant men I had known were already lost at sea.

In early 1940 I was invited to help crew *Thunderbird*, a 43-foot Cape Breton schooner built on the lines of the famous *Bluenose*. Candidates for the male crew had been called into Canadian military service, and the owner, Jack Shark, resorted in desperation to a female crew—Mavis

Wilcox of Vancouver, BC, and myself. We were to sail from Lunenburg, NS, along the Atlantic coast, through the Panama Canal, and to Vancouver. "There won't be any war in the Pacific," Jack assured us. After weeks of preparation we sailed into the Atlantic and three nights later, during a storm, we were wrecked on an offshore island near the fishing village of Seal Harbour. Jack returned to work in a Yukon gold mine. Mavis and I walked and hitchhiked 125 miles to Halifax.

There I found work as a waitress in a waterfront café while Mavis searched for a better job. We became Halifax's first "Gas Gals," working at a Texaco station near the Citadel. Convoys of ships came and went from the harbour, and wounded men and damaged vessels were common sights. I went aboard Norwegian whaling ships that had escaped from the Antarctic, also a few of the 50 overage US Navy four-stack destroyers that steamed into Halifax to be turned over to the Royal Navy in exchange for bases in Bermuda. Halifax was crowded with servicemen from many Allied nations.

In November 1940 I departed Halifax by ship to Boston, where I visited friends I had met in Alaska. Then the long train ride to Seattle. While waiting to change trains in Chicago I met Neil G. Carey, of the USS *Colorado*.

In the spring of 1941 I signed a two-year contract with National School Assemblies to speak at schools, universities and civic groups throughout the western States about my experiences at sea and in Halifax. I was in Arizona on December 7 when Pearl Harbor was attacked, and nearly home for Christmas when I learned that *Colorado* was in Bremerton, Washington, the only Pacific Fleet battleship not at Pearl. Neil and I were married the day after Christmas. Too soon he left for the South Pacific and I returned to the lecture circuit. Although gasoline was rationed, the Treasury Department determined that my speeches contributed to the war effort and authorized all the gasoline and tires required to drive approximately a thousand miles a week.

Neil was ordered to Washington, DC, early in 1943. I drove out to meet him after completing my spring contract, then we drove to US Naval Training Station, Farragut, Idaho, where Neil was a gunnery instructor. Our sons George and Gene were born during the war. I was now a mother and navy wife, following Neil to west coast ports, to Hawaii and, during the Korean War, to Japan.

During those years I augmented my journalism degree with graduate work at the University of California, Berkeley, and the University of British Columbia.

Neil resigned his commission in August 1953 and we prepared to search for a home in an isolated area of the Northwest. In June 1954 the four of us set out in an outboard-powered 19-foot Grand Banks codfish dory to circumnavigate Vancouver Island, camping ashore at night and exploring by day. After 91 days we decided the island was too crowded for us.

In May 1955 we departed Anacortes in our dory, destined for the remote Queen Charlotte Islands. The Charlottes lived up to their misty reputation—during July we saw the sun only as a white orb through mist, fog and rain. But we did find two lovely isolated sites on the west side of Moresby Island during our 120-day exploration.

Seven years later, our son Gene and I loaded *Bijaboji* aboard *Skeena Prince* at Prince Rupert and crossed to Jedway, an iron mining camp on Moresby Island. Our plan was to revisit the two possible home sites we had seen in 1955. Contractors working on St. James Island were short-handed and Gene was shanghaied, so I continued alone to Gilbert Bay, one of our chosen sites. After camping overnight amidst the weathered totems of Ninstints, a hauntingly beautiful abandoned Haida village on Anthony Island, I headed northward along Kunghit Island's magnificently rugged west coast to the lagoon that we later leased and named Puffin Cove. I then went on to Tasu Sound, where exploratory drilling was being conducted. The modern iron and copper mining town of Tasu was just starting to be developed. *Bijaboji* and I ended our trip at Sandspit, site of the Charlottes' airport.

In April 1963 we met the Forestry Vessel *Hecate Ranger* in Masset, which took us around the Charlottes to stake the two home sites. Of the eight people aboard, Neil and I were the only ones who had seen the Charlottes' west coast.

We left *Hecate Ranger* in Prince Rupert. Neil returned to California; I stayed in the north and a few weeks later *Bijaboji* and I commenced

Betty Lowman Carey and Bijaboji *three decades later, leaving the ancient Haida Village of Ninstints, Queen Charlotte Islands —now a World Heritage Site. Even after she became a grandmother, Betty continued to explore and enjoy British Columbia's magnificent coast.*

the return trip from Ketchikan to Anacortes. I was 49 years old, and I took no rides and few side trips. By working the tides I sometimes covered as much as 40 miles a day. The scenery was as magnificent as ever and the weather was just as full of surprises for this canoeist without a watch, compass or radio. Changes had occurred during the intervening 26 years. There were fewer handloggers and A-frame logging camps. Many salmon canneries had been abandoned. Japanese people, afloat or ashore, were rare since the internment during the war. Shipping traffic had increased so greatly that I was seldom out of sight of one or more vessels. Tugs were now more likely to be towing barges than log booms.

In 1964 Neil and I departed from Anacortes in a 26-foot converted World War II lifeboat, loaded with tools and other items we would need to build a small home. We also carried *Bijaboji* aboard, as our shore boat. We had arranged to have materials for a pre-cut home shipped to Sandspit. Our sons arrived by air in time to help clear our lot and pour a concrete foundation. The building materials were late, so Neil returned to work and the boys and I put our small cabin together in a day. They then returned to their universities in Arizona and California.

By mid-summer of 1965 Neil had completed his naval reserve service, resigned his position at the Naval Missile Test Center, Point

Betty and Bijaboji *at the Sandspit airport where the little red canoe is now on permanent display.*

Mugu, California, and had come to Sandspit. We commenced nearly 30 years of cruising around the Charlottes in all months and began building a cabin at Puffin Cove, which was better than any cabin I had seen or envisioned during my dugout canoe trips. We had a grand view of the North Pacific from our well-sheltered lagoon.

During our years of cruising the Charlottes we transported scientists from Canada, Europe and India, as well as sport fishermen. We even rescued a stranded hiker. Two US TV stations and two CBC film crews documented our activities for TV.

I continued to take trips with *Bijaboji* along the ragged coasts of the Charlottes. In the fall of 1993, when both of us were in our seventies, we left Puffin Cove and our life at sea. We had enjoyed nearly three decades of life free of crowded highways and tight schedules, but full of varied activity and endless surprises. *Bijaboji* and I made short trips until the spring of 1999, when the manager of the Sandspit Airport asked if I would allow *Bijaboji* to be displayed in the new air terminal and visitors' reception centre for a couple of weeks. Now, four years later, my dugout is still there, attracting and delighting passengers coming and going from the Charlottes.

All of this has happened because as a teenager I had an overwhelming desire to get to Alaska, and my father gave me the best birthday present of my life—*Bijaboji*, a superb Indian dugout and, to me, the world's best and most beautiful sea-going vessel.

Index

.22 pistol, 21, 26, 36, 37, 38, 54

Aaltanhash Inlet, 183
Addenbroke, 148–149, 154, 256
Addenbroke Lighthouse, 148, 177
Agamemnon Channel, 13, 40–41, 43, 45, 47, **48**, 49, 51, 53, 55
Alaska Life, 29, 150
Alaskan lighthouse construction, 265
Alaskan–Pacific Airways, 156
Alert Bay, 72, 93, 97–98, 100, 102–103, 109, 112, 116, 118–119, 121, 126, 176
Allison Harbour, 105, 113, 116, 132, 134, 136–137, 141
Alpine Fir, 196–197, 202, 204–206, 243
Anacortes, 15, 18–19, 27, 36, 53–54, 93, 108, 201, 208, 237, 269, 271, 276–278
Anacortes Mercury, 102, 274
Anderson, Alfred, 219–220
Anderson, Helen 70, 71
Anderson, Peter 70
Andrew Foss, 180
Annette Island, 265–266
Anthony Island, 276
Associated Press, 240
Atrevida Reef, 66
Avon, Wash., 156

Baker Inlet, 226
Barrymore, John, 223
Beaver Cannery, 147–148, 150
Behm Canal, 266
Bella Bella, 140, 146, 150, 156–157, 159–160, 164–166, 168, 176, 197, 222
Bella Bella Mission Hospital, 146, **165**, 197
Bella Coola, 222
Bellingham, Wash., 19–20, 268
Bellingham Channel, 19–20
Bijaboji, **25**, **37**, **66**, **121**, **144**, **213**, **277**, **270**, **278**
Big Bay, 247
Black Rock, 264
Blubber Bay, 44, 61
Bluenose, 274
Blunden Bay, 136
Blunden Harbour, 129–130, 159
Boat Harbour, 33, 269
Boathouse Harbour, 148, 154
Boswell Cannery, 140
Boundary Pass, 29
Boxer Reach, 189
Boy Scouts, 22, 39, 85, 99, 102, 118
Bramham Island, 135
British Columbia Coast Pilot, 75, 90, 92, 106, 182
Brunswick Cannery, 140, 145–146
Bucknell, Roy, 36, 39, 156
Bull Harbour, 92, 94

Burnett Bay, 136

Bute Inlet, 85, 142

Butedale, 170, 183–185, 187–188, 194, 201, 212

Butedale Cannery, 184, 188

California, 62, 68, 148, 159, 195, 253, 259, 273–274, 276, 278–279

Calm Channel, 84–85

Calvert Island, 141, 148–149, 151

Camp Point, 216

Canadian Home Journal, 215

Canoe Rock, 137, 139, 141

Cape Breton, 274

Cape Caution, 123, 132, 134, 136

Cape Fox, 252, 256–258

Cardena, 103, 157, 176–177, 183, 188

Casper, Herman, 51

cedar chest, 250–251

Chancellor Channel, 89, 91

Charlotte Bay, 105–106, 109–110, 132, 134

Chatham Sound, 237, 245–246, 248

Chatterbox Falls, 52

Chinook, 138

Chinook language, 158

Church, Captain Art, 35, 46, 51, 112

Clarence Strait, 271

Claxton Cannery, 218, 231–232

Coast Guard,
American, 15, *74*, 79–80, 108
Canadian, *74, 77, 79*

Coghlan Anchorage, 216

Columbia, 112, 113, **114**, 140

Codville, Annie, 157–**158**, 159, 160

Codville, Ben, 157–**158,** 159, 160

Cone Island, 175

Copeland Islands, 68

Coqualeetza Indian Institute (residential school), 190

Cordero Channel, 89

Cormorant Island, 100

Cortes Island, 68–69, 71–72, **73**, 84
Squirrel Cove, 62, 68, 72, **73**, 79, 85

Costello, Dolores, 223

Crab River, 190

Customs and Immigration, 20, 34–35, 37

Cypress Island, 18, 20–21

Daily Colonist, 69, 84, 216

Daily News, 240, 247

Daily Province, 191, 232

Darby Channel, 148

Deer Passage, 84

Deserters Group, 104

Desolation Sound, 71

Devastation Channel, 189–190, 194–195

Dixon Entrance, 245–246, 252, 255, 258, 266

Dodd Narrows, 32–33

Dominion Day (July 1), 89, 249

Douglas Channel, 165, 196–197, 201–203, 205, 207, 209, 211, 213–215, 219, 229, 233, 239, 258, 265, 273

Darby, Dr George, 132–133, 135, 137, 139, 140, 141–150, 160–161, 164, 165

Drayton, Steve 61, 62, 63, 64, 75,

77–78, 82–83

Drayton, Walt 61–62

Drumlummon Bay, 197, 199, 203

Dundas, 245

Earhart, Amelia, 97, 107, 119, 122, 134–135, 198, 208, 228, 245

Eskimo, 261, 264

Eva Point, 195

F.K., 95, 98, 101

False Egg Island, 137

Finlayson Channel, 175

Finlayson Island, 247

Fisheries Department, 223, 228

Fisheries Patrol, 183, 185, 260

fishing,
  purse seine, 72, 101, 103, 122, 124, 136, 179, 183, 213

Fitz Hugh Sound, 141, 148–151, 153–155, 157, 159, 161, 163, 165, 167, 169

Five Cone Islands, 20

Flewin Point, 248

Florence Steele (Flo), 19–24, 26–29, 31–40, 43, 45–54, 66, 75, 97, 103, 113, 122, 147, 190, 271

Foch Lagoon, 197, 203, 205, 210

Foggy Bay, 258, 260–261, 263–264

Foggy Point, 257

Fourth of July, 104, 107–108, 111

Fraser Reach, 187, 189

Fraser River, 138, 190

Garden Bay, 54, 56–57, 59, 61, 63, 65, 67, 177

Gardner Canal, 185, 187–189, 191,

193–195, 197, 199

Gibson Island, 230

Gillard Pass, 89

Gilttoyees Inlet, 203

Godfrey (Captain), 112

Goose Bay, 138, 141–142, 145, 155

Graham Reach, 180, 182–183

Greene Point Rapids, 89

Grenville Channel, 164, 194, 197, 201, 214–216, 218, 223–226, 228–230

Coast Guard, 74, 77, 79–80, 108

Grey Rock, 41

Grief Point, 60

Guemes Channel, 18

Guemes Island, 18–19

Gulf of Alaska, 274

Gunboat Passage, 161

Haida (First Nations), 143, 235, 244, 276–277

Hakai Passage, 154

Halliburton, Richard, 86

Hammond Bay, 40, **42**

Hartley Bay, 212, 218

Harwood Island, 65

Hawkesbury Island, 195

Hecate Ranger, 276

Henry Island, 18

Hernando Island, 61

State of Hesse, Germany, 256

Hiekish Narrows, 180

Híkusam, 95, **96**

Hogan Island, 248

Hoop Bay, 136

Horan, Jack, 141, 145–146, 148, 155–156, 176

Hudson's Bay Company, 223, 248
Hume, Don, 33
Hurtado Point, 67

Indian Cove, 136
Indian Reserves, 58, 130
Inside Passage, 18, 66, 108, 128,
    207
Inverness Cannery, 177, 233–234
Irene R., 50, 54
Irvines Landing, 44
Ivory Island, 166–167

Jackson Passage, 169, 173–174,
    176
Japanese Fishermen, 99, 193
Jervis Inlet, 13, 39, 46–48, 50, 57,
    59
Johns Island, 23–24
Johnstone Bluff, 85
Johnstone Strait, 91, 98, 100, 117,
    194
Jones Cove, 136
Juan de Fuca Strait, 15, 23

Kaien Island, 237, 239
Kasaan, 266, 268, 273
Kasaan Canning Company, 268
Kassan Bay, 271
Kelly Raft, 80, 82
Kelly, Dr. Peter, 143
Kelsey Bay, 92, 98–99
Kemano, 212
Ketchikan, 13, 18, 62, 127, 160,
    165, 219, 234, 245–246, 249, 251,
    255, 259–261, 263–265, 268–270,
    273, 277

Ketchikan Creek, 269
Khutze Inlet, 183
Kildala Cannery, 144
Kincolith, 250–251
Kitamaat Village, 191
Kitgore, 212, 214–215, 219
Kitimat, 191, 196–198, 204, 206,
    212, 214
Kitimat Arm, 197
Klekane Inlet, 187
Klemtu, 168–169, 173, 175–176,
    179, 207, 229
Klewnuggit, 220, 224–226, 229
Klewnuggit Inlet, 224–225
Klewnuggit Light, 225
Koeye River, 154
Kumealon Inlet, 226
Kuper Island, 32
Kwan Lamah, 23
Kxngeal Inlet, 226

Lake Como III, 122, 124–125
Lama Passage, 157, 159, 165
Lasqueti Island, 39, 43, 147
Lazy Lou, 255, 269
Leaping Lena, 80
Lee, Mrs., 46–47
Lewis Channel, 72, 75, 84
Lewis Rocks, 129
logging,
    A-frame, 72, 170–172, 195,
        278
    Davis Raft, see also Kelly Raft
        80, **81**
Lord Tweedsmuir, 198, 222, 244
Lowe Inlet, 215, 218, 224, 227–229,
    240

Lowman, Charlie ("Daddy"), 16, 18, 38, 64, 74, 136, 155–156, 163, 168, 184, 207, 213, 222, 227, 232, 240, 245, 260, 265, 268–269, 271–272, 253, 256

Lund, 66–67, 69

Lunenburg, 274

McConnell, Rev. F., 197, 198, 199, 200

Macdonald, James "Mac", 52

Maclean's, 212

Maisonville, Shorty, 123, 125, 130

Haddock (Major), 50–51, 54

Malaspina Hotel, 34, 35

Malaspina Inlet, 71

Malaspina Peninsula, 68

Malaspina Strait, 13, 59

Malcolm Island, 121, 124, 127, 213

Mary Island, 264–266

Mathieson Channel, 163, 167, 169, 173, 241

McCracken Point, 18

Metlakatla, 246

Milbanke Sound, 166–168, 175

missionaries, 126–127, 196–197, 251

Moresby Island, 29, 276

Mount Baker, 18

Mount Vernon, 159

Mountain Point, 269

Mussel Inlet, 170

Nakwakto Rapids, 105–106, 109, 132

Namu, 128, 155–156, 164

Nanaimo, 20, 22, 27, 32, 34–35, 38, 40, 42, 46, 147

Nanaimo Free Press, 38, 40

Nass River, 235, 250

National Geographic Society, 126

Native Graveyard, 101

Native Villages, 72, 95, 130, 156, 160, 168, 198, 212, 214

Nelson Island, 13

Nettle Basin, 219, 224

Nimpkish Hotel, **117**

Ninstints, 276–277

Nose Point, 29

Numas Island, 128–129

Obstruction Pass, 21

Ocean Falls, 160–164, 207

Office of Strategic Services (OSS), 274

Ogden Channel, 229, 231

Olga (summer resort), 21

Orcas Island, 20–21

Pacific American Fisheries, 271

Pacific Fleet Battleship, 275

Payne, Mel, 90

Pearl Harbor, 275

Pearse Canal, 249

Pender Harbour, 13, 43, **44**, 45, 51–52, 54, 141

Peterborough Canoe, 61

Petersburg, 54

Pine Island, 98, 100–101, 140

Pioneer Square, 235

Pitt Island, 216, 225–226, 229, 231

Point Alava, 266

Pointer Island Lighthouse, 157–158

Poison Cove, 170

Pomona College, 39, 53, 129, 190, 253, 273

Port Kusam, 91–92, 101

Port Simpson, 235, 245–248

Port Tongass, 253

Portland Canal, 245

potlatch, 114

Powell River, 59–61, 63–65, 68, 75, 77, 87, 162, 164, 181

Powell River News, 64–65

Prince of Wales Island, 273

Prince of Wales Reach, 47

Prince Rupert, 138, 159, 164, 173, 176, 178, 183, 185, 201, 206, 212, 233, 235, 237, 239–242, 245–246, 252, 276

Prince Rupert Daily Province, 232

Prince Rupert Yacht club, 178, 236

Princess Louisa Inlet, 34, 50, 99

Princess Royal Island, 170, 180–181

prohibition, 80

Pryce Channel, 85

Puffin Cove, 276, 279

Puget Sound, 16, 23, 36, 53–54, 68–69, 92, 131, 140, 168, 274

Pulteney Point, 104, 123–125, 127–128

Quadra Island, 93

Queen Charlotte Islands, 137, 235, 244, 276

Queen Charlotte Sound, 64, 85, 90, 122, 127, 132, 135, 138, 155, 158

Queen Charlotte Strait, 98, 101–102, 104, 113, 116–119, 121–125, 127–129, 131–132, 140, 159, 266

Queens Reach, 50

Reade, Gordon, 160

Redcliff Point, 184

Reid Passage, 167

Rendezvous Islands, 85

Revillagigedo Channel, 264, 266

Richards, "Scoop," 65

Ripple Passage, 104

Rivers Inlet, 127, 137–138, 140–143, 145, 155, 234, 243

Robinson Island, 130

Roosevelt, President, 274

Royal Northwest Mounted Police, 113

Safety Cove, 141

Salmon River, 95, 100

Saltspring Island, 29

Sandspit airport, 279

Sarah Island, 179–180

Sarah Point, 68, 71

Saturday Evening Post, 80

Savary Island, 67

Schooner Channel, 105, 148

Schooner Passage, 141, 148

Scotch Mist, 19, 197, 265

Scots, 31–32, 78, 119, 146

sea anemones, 30, 92

sea lions, 149, 193

sea urchins, 92

Seaforth Channel, 166, 168

Seal Harbour, 275

seal, "Christopher," 21, 24

Seattle, 22, 36, 39, 54, 85, 91, 116, 125, 156, 158–159, 180, 191, 235, 249, 275

Seattle Chamber of Commerce, 274

Seattle Star, 158, 237

Sechelt, 45, 56, 176

Sechelt Peninsula, 45

Seymour Inlet, 104, 106, 109, 127

Seymour Narrows, 61

Seymour River, 109

Seymour the Kidnapper, 199, 203

Shaw Island, 21, 23

Sherman, 215, 218–220, 225

Shields, Billy, 56, 59, 177

Sidney W., 179, 229, 231–232

Skagit County, 156

Skagway, 159

Skeena River, 99, 177, 227–228, 230–231, 234

Skowl Arm, 18–19, 125, 245, 269, 271, 273

Sliammon, 65–66

Slingsby Channel, 112, 114, 140

Smith, Barney, 62, 64, 75–76, 82

Smith Inlet, 85, 89, 97, 101, 132, 136–137, 140

Smith Sound, 132, 136–137

Sointula, 121–124, 126, 196, 213

Spieden Channel, 24

Spieden Islands, 23

Spokane Radio Station, 74

Stewart Narrows, 216

Stillwater, **60**

Stonjalskys, 132

Strait of Georgia, 34, 39, 43, 65

Stuart Island, 25, 27–29, 84–85, 89, 142

Sunset Cove, 26

Surf Inlet, 214

Sutil Channel, 84

swamping, 40, 176, 189

Swanson Bay, 178–179, 183

Swanson Channel, 29

Table Island, 137–138

Tanaka (Captain), 227–228

Teakerne Arm, 62, 64, 69, 71, 73–75, 77–79, **81**, 83, 87

Texada Island, 13, 45, 59, 61

Thetis Island, 33

Thomas Basin, 269

Thorne Arm, 268

Thomson, Sheff, 239, 242, 244

Thulin Passage, 68

Thunderbird, 274

Thurlow Island, 90–91

tidal wave of 1923, 113

Toba Inlet, 72, 85

Tolmie Channel, 179–180

Tongass Island, 253, 255, 257

Tongass Narrows, 269, 271

Tongass Passage, 252

totem poles, 101–102, 160

Tree Point, 253, 256–259

Tree Point Lighthouse, 253, 256, 258–259

Tremble Island, 106

troller, 41, 45, 68, 105–106, 116, 125, 164, 167

Tsimpsean Peninsula, 246

Turn Point, 28–29

Turner's Cove, 69, 71

Turret Rock, 106

Tyee Scout, 22, 34–35, 38, 44–46, 50–51, 72, 93–94, 97, 100–103, **104**, 105–107, 109–115, 117, 132, 140–141, 185

Una Mae, 232, 268–269, 271–**272**–273

United States Army, 61

University of British Columbia, 276
University of California, Berkeley, 276
University of Washington, 17, 31, 33, 135
Ursula Channel, 189
US Customs, 244
US Navy, 125, 275
USS *Charleston* (breakwater at Powell River), 65
USS *Colorado*, 275
USS *Swallow*, 121

Vancouver, 45, 49, 54, 105, 128, 134, 139–142, 148, 155, 157, 159–160, 193, 241, 255, 274–275
Vancouver Island, 33, 40, 65, 67, 71–72, 91, 104, 108, 121, 125, 136, 276
Vancouver, Captain George, 170
Vancouver Radio, 142, 159
Venture, 134, 139, 141
Verney Passage, 189, 194
Village Island, 247

Wales Island, 235, 246, 248–251, 273
Wales Island Cannery, 235, 249
Wales Passage, 248

Walker Hook, 32
Walla Walla, 102, 113
War:
    World War I (Great War), 51, 92–93, 97, 151–152, 158, 174
    Spanish American War, 145,
    World War II, 274–276, 278
    in the Pacific, 275
Washington State, 17, 31, 33, 36, 56, 104, 106, 132, 135, 156, 159, 195, 207, 251, 255, 268, 275
Washington Post, 56, 132
Watts Narrows, 226
Weaver, Gwen, 221, 223–224, 228, 240
Weaver, Len, 223, 228
Wells Pass, 129
West Thurlow Island, 90–91
Westview, 61–62
Whirlpool Rapids, 89
wood ticks, 89, 96, 102, 142
Wright Sound, 194, 216, 218

Yakutat, 271
Yanagi, 227
Yucultas Rapids, 61, 64, 72, 75, 83–85, 87, **88**, 89–91, 93, 95, 97, 99, 101
Yuculta Traders, 85, 88

OTHER GREAT BOOKS FROM HARBOUR PUBLISHING

Visions of the Wild: A Voyage by Kayak Around Vancouver Island
Maria Coffey and Dag Goering
Brimming with breathtaking colour photos and compelling journal entries, an inspiring
chronicle of the adventure of a lifetime.
1-55017-264-6 • 8 x 9¹/₂ • 192 pages • colour photos • $36.95

Snowshoes and Spotted Dick
Chris Czajkowski

Chris Czajkowski chose to build her life and small ecotourism business on the shore
of a high-altitude lake near the southern tip of Tweedsmuir Provincial Park. In these
fascinating letters, Czajkowski details her often-solitary life in the wilderness and her
challenges and triumphs as she tries to finish her cabin.
ISBN 1-55017-279-4 • 6¹/₂ x 8 • 304 pages • b&w photos and illustrations • $24.95

The Last Island: A Naturalist's Sojourn on Triangle Island
Alison Watt

Twenty-three year old Alison Watt spent an unforgettable summer studying puffin
populations on a remote island north of Vancouver Island. Her award-winning memoir
is filled with adventures and revelations and illustrated with delightful watercolour
paintings, The Last Island is a beautifully written testament to the environment, friend-
ship, and the endurance of the human spirit.
ISBN 1-55017-280-8 • 6¹/₂ x 9¹/₂ • 226 pages • 40 colour illustrations • $34.95

The Remarkable Adventures of Portuguese Joe Silvey
Jean Barman

British Columbia is known for the colourful pioneers who helped build and shape
the character of this weird but wonderful province. And few were as colourful as
Portuguese Joe Silvey-a saloon keeper, whaler and pioneer of seine fishing in British
Columbia.
ISBN: 1-55017-326-X • 8¹/₂ x 11 • 80 pages • b&w photographs • $17.95

Full Moon, Flood Tide: Bill Proctor's Raincoast
Bill Proctor and Yvonne Maximchuk

Bill Proctor has lived and worked by the full moon flood tides for all his life. A natural
storyteller who has lived in the Broughton Archipelago for decades , he points the
way to hidden waterfalls and abandoned Native village sites, knows the best coves for
shelter in a sou'easter and shared the compelling and often funny stories of the Natives
and settlers who loved this place.
ISBN 1-55017-291-3 • 6¹/₄ x 7³/₄ • 288 pages • b&w photos and maps • $24.95

These titles are available at bookstores or from:

Harbour Publishing
Box 219, Madeira Park, BC V0N 2H0

Toll free order line: 1-800-667-2988
Fax: **604-883-9451** • Email: **orders@harbourpublishing.com**